Indian and Intercultural Philosophy

Bloomsbury Studies in World Philosophies

Series Editor:

Monika Kirloskar-Steinbach

Comparative, cross-cultural and intercultural philosophy are burgeoning fields of research. Bloomsbury Studies in World Philosophies complements and strengthens the latest work being carried out at a research level with a series that provides a home for thinking through ways in which professional philosophy can be diversified. Ideal for philosophy postgraduates and faculty who seek creative and innovative material on non-Euroamerican sources for reference and research, this series responds to the challenges of our postcolonial world, laying the groundwork for a new philosophy canon that departs from the current Eurocentric sources.

Titles in the Series:

Andean Aesthetics and Anticolonial Resistance, by Omar Rivera
Chinese Philosophy of History, by Dawid Rogacz
Chinese and Indian Ways of Thinking in Early Modern European Philosophy, by Selusi Ambrogio
Indian and Intercultural Philosophy, by Douglas Berger

Indian and Intercultural Philosophy

Personhood, Consciousness, and Causality

Douglas L. Berger

BLOOMSBURY ACADEMIC
LONDON • NEW YORK • OXFORD • NEW DELHI • SYDNEY

BLOOMSBURY ACADEMIC
Bloomsbury Publishing Plc
50 Bedford Square, London, WC1B 3DP, UK
1385 Broadway, New York, NY 10018, USA
29 Earlsfort Terrace, Dublin 2, Ireland

BLOOMSBURY, BLOOMSBURY ACADEMIC and the Diana logo are trademarks of Bloomsbury Publishing Plc

First published in Great Britain 2021
This paperback edition published 2023

Series design by Louise Dugdale
Cover image © Olga Kurbatova/Getty Images

A catalogue record for this book is available from the British Library.

Library of Congress Cataloging-in-Publication Data
Names: Berger, Douglas L., 1970- author.
Title: Indian and intercultural philosophy: personhood, consciousness, and causality / Douglas L. Berger.
Description: London, UK; New York, NY, USA: Bloomsbury Academic, 2021. |
Series: Bloomsbury studies in world philosophies | Includes bibliographical references and index. |
Identifiers: LCCN 2021004175 (print) | LCCN 2021004176 (ebook) |
ISBN 9781350174177 (hb) | ISBN 9781350174184 (ebook) | ISBN 9781350174191 (epdf)
Subjects: LCSH: Philosophy, Indic. | Philosophy–India. | Philosophy, Comparative.
Classification: LCC B131 .B438 2021 (print) | LCC B131 (ebook) | DDC 181/.4–dc23
LC record available at https://lccn.loc.gov/2021004175
LC ebook record available at https://lccn.loc.gov/2021004176

ISBN: HB: 978-1-3501-7417-7
PB: 978-1-3502-5399-5
ePDF: 978-1-3501-7418-4
eBook: 978-1-3501-7419-1

Series: Bloomsbury Studies in World Philosophies

Typeset by Deanta Global Publishing Services, Chennai, India

Contents

Acknowledgments vi

Introduction 1

Part I Brāhmiṇical Traditions

1 Shedding Light on the Matter: Śaṅkara's Dualistic Theory of Cognition 15
2 The Abode of Recognition: Memory and Selfhood in Classical Nyāya Thought 24
3 How Do We Sense?: Imagination in Buddhist and Nyāya Thought 41

Part II Madhyamaka Buddhism

4 What Kind of Designation Is "Emptiness"?: Reconsidering Nāgārjuna's MMK 24:18 57
5 "The Social Meaning of the Middle Way": B. S. Yadav and the Madhyamaka Critique of Indian Ontologies 101
6 Deconstruction, *Aporia* and Justice: In Nāgārjuna's Empty Ethics 125

Part III Indian and Intercultural Philosophy

7 Early Brāhmiṇical and Confucian Ideas of Duty 149
8 Indian and Chinese Notions of Luminous Awareness 174
9 The Unlikely Commentator: The Hermeneutic Reception of Śaṅkara's Thought in the Interpretation of Dārā Shukøh 188
10 The Pivot of Nihilism: Buddha Through Nietzsche's Eyes 197

Bibliography 215
Index 223

Acknowledgments

It is an incredible honor to have been invited to contribute a volume of my essays on Indian and Intercultural Philosophy to the Bloomsbury series in *World Philosophies*. I am deeply grateful to the series editors, Monika Kirloskar-Steinbach, Leah Kalmanson, and Sarah Mattice, for the opportunity to add this book to their highly valuable collection. I also extend sincere thanks to Colleen Coalter and Becky Holland at Bloomsbury for their most helpful assistance in taking this manuscript through the publication process. I am also enduringly grateful to Dr. Agnieszka Rostalska for her proofreading of these essays and assistance in editing and preparing this manuscript for publication.

I have been the recipient of almost unbelievable good fortune in learning about and receiving the mentorship of this generation's most extraordinary guides into the Indian philosophical tradition for Western philosophers. Their patient and illuminating instruction, priceless assistance, and sound advice are what have made my journeys in Indian thought possible. Some of them are no longer with us, but all have been enormously influential to my reflection and work. I can only express my heartfelt gratitude to Professors Bibhuti Singh Yadav, J. N. Mohanty, Bina Gupta, Wilhelm Halbfass, Timothy Cahill, Chakravarthi Ram-Prasad, Purushottama Bilimoria, and Arindam Chakrabarti. For anyone wishing to learn from the Indian tradition, hard-work and ceaseless study are of course required. But there is simply no substitute for being in the right time and place. That all of these brilliant figures were present during the same decades was a blessing that I, and many others, cannot begin to adequately reckon.

As an essays collection represents something of a milestone in one's career, I would like to take this opportunity to devote this volume to my late mother and father, Ann K. Weinschrott Berger (1924–2017) and Raphael J. Berger (1915–1990). Both were children of immigrants to the United States, grew up on wheat farms in the area of Lefor, North Dakota, endured the years of the Great Depression and the Second World War, and ended up raising seven boys together. My mother was a master of German pastries and a homemaker, who cheered her sons on in whatever paths through life they chose. My father, a

Catholic seminary student in his youth, returned from the war to become an electrician, and always encouraged study and intellectual curiosity. They nursed me through childhood illness and disability and provided me the values and courage I needed to turn to a career that they would not have anticipated. All the things I have been able to achieve are their achievements, and so I dedicate this book to them.

Introduction

As I sit down to write this introduction, a memory has sprung up from my youth. It was a little over twenty-five years ago when I, as a graduate student doing a year's worth of exchange research in Germany, sat outside of Tübingen University's library and read through J. N. Mohanty's *Essays on Indian Philosophy*. What a landmark it is for one's career as a scholar, I thought to myself, for an entire volume to be devoted to one's lifelong ruminations on a wide range of figures and topics in Indian thought. As I was officially enrolled at Temple University, I could only hope that Professor Mohanty would stay on long enough for me to learn directly from him and gain the benefit of his feedback on my envisioned dissertation project. That aspiration, to my immense good fortune, was fulfilled. And now, a quarter-century later, the *Bloomsbury Series in World Philosophies* has granted me the honor of publishing my own collection on Indian and intercultural philosophy. My journeys through the penetratingly brilliant and abundantly rich heritage of South Asian philosophical reflection have, from their beginnings until now, indeed been blessed by beneficent mentors and transforming discoveries.

There are, to be sure, many exemplary collections on Indian philosophy already in print, penned by the last several generations of scholars who have achieved monumental successes in making classical and modern Indian thought accessible to and most relevant for intercultural philosophical discussion today. And so, in putting forward my own assemblage of republished and original chapters here, I am obligated to set forth for the reader what is distinctive about these contributions. I will do so in three steps. First, I will rehearse in brief outline my own autobiography of learning in Indian philosophy in order to narrate who my teachers and greatest influences were, as well as what topics and issues in Indian and intercultural philosophy have been most important to me. Next, I will provide a skeleton review of the parts and chapters found in this volume, to give the reader a glimpse at which problems I have been most concerned to resolve in these fields. Finally, I will attempt to accentuate the most important discoveries I have so far made as a result of my encounters with Indian philosophical traditions. These discoveries not only relate to important aspects of India's traditions, but have to a great degree shaped my own philosophical views.

That a teenager from the small city of Dickinson, North Dakota, which was comprised of about 20,000 people and had a state university but was historically an agricultural supply town, would become fascinated by Indian philosophy in the 1980s was, to say the least, unlikely. Though the expansive horizons of the Dakota plains beckoned to worlds beyond them, not much information on India was available to me then. In fact, that I turned toward the study of philosophy at all resulted from an unplanned series of events. Burdened with a visual disability from birth, I worried about what kind of career I could have as an adult. During my junior and senior years of high school, I found some affinity for computer programming, and wrote sports statistics-keeping programs for our football and wrestling teams. I entered college fully intending to major in computer science and become a programmer, in the heady days of groundbreaking operating systems and graphical interfaces and the budding years of Artificial Intelligence. I was actually only about a year or so from completing all the requirements for this degree. But as a freshman, I had taken an Introduction to Philosophy class with a Hume scholar who eventually retired from Fairbanks, Mark A. Box. The challenges that Hume's thought laid at the feet of my inherited Catholic faith prompted me to immerse myself in philosophy reading and take all my Humanities electives in philosophy, religious studies, literature, history, and German. After a few years, I read the works of the nineteenth-century German philosopher Schopenhauer and the writings of the mythologist Joseph Campbell. It was these authors who began, in what I would come to appreciate were their quaint Orientalist fashions, to open up the world of ancient India to me. Just before my junior year of college began, and just after I turned twenty, my father passed away. The mourning period got me to thinking about what I would do with this one relatively short life that I have. By then somewhat bored with computers but highly motivated by philosophical reading, I decided to change my course of study. I transferred to the University of North Dakota in Grand Forks and completed a combined major in Philosophy and Religious Studies in 1993. And, from there, off I went to graduate school at Temple University in Philadelphia.

Even in the early 1990s in the United States, it was not easy to find a Philosophy graduate program in which to specialize in anything other than European or Anglo-American thought. The few that did exist either did not accept my applications or were prohibitively expensive for me. If one wanted to concentrate on some area of Indian and intercultural philosophy, one normally had to go to a department of Religious Studies. This is what I did, and in my case, the outcome was most fortunate. To take Professor Mohanty's courses on India, in which one studied primarily Nyāya and Advaita Vedānta, all I had to do was walk up one flight of stairs to Philosophy. In the Religious Studies program, Indian traditions, particularly the Madhyamaka Buddhism of Nāgārjuna and Cadrakīrti, were taught by the brilliant and charismatic professor Bibhuti Singh Yadav, to whom a chapter in this volume is devoted. Though my classes on Indian thought were tightly and superbly focused on topics such as Nyāya theory of knowledge, Advaita debates on consciousness and Madhyamaka critiques of metaphysics, my abiding interest remained unpacking the complex, problematic but still fascinating details of Schopenhauer's appropriation of Upaniṣadic, Vedāntic, and early Buddhist ideas. For more background and methodological preparation for my dissertation on Schopenhauer, I engaged in a year's worth of conversations with Wilhelm Halbfass across town at the University of Pennsylvania and took courses on hermeneutics with Thomas J. Dean at Temple, who was to be my advisor. Though both professors Yadav and Halbfass died only a few months before my dissertation defense, the project was deemed a success and, after some revision, was published as my first monograph in 2004. I had gone into my graduate career interested in the problem of how, or whether, classical Indian Brāhmiṇical and Buddhist authors could be considered "idealists" in the Continental European sense of that term, which is to say, as precursors to thinkers like Kant and Schopenhauer. By the end of my PhD work, I was convinced that this was not a viable comparative connection, and turned my attention within the Indian tradition to debates between Madhyamaka and Nyāya about the possibility of *pramāṇa* theory and what this debate could offer Western discussions between epistemological skeptics and realists. Still, I remained fascinated by the problems posed to us by intercultural hermeneutics, and how, if possible, to separate the study of Indian thought according to its own categories and frameworks from the temptation to distort these in the name of comparative philosophical pursuits.

One of the difficulties of my dissertation project and how it bore on my early career, however, was the degree to which it put me on the borderlines, rather than at the center, of several fields. I had trained myself to be a specialist in classical Indian thought, but had written a thesis on Schopenhauer. I was claiming to be a philosopher, but graduated from a department of Religious Studies. This made landing a position even more challenging than the normally strained circumstances of the philosophy market in the United States made it. After a half-year of postdoc research in Tübingen and two years of term-contract teaching at Temple University's branch campus in Tokyo and main campus, I finally did accept a tenure-track position at Oakton Community College in a northern suburb of Chicago. Despite the heavy teaching load at Oakton, I continued to write essays on debates between Nyāya and Madhyamaka and published my dissertation. It was at this point that I began to attend University of Hawai'i workshops on Chinese philosophical traditions, which by this time I had been given significant teaching duties in.

In the fall of 2006, I was offered a position in the Philosophy department at Southern Illinois University in Carbondale, which had long-standing commitments to Asian traditions at both the undergraduate and PhD levels, but which was also the nation's hub of American pragmatism. For the next eleven years, I would teach classes and advise projects in both Indian and Chinese philosophies (and a few on Japanese thinkers) and enjoyed significantly more time to develop my research. Here, I continued somewhat closer interpretive work on Nāgārjuna but also began to embark on attempting to create some dialogue between classical Nyāya and contemporary philosophy of mind. In the latter venture, I found myself strenuously challenged by leading figures in the contemporary field, primarily Chakravarthi Ram-Prasad, Arindam Chakrabarti, and Purushottama Bilimoria, who rightly admonished me to focus more intently on the specific categories used by classical Indian thinkers. This would allow me to tease out their own formulations of the relationship between consciousness, embodiment, and personhood instead of artificially grafting their debates onto issues related to reductionism and emergentism in Western thought. It was yet another important reminder of how insidiously covert the Orientalist legacy can be for scholars.

At the same time, during my tenure at SIUC, I was more and more drawn into classical Chinese Confucian, Daoist, and Mohist thought as well as Tang and Song Dynasty Chan Buddhist writings. I grew ever more fascinated with notions of personhood and embodied consciousness in these lineages of reflection and debate, and began working on more projects that brought South and East Asian traditions into conversation. Institutionally, I tried to foster such avenues of intercultural debate through my service as vice-president and president of the Society for Asian and Comparative Philosophy from 2012 to 2016. In my own published work, I collaborated with Liu JeeLoo at California State University Fullerton on a co-edited collection of essays, bringing the work of twenty-one scholars together on notions of "nothingness" in South and East Asian thought. I also produced my own second monograph during these years, on how conceptions of consciousness were transformed in the migration of Buddhism from India to China, and how these transformations in turn reshaped Chinese philosophical thematizations of consciousness at large. My years at Southern Illinois University then in several respects deepened my appreciation of Nyāya realism and Buddhist causalism. But they also witnessed the expansion of my vision of the possibilities of intercultural philosophy to the prospects of bringing Asian traditions into greater, and renewed, dialogue with one another, rather than having the West serve as the center of gravity of and standard for so-called comparative philosophy.

In 2017, I accepted an offer to move to the Institute for Philosophy at Leiden University in the Netherlands, which had jumped on the outstanding opportunity to create first undergraduate and then graduate specializations in Global and Comparative Philosophy. This program was the first of its kind in the Netherlands, and still a rarity in Europe. The program's undergraduate enrollment quickly grew. Its faculty and the areas of global philosophy it covers were broadened to include not just Indian and East Asian traditions but Arabic and Persian as well as African philosophy. It is from this post that I have received the chance to release this collection.

The three parts of chapters into which this volume is divided correspond closely to the three major areas of my research and deliberations on classical Indian thought. Part I on classical Brahmiṇical philosophies in some fundamental ways recaps the reasons for my first major change in allegiance between early schools of Buddhism and Advaita toward Nyāya. Chapter 1, "Shedding Light on the Matter: Śaṅkara's Dualistic Theory of Cognition," was originally written as a conference presentation in 1998, and has been entirely rewritten for this book collection. Here, I take a cue from the late Daya Krishna, but push his arguments much farther than he had intended them to go. While the seminal eighth-century promulgator of Advaita Vedānta, Śaṅkarācarya, set out to establish a unitary theory of the innermost self, that very theory inextricably relies on a persistently dualist Sāṃkhya metaphysics. Śaṅkara's Advaita should therefore properly be considered a monism of *ātman* rather than a monism of the entire cosmological order. Chapter 2, "The Abode of Recognition: Memory and Selfhood in Classical Nyāya Thought," first appeared in 2012. It argues that the description of memories that is found in the early Nyāya authors Vātsyāyana and Uddyotakara does much more justice to the subjectivity and agency of our experience of remembrance than does the minimalist account we find in Buddhist authors such as Vasubandhu and Ratnakīrti. The Buddhist frameworks eviscerate not only real subjectivity from our memories but the experience of subjectivity as well. The last chapter in Part I, entitled "How Do We Sense?

Imagination in Buddhist and Nyāya Thought," was composed for several talks I gave in 2015 and 2019 but has been entirely rewritten here. The chapter argues that the sharp distinction we find between non-imaginative and imaginative perception given by the pivotal Buddhist philosophers Diṅnāga and Dharmakīrti calls into question the very cognitive value of the former. By contrast, the tenth-century commentary on Nyāya by Vācaspati Miśra offers us a robust description of how imagination and memory do not solely distort our perceptions but often aid us in accurately recognizing what we sense. The chapters in Part I mark key moments in my own reflection during which I moved away from early attractions to Advaita and Buddhist views of consciousness. I found myself more and more compelled by Nyāya accounts of cognition and experience, even if early Nyāya metaphysics proves to be too extravagant.

Despite my growing sympathy for Nyāya thought, the second- and third-century Madhyamaka Buddhist pioneer Nāgārjuna has remained a major focus of my work. His particular philosophical formulation of *pratītya samutpāda* or "causally conditioned co-arising" continues to impress me as a unique watershed in the history of Indian thought, proffering as it did a relational metaphysics of causal interdependence. The first chapter in Part II is a complete reworking and further development of the most controversial of my essays that originally appeared in 2010. Here, I correct some of its errors of my first salvo but greatly expand its arguments. In "What Kind of Designation Is 'Emptiness'?: Reconsidering Nāgārjuna's MMK 24:18," I challenge foregoing translations and readings, which follow the seventh-century exegete Candrakīrti, of what has been called the "central verse" of Nāgārjuna's *Mūlamadhyamakakārikā*. I argue that the textual details, balance of commentarial literature, historical circumstances, and logical implications of this verse lead to the conclusion that Nāgārjuna considered the notion of "emptiness" to be merely a synonym of conditioned co-arising and not an ultimately metaphysically false conventional label. The next two chapters of Part II explore various implications of Madhyamaka ethics. "'The Social Meaning of the Middle Way': B. S. Yadav and the Madhyamaka Critique of Indian Ontologies" presents an assessment of Nāgārjuna's philosophy by my late teacher, Bibhuti Singh Yadav (1943–1999). For Yadav, the "deconstructive" aims of Nāgārjuna and Candrakīrti, which assailed the realist "essentialism" of Nyāya and Advaita, constituted a fundamental attack on their social elitism and casteism, demanding a social transformation of human practices. Chapter 6 is a reprint of a paper that originally appeared in 2007. "Deconstruction, *Aporia* and Justice: In Nāgārjuna's Empty Ethics" goes somewhat against a progressively popular grain in intercultural scholarship of seeing Nāgārjuna as a kind of

South Asian deconstructionist. The chapter closely examines the later ethical writings of Jacques Derrida along with extended passages on *karma* and praxis in Nāgārjuna's *Kārikā*. It finds in the latter not Derridian aspirations for a generative but "impossible" gift-giving, but rather a really efficacious program of cultivation and boon-bestowing. These three chapters on Nāgārjuna then illustrate what I have come to believe are deeply Buddhist theoretical and practical commitments to interconnectedness and ethical cultivation that can be found in his most seminal of works. Nāgārjuna offers us profound insights into the multidirectionality and socially transforming valences of causality which, it seems to me, are in their detail unique in the Indian tradition.

The final four chapters in this volume offer a vision of the many different intercultural resonances that Indian thought has had and continues to have across the globe. Chapter 7, "Early Brāhmiṇical and Confucian Ideas of Duty," is based on a short paper of mine which was first published in 2007 but has been vastly expanded and completely rewritten for this venue. This chapter attempts to create a vibrant dialogue between the authors of the perennially vital Bhagavad Gītā and the fourth-century BCE Chinese classic *Mengzi* or *Mencius*. The new essay here was sparked by a recent debate among Chinese philosophers about the value of *xiao* or family dependability and a rereading of the Gītā's call to social duty beyond family loyalty by Geoffrey Ashton. I weigh the relative weaknesses and strengths of these contrasting views. Ultimately, I find that their respective positions are grounded in contrasting theories of personhood and its social consequences, and argue for the qualified preferability of Mengzi's moral vision over the Gītā's. In Chapter 8, "Indian and Chinese Notions of Luminous Awareness," original to this collection, I attempt to evaluate the various notions of *prabhāsvaram cittaṃ* in the Indian Vijñānavāda Buddhist Vasubandhu and its reception and alteration in Paramārtha's / Zhen Di's Chinese Wei Shi as well as in various Chan Buddhist authors. In the end, I find the philosophical formulation of luminous awareness in Vasubandhu, while cryptic, more palatable than alternative metaphysical models, but nonetheless see possibilities in the more metaphysical renditions that could prompt deeper reflection on human potentiality. Chapters 7 and 8 are efforts to respectively instigate or revive philosophical debate between Indian and Chinese philosophers. Chapter 9, reprinted from 2015, is entitled "The Unlikely Commentator: The Hermeneutic Reception of Śaṅkara's Thought in the Interpretation of Dārā Shukøh." It examines the exegetical, interreligious, and political aims of the seventeenth-century Mughal prince in his commissioned Persian translations of and personal commentary on the *Upaniṣads* accompanied by the interlinear elucidations of Śaṅkara. This work not only brings together Dārā's Qādari Sufi syncretism and classical Vedānta but also portends the extension of what was a quite controversial brand of Mughal interreligious syncretism which, tragically, did not succeed. It turned out to be a moment of lasting cultural value though, for it was Dārā's Persian translations of the *Upaniṣads* that, through the early 1800s Latin recension of Aquetil Duperron, was to become Schopenhauer's nightly reading throughout his life. Chapter 10 is a reprint of a 2017 essay which offers a criticism of Friedrich Nietzsche's understanding of early Buddhist thought. In "The Pivot of Nihilism: Buddha Through Nietzsche's Eyes," the nineteenth-century German philosopher's simultaneous respect of and contempt for the "nihilistic" vision of the Buddha is critiqued through an examination of early Theravāda discourses. As it turns out, in the self-understanding of awakening that is presented in the Buddha's words, "nihilism" is really an amoralistic attachment to worldly desires that is to be avoided, a view that represents a conspicuous rebuke of Nietzsche's thought. The papers that have been arranged into this section reveal the global relevance of classical Indian thought, in its real and possible import for classical Chinese, medieval Persian Islamic, and modern European thought. The section is also meant to emphasize my conviction that intercultural philosophy should be truly intercultural, and not merely place various traditions in one-on-one interfaces with Western thought, which has been provincially and wrongly treated as the fulcrum of all philosophical reflection.

The career which I have spent learning and deliberating about classical Indian philosophical traditions has facilitated what might be called a few major "conversions" on my part. These conversions have been less dramatic than those of the religious sort and, given what Westerners often expect from Indian thought, surprising. As noted earlier, I initially approached the Indian tradition as a somewhat cynical young man who was an acolyte of Schopenhauer. Indeed, many nineteenth-century thinkers, philosophers like Nietzsche and Orientalists like Paul Deussen, were convinced that Schopenhauer's broadest impressions of early Brāhmiṇical and Buddhist traditions were quite accurate. Those impressions included the determinations that Indian thought as a whole was idealist in the Kantian sense and pessimistic about worldly life in the Schopenhaeurian vein. That our experiences of worldly difference from other phenomena and beings was a function of the projections of consciousness was, Schopenhauer insisted, a doctrine found both in Kant's *Transcendental Aesthetic* and in the conversations between Uddālaka Āruṇi and Śvetaketu in the *Chāndogya Upaniṣad*. That all things and persons are epiphenomenally manifestations of one unitary and homogeneous metaphysical ground could, for Schopenhauer, be found not only in the Platonists but also in the Gītā. That this world is the worst of all possible worlds and should be escaped through mystical practices was, according to Schopenhauer, a truth that could be found not just in Euripides, the Christianity of the Desert Fathers, and Shakespeare but in Jain and Buddhist thoughts too. And so, my early ventures in Indian thought tended to look for confirmations of all these perspectives, from Mādhyamika and Vijñānavāda refutations of realism to Śaṅkara's formulation of *adhyāsa* and his extrapolation of the meaning of *tat tvam asi*. While I had no proclivities for mystical or meditative practices, I did think Schopenhauer's ethic of compassion, which in very loose ways followed from his metaphysics of will, would adequately address the ethical and social dilemmas of our lives. I first approached India, then, as many Westerners still do, in the unwitting Orientalist manner, through the eyes of another Westerner who believed that his interpretation of Indian thought, though steeped from the beginning in European conceptual vocabulary, was the last word.

Happily, as I continued to delve into the inconsistencies in Schopenhauer's own system as well as learn about the history of the intertwined projects of colonialism and Orientalism, these early convictions began to loosen. Guided through the structures and content of the early Indian tradition by some of the most able teachers of the last several decades, I discovered that the debates between the classical *darśana*-s were often focused on very different matters and had quite diversely different agendas than I did. However, the fundamentally idealist proclivities I initially held were deeply rooted. In an overarching sense, I did not think epistemological or metaphysical realism had much purchase. Although I was an ardent admirer of science from my early youth on, it seemed to me that contemporary quantum theory had undermined both the notion of ourselves as observers of an independent reality as well as the classical conceptions of causation. Indeed, I had come to believe that Hume had successfully uprooted any reasonable belief in regular causation in the 1700s. And, from every other philosophical corner, from Nāgārjuna's attack on *pramāṇa* theory to Kant's transcendental arguments about space and time to the Positivists' failure to formulate a satisfactory theory of verification, it seemed to me realism was a philosophical non-starter of the most naïve variety. The balance of discussion in the classical Indian tradition, I thought, had dispensed with realist principles.

Then, in the midst of my graduate studies, I was assigned the remarkable 1986 treatise of B. K. Matilal, *Perception: An Essay on Classical Indian Theories of Knowledge*. Over the course of several years, to put it quite simply, Matilal, along with accompanying readings of the classical authors, converted me to a qualified version of Nyāya realism. On prolonged and more careful consideration, I was compelled to the conclusion that Nyāya thinkers could rebut Nāgārjuna's and Śriharṣa's regress, circularity, and relation arguments that were brought against its portrayal of knowing cognitions. Further, and more positively, detailed Nyāya accounts made better sense of our experiences of memory and the complex but intelligible relations between perceptual and conceptual cognitions. In like manner, as is made clear by Vivekananda's nineteenth-century letters urging Nyāya paṇḍits to stop teaching logic in deference to Westerners' interest in Vedānta, realistic philosophy in India was not so much defeated in debate as it was overshadowed by what Ashis Nandy has called the neo-Vedāntic embrace of its "intimate" colonial "enemy." I certainly could not endorse the wildly overfurnished Nyāya ontology, nor could I ascribe to its eternalist formulations of selfhood. And yet, studying Nyāya thinkers such as Vātsyāyana, Uddyotakara, to a lesser extent Udayana, and the independent commentary of Vācaspati resulted in the discovery of good arguments for realist models of relation and cognition. As unexpected as it may have been for a young scholar looking to India to confirm idealist aspirations, what nonetheless emerged from my engagement with Indian thought was a limited and yet robust turn to realism. But Nyāya's brand of realism is not naïve. It is not a bland and static certainty about an objective world that is altogether independent of and indifferent to us. Instead, Nyāya's realism is fallibilistic, recognizing that our present confidences may be upended by future discoveries and innovations. It has an eye to providing standards, not fixed and immutable but malleable yet reliable ones, according to which we can make practical decisions, about the planting of our crops, the success of our ventures, the evaluations of our social relations, and even about our religious convictions. It is also a restorative kind of realism, situating our experiential lives in their concrete environments, wedding our subjectivities to our embodiments and histories, and keeping us attuned to the consequences our acts have for ourselves, others, and our world. As a system which is committed to the view that both *pratyākṣa* and *kalpanā* shape our sensations, reflection, and aims, Nyāya has never recognized a time when realism lacked a human face.

In just as important a respect, I have experienced something of a "conversion" in my estimation of the Madhyamaka logician Nāgārjuna's thought. Branded, even by rival Indian Buddhists, as a "nihilist," hailed by East Asian Buddhists as a philosopher of "nothingness," and resurrected in modern scholarship on behalf of anti-essentialist and deconstructionist causes, I have come to see Nāgārjuna differently. Nāgārjuna, in a profound and far-reaching manner, re-envisions the Buddha's teaching of *pratītyasamutpāda* not merely as a doctrine of causal conditions, insisting that definite effects are brought about by definite causes, but, in addition to that, as revealing a thoroughgoing material and moral interdependence. Where Indian Buddhist reductionists see at the ground of transient and impermanent wholes a set of fixed and unanalyzable *dharma*-s, Nāgārjuna sees unceasing dynamic interaction between the activity of structuring and that which is structured. Where Buddhist moral theorists wish to make categorical distinctions between deeds that tighten the bonds of attachment and deeds that liberate, Nāgārjuna reveals how the very pains of our bondage help facilitate our journeys to freedom. Where Buddhist meditational adepts point to the living Buddha as model and the released Buddha as indescribable, Nāgārjuna reminds us that awakening is a praxis and its description is the process of cultivation. And where Brāhmiṇical epistemologists aspire to specify a limited set of conditions according to which the object of a cognition becomes something known, Nāgārjuna reminds them that these conditions will be just as specific to each circumstance as are the object and cognition to be considered. In this light, Nāgārjuna's thought does not force us to choose between a set of mere social conventions that can never touch reality and a sagely ultimacy that must keep silent lest it be misunderstood. Nor does his system identify these two artificially abstracted poles with one another in some elusive mystery. On the contrary, in hacking away so mercilessly at our habits for drawing distinctions, he wishes to show us how the things we distinguish depend on one another. In so doing, he strives, as B.S. Yadav believed, to return the Buddha back to Buddhists and, as I would add, to illuminate how the cosmos and human commerce are themselves a great *saṅgha*.

In certain respects, a number of the chapters in this volume will, when compared to standard readings and evaluations of classical Indian thought, strike some readers as controversial and provocative. There are, for instance, not many students of Indian philosophy who would, after more than a quarter-century of study, claim that Śaṅkara was a metaphysical dualist, that Vācaspati Miśra handled the topic of the concept's relation to sensation better than most devoted Naiyāyikas, that Nāgārjuna did not think the term "emptiness" was an anti-metaphysical convention, that the Gītā may well have a flawed conception of moral duty, and that in some cases Chinese Buddhists outdid Indian Buddhists in making consciousness an ultimate reality. However the reader may adjudicate these matters for herself or himself, it is hoped that the chapters in this volume will at least deepen and broaden discussion of the incredible contributions the Indian tradition has made to the philosophy of consciousness, personhood, and causality. And it is further hoped that this presentation will enhance the scope of the relevance of classical Indian philosophers to intercultural philosophical debate at large.

Still, though I hope to have arrived at some unique and helpful insights in these pages, that hope is incalculably outweighed by my gratitude. I have enjoyed the immense good fortune to have learned from the many teachers, official and unofficial, mentioned earlier, as well as from a host of other scholars and philosophers inspired by the classical Indian tradition in our time. I can say in resounding unison with all other students of Indian thought, as well as with complete honesty, that all the virtues of these chapters have come from my teachers, and all their mistakes are mine.

Part I

Brāhmiṇical Traditions

1

Shedding Light on the Matter

Śaṅkara's Dualistic Theory of Cognition

It remains common in contemporary scholarship on the eighth-century Śaṅkarācarya to brand him as the seminal shaper of "non-dualistic" Vedānta, as "non-dualism" remains the preferred translation for Advaita. As Eliot Deutsch proclaimed in the first modern English-language seminal treatment, Śaṅkara's philosophy of the self was in all respects dedicated to establishing the "oneness of reality" and human existence (1973: 47). Modern advocates of Advaita have continued to make this case. Bina Gupta, in her survey of classical and modern construals of Advaita, holds that the "non-dualism" of the school consists in its commitment to the conclusion that, because consciousness is the locus of material projections as well as their false object, "being and consciousness are one" (2003: 115). That the entire metaphysical scheme of Śaṅkara's system has not been convincing either to rival classical schools of Vedānta or to many modern thinkers is, given the radicality of this supposed "non-dualism," not surprising. None of the early centuries of Advaita commentators, from Padmapāda to Vācaspati to Madhusudana Sarasvati, according to J. N. Mohanty, ever successfully explained how a supposedly changeless *ātman*, which never performs any actions, could objectify itself into finite persons (1993a: 73). The hard nub of Advaita Vedānta then presumably rests on its ability to explain how a completely unitary and static self could ever have become the basis (*āśraya*) for a world of fleeting material transformations and discreet cognitions owned by heterogeneous *jīva*-s.

In his highly provocative and brilliant collection of essays released in 1991 entitled *Indian Philosophy: A Counter-Perspective*, Daya Krishna included a brief but incisive paper hypothesizing that Śaṅkara's Advaita, in the way it formulated the fundamental problem of mistaking a unitary spiritual self for an empirical ego, took a Sāṃkhya philosophical departure from the very start. That is to say, when, in the *Brahmasūtrabhāṣya*, Śaṅkara claims that the fundamental error of all consciousness is *adhyāsa*, the "displacement" of empirical qualities on a spiritual subjectivity, he is describing a process with which a Sāṃkhya dualist would be in full agreement. This creates a dilemma, for if this is the case, Śaṅkara is basing a non-dualistic perspective on a dualistic distinction. Ultimately, Krishna argues, this problem is overcome by Śaṅkara, because in defining the *ātman* as ultimately completely devoid of difference, he can, contrary to Sāṃkhya, deny all metaphysical identity and difference and be a true Advaitin (1991b: 161).

I believe, however, that Krishna's brilliant diagnosis of Śaṅkara's dualistic formulation of *adhyāsa* has greater implications than he was willing to countenance. What we have in Śaṅkara's system, I contend, is not an overarching metaphysical "non-dualism" at all. On the contrary, Śaṅkara constructs a worldview according to which a distinctly Sāṃkhya dualism continues to obtain between the eternally pure and homogeneous self and ever-changing, transforming, and finite matter. The only estimable philosophical difference between Advaita and Sāṃkhya lies in the fact that, for the latter, there are multiple and individuated spiritual selves while, for the former, there is only one transcendental self in all beings. However, for Śaṅkara, there is still a persisting difference between self and material existence. And this can be seen not only in the way Śaṅkara formulates *adhyāsa*, but in how he describes the perceptual and cognitive processes as well. What Advaita then really denotes is the fact that the singular spiritual *ātman* is not two things, is not both transcendental self and bodily ego. If Śaṅkara's Advaita is a monism, it is a monism of the self alone, and not a monism that envelopes all beings. This depiction of Advaita does not in any way solve the philosophical conundrum of how such a unitary self can be related to the world of difference and change; it only clarifies what the distinction of Advaita is describing for Śaṅkara. I will in this brief chapter illustrate why I take this implication to be the case. I will do so first by rehearsing and supplementing a few of Daya Krishna's arguments, and then add a few of my own.

Śaṅkara's commentary on the *Brahmasūtra* begins with the assertion that the "notion of this" (*asmadpratyaya*) and the "notion of the other" (*yuṣmadpratyaya*) are as different from one another as light is from darkness. By the former term, Krishna rightly points out, Śaṅkara clearly means the unitary and eternally pure spiritual self (*ātman*), while by the latter he means both all material plurality and relation and all distinctions between individuated egos (1991a: 157–8). Therefore, to attribute the features of the latter, physical, changeable, and heterogeneous, onto the former is a special Advaitic species of *adhyāsa*. Often translated as "superimposition" or "projection," *adhyāsa* really means to place (*as*) one thing in the locus (*adhi*) of another thing. This process of misattribution, according to Śaṅkara, enables us both to have individuated awareness, in the form of continuous ego-identities, and to be subjects of knowledge. When we identify our continuous selves with the body and all its specific distinctions, activities, and dispositions, as in "I am short," "I am old," "I am a teacher," "I love my home," and so on, we wrongly locate bodily, causal, and psychological habits upon the actual source of our continuous self-awareness, the spiritual self. Similarly, when we undergo the cognitions "I see this," "I taste this," "I infer this," and "I remember this," or even "I do not know this" or "I don't recall this," we take specific and limited cognitive states that are brought about by constrained and contingent circumstances and locate them in the ever-unchanging and tranquil *ātman*.

This procedure is further described by Śaṅkara as *adhyāropa apavādanyāya*, or the logic (*nyāya*) of invoking an exception (*apavāda*) for a misplaced form (*adhyāropa*). In normal circumstances, it is simply wrong for us to mis-predicate a feature to a substance to which it does not belong, taking something to be a snake because it is long and winding when it is actually a rope, for example. But in the case of our lived and embodied experience, we cognitively "invoke an exception" (*apavāda*) for the error of projecting empirical forms unto pure subjectivity, because if we didn't, we could not live active and conscious worldly lives. There is then a pragmatic sort of logic (*nyāya*) to the "fundamental incomprehension" (*mūlāvidya*) of reifying our spiritual selves, since that is how we can become individual persons (*jīva*-s). Here, Krishna quite correctly observes, despite the metaphysical disagreement between Advaita and Sāṃkhya on whether there is one spiritual self or many, the way that Śaṅkara has described the process of mistaking spirit for matter "is pure and unmitigated Sāṃkhya doctrine" (1991a: 158). After all, the Sāṃkhya philosopher would and does offer precisely this description of our everyday misidentification of the spirit (*puruṣa*) with the primordial materiality (*prakṛti*) of the body. Śaṅkara has then, according to Krishna, launched his presumably non-dualistic Vedānta with an argument that can, as such, easily be accepted by an unabashed dualist (1991a: 160).

We should dwell upon this on a more basic level for a moment, just to make what is being presently discussed clear. A standard form of "non-dualism," which might otherwise be characterized as a "monism," would hold that all things, in some fundamental respect, have the same nature. If all things in the world, no matter how different they may be in many respects, nonetheless share a more fundamental commonality among them, then at least in that respect, they are "one" in exhibiting that fundamental feature. This is of course how the *mahāvākya* or "great pronouncement" of the *Chāndogya Upaniṣad* is often understood. In that text, Uddālaka teaches his son Śvetaketu that, since the existence (*sat*) of all things lies in a uniformly invisible source, Śvetaketu should consider himself to be the same in essence with all things. That is the meaning of the formula "*tat tvam asi*" ("that is you"). But this conventional interpretation of *tat tvam asi* was not held by Śaṅkara. Instead, Śaṅkara holds that there is an irreducible distinction, and not a reducible unity, between *ātman* and the material world. And so, for Śaṅkara, the "great pronouncement" *tat tvam asi* identifies the source of the embodied person's consciousness, and not their separate material existence, with *ātman*. For a metaphysical non-dualist, then, distinguishing between the self and the world is misguided, while for Śaṅkara, it is the identification of self with world that is the great root of all error.

Krishna goes on to argue, however, that Śaṅkara manages to push this Sāṃkhya premise of his argument toward a genuinely Advaita conclusion. Krishna contends that Śaṅkara holds normal states of conventional cognitive truth to be in the ultimate sense just as erroneous as states of conventional cognitive error. This is so because both wrongly objectify the *ātman*, and enmesh it with all its differentiation. But this forced identity in both empirical error and empirical truth is always denied in his Advaita (Krishna 1991: 160–2). It is, therefore, not as if Śaṅkara ever really believed that empirical qualities and transformations were real features of existence that were being projected by *adhyāsa* onto a transcendental self, but instead, empirical features of existence are all ultimately illusory to begin with. Because Śaṅkara, unlike Sāṃkhya philosophers, does not believe that *prakṛti* or material existence is ultimately real, he can rightly claim a non-dualistic stance. However, even here, according to Krishna, we must be precise about what non-dualism means for Śaṅkara. "It is not an answer to the question of whether reality is one or many. It is an assertion that the real is the realm where . . . duality . . . does not apply" (Krishna 1991: 161). But is this the case? Do Śaṅkara's frameworks for cognition in general and epistemology in particular enable him to reclaim non-dualist ground after having initiated his philosophical project with a dualistically formulated problem? It does not, as we shall now learn, seem so. Indeed, Daya Krishna let Śaṅkara off the hook too easily.

According to Śaṅkara, the living body has the standard Indian philosophical compliment of five external sense organs and the "inner instrument" (*antaḥkaraṇa*) of mental states. While later Advaitins like Vidyāraṇya tried to erect subtle arguments denying that these sense organs were physical or directly causal, there is no evidence from Śaṅkara's *corpus* that he conceived of them in any such subtle ways (Mayeda 1992: 29–30). Śaṅkara describes the senses as going out from the body in the direction of external objects (*bahirmukha*), and notions (*pratyaya*) of those external objects are brought about in the *antaḥkaraṇa* by those external forms (*bāhyākāranimittatva*) (Mayeda 1992: 35). Now, it is certainly the case for Śaṅkara, as it was for all Brāhmiṇical systems, that this process of outer and inner sensation was not sufficient for consciousness, since material processes and interactions were for these thinkers by definition unconscious. Only the *ātman*, for Śaṅkara, is cognitively luminous (*prakāśa*), and it is the self's luminosity that makes the external forms and internal sensations take a false coupled appearance (*ābhāsa*), manifesting themselves as the grasped (*grāhya*) and grasper (*grāhakā*) in our experience. And, again, later Advaitins would continue to stress that both the forms of things and the cognitive luminosity of the self were only experienced together internally, in the illuminated space of the "inner instrument," and so we should not think of perception proper as involving external contact (Mayeda 1992: 34). However, we should not let all of the special pleading of Advaita authors and commentators distract us from details of the perceptual process as they describe it. In order for us to be conscious, we need the *prakāśatva* of *ātman*, surely. But in order for *ātman* to be conscious of anything else, it must "light up" the *antaḥkaraṇa*, and in order for this "inner instrument" to form "notions" of external or internal features, it must be stimulated by external or internal senses which are in contact with their objects. No dreams, no memories, no perceptions, and no sensations will be experienced without physiological or physical activities taking place. The "inner instrument" is but a locus where spirit and matter must come together in order for us to have embodied experiences. And, if Śaṅkara is to be believed, all the causality involved in these processes must come from the side of the physical and physiological, for nothing whatsoever is caused or brought about by the self.

The requirements that both spiritual luminosity and physical causality are necessary in order to give rise to individuated and embodied experiences are, then, held very much in common by Sāṃkhya and Advaita. And the details of their fundamental agreements go farther still. Because his cosmology insulates *brahman* from all causal interactions as well, Śaṅkara must posit the existence of an "unevolved name-and-form" (*avyākṛte nāmarūpe*) from which material nature (*prakṛti*) arises. And because Śaṅkara provides us with no explanation of his mere claim that "unevolved name-and-form" itself evolved from *brahman*, his cosmology differs from the Sāṃkhya dualism between spirit and nature only in minor detail (Mayeda 1992: 22). On top of this, Śaṅkara's portrayal of the way the "inner instrument" (*antaḥakaraṇa*) is first illuminated by *ātman* and then reflects back to *ātman* a false appearance of its own subjective agency corresponds very closely with descriptions given of the *buddhi* in late Sāṃkhya commentaries (Rukmani 1988: 367–76). The unavoidable need for both spirit and matter in explaining cosmic evolution and human cognition in Śaṅkara's Advaita perpetuates, and does not negate, its dualistic formulation of *adhyāsa*.

This feature also applies to Śaṅkara's technical epistemology. It is here where Krishna believed Śaṅkara extricated himself from the dualistic implications of his other ideas because, ultimately, he held physical and differentiated things to be *māyā*, cognitive "magic." But in fact, Śaṅkara was not quite so categorical about the ontological status of material objects. It is true that he glosses the *māyā* of the *Upaniṣads* with the more technical term *avidyā* or "incomprehension." But close attention must be paid to how he writes about the latter. It is assuredly the case that Śaṅkara does not believe the paramount truth (*paramārthasatya*) of the identity between *brahman* and *ātman* can be gleaned from any of the widely recognized "means of knowledge" (*pramāṇa*-s) of the philosophers, but only through scripture and direct insight. However, this by no means entails that the "means of knowledge" should simply be ignored. In fact, Śaṅkara is not hesitant to assert that the "means of knowledge," such as perception, inference, and testimony, are directed toward materially existing objects (*yathābhūtaviśaya*) and are based on externally existent phenomena (*vastutantra*) (Mayeda 1992: 47). In addition to this, it is crucial to keep in mind how Śaṅkara describes the ontological status of external objects. They are not, he tells us, illusory or false, but instead are *anirvacanīya*, or "incapable of articulation," such that we cannot determine their ontological status with any verbal precision. In one sense, we cannot say, given Śaṅkara's lofty standards, that empirical things in the world have existence (*sat*), since they are limited in spatial extension and temporal duration and their deprivation and loss leaves us with dissatisfaction. On the other hand, neither can we say that empirical things should be held not to exist (*asat*), since we experience them, interact with them, and, in terms of our ego-sense and desires, often identify with them. This was a position staked out by Śaṅkara with a view to avoiding the dangers he believed were explicit in Vijñānavāda Buddhism. As far as Śaṅkara was concerned, Vijñānavāda proffered the view that all presumably material objects were merely products of the imagination (*abhūtaparikalpa*). For the Advaitin, however, we can make distinctions between cognitions that have been caused by objects and cognitions that are either erroneous or encountered in dreams (Gupta 2003: 105–6). And so, it would simply be misleading to construe Advaita as rejecting the concrete materiality and pluralism of the physical world in deference to the singular reality of *ātman*/*brahman*, since cognitions may either fail to comprehend something in the external world or actually reveal them (Gupta 2003: 110). Śaṅkara has, therefore, thematized an epistemological framework that cannot hold good without the reality of external objects, however less noble these external objects may be than *ātman*. We can only conclude then that Daya Krishna, in his extended evaluation of Advaita, was mistaken in claiming that Śaṅkara recovered non-dualism from the implications of his initial representation of *adhyāsa* by positing that external objects are ultimately unreal. In this assessment, Krishna took Śaṅkara's elevation of the self over the world too strongly and his affirmation of the physical reality of the world not strongly enough. In his epistemology, Śaṅkara does not dissolve the heterogeneity of the self and the world; on the contrary, Śaṅkara strongly and intentionally perpetuates this heterogeneity.

Where does this all leave us? Let us tally up our observations. First, Śaṅkara begins his exegetical efforts to reveal the truths of the *Brahmasūtra* by claiming that the true self and the material world of things and individuated beings are as different from one another as light and darkness, and cannot be identified with one another. He then rolls out a cosmological theory according to which *brahman* is, at best, an indescribably indirect cause of the material world, but should not be mistaken for the latter. After that, he describes a psychology of cognitions in which there must be modification of the "inner sense" either by sense-organ contact with external objects or internal feeling or deliberation in order for the self to be cognizant of anything other than itself. Next, Śaṅkara formulates an epistemology that strictly ties knowing cognitions to external things and sharply distinguishes between this supposedly correct view of *pramāṇa*-s from those who would deny that there are objects outside the mind.

All these positions, taken together, cannot in any respect support the view that Śaṅkara was some sort of overarching metaphysical monist. In fact, his metaphysics is a dualism, par excellence. There is a uniform, eternal, and spiritual *ātman* that is entirely devoid of internal or external differentiation, change, and relation. There is also the world of physical existence, characterized by pervasive differentiation, change, and causal connection. The latter may be impermanent and the former may be eternal, but that does not mean the material heterogeneity of the world can be disregarded, either for the everyday person or the Vedic expert seeking release. So, Śaṅkara's Advaita is not a thoroughgoing metaphysical "non-dualism" or "monism" at all. It is, instead, a commitment to the idea that the *ātman*, the self, is never two things. This means that there is not more than one self in all reality, which is the light that is shed on all the states of awareness in all sentient beings, and which is in no fashion internally structured. For all of his protestations about Sāṃkhya thought, Śaṅkara has borrowed Sāṃkhya terminology, maintained Sāṃkhya categorical distinctions with only some adjustments, and used Sāṃkhya arguments in some of the most crucial junctures in his interpretive works. In fact, Śaṅkara's only fundamental philosophical disagreement with Sāṃkhya regards the latter system's claim that spiritual consciousnesses are many (*puruṣa bahutva*). The *Sāṃkhyakārikā* argues that this must be the case because different individuals are born and they die at different times and exhibit different karmic capacities, but all are beings with consciousness. Śaṅkara denies that a plurality of many selves can be supported by scriptural interpretation, and argues that differentiation must be external and not internal to spiritual substance. After all, spiritual substance, in order to be eternal, can admit of no composition. However, besides this disagreement, Śaṅkara holds fast to the thoroughgoing difference between self and matter. Śaṅkara's Advaita is, in a variety of ways, a kind of Sāṃkhya with a transcendental and unitary *ātman*.

This conclusion is, I realize, bound to be a provocative one, though I think it is fully supported by all that Śaṅkara argues. However, I would now hastily add that I do not believe this fact dilutes the philosophical radicalism of either Śaṅkara's own thought or the developing tradition of Advaita in the larger context of Indian philosophy. The radicalism of Advaita, even when recast as I am suggesting here, operates on several levels. For one, the view that there is only one unitary *ātman* and not one in a real plurality of spiritual selves was a decidedly minority one in Brāhmiṇical circles. Not only was the plurality of spiritual selves staunchly defended by practically every other school of Brāhmiṇical thought for centuries by then and after, but several other major schools of Vedānta were established in part to make greater accommodations to this plurality than the Advaitins did. Second, there were some fairly daunting implications for both the traditional Brāhmiṇical notion of *karma* and for the character of *mokṣa* or liberation that followed from Śaṅkara's formulation of *ātman*. Included in these implications were the inferences that *karma* and rebirth must in the final sense be metaphorical teachings and that the *ātman* itself was never actually imprisoned in reborn and re-dying bodies, but was always free (Deutsch 1973: 67–80). Added to all of this were the considerable philosophical difficulties with Śaṅkara's formulation of the self, only a few of which are mentioned here. Many centuries of Advaita commentary were required to further refine the Advaita view of the relation between *ātman*, mind, senses, and world that rarified the former enough to allow it to be plausibly considered a unitary and indivisible reality. And so, considering Śaṅkara to be an overarching metaphysical dualist, as I do, does not in any way diminish the ingenious and profound ways in which he proclaimed that all of us share, at bottom, one and the same subjectivity. My inquiry in this chapter only seeks to make necessarily lucid what meaning the term "Advaita" has for Śaṅkara's thought. For him, what is "not two things" is the self alone, not the irreducible opposites of spirit and matter. Here, I am in basic agreement with the way Daya Krishna qualified the meaning of "non-dualism" in Śaṅkara's Advaita, even though I think those qualifications go farther than he did.

Philosophically speaking, I don't think that the system of Advaita, whether it be Śaṅkara's version or those of his successors, is viable. For one thing, as Mohanty and many others contend, Advaitins provide us with no satisfactory explanation of how the world of multiplicity, activity, and finitude could have either unfolded or appeared from a unitary, causally inert, and eternally changeless self. If one is going to be a dualist, the Sāṃkhya philosopher, who sticks to their guns in maintaining the almost complete and inexplicable independence of both spirit and the physical world, is at least more consistent. Moreover, even if it was once possible, in many though certainly not all philosophical traditions, to defend the complete distinctness of consciousness and the body, I don't think this can be credibly accomplished anymore. Even other Brāhmiṇical schools had more nuanced positions on this issue than the Advaitins did. But to deny that physical development and physical limitation or trauma themselves produce and attenuate consciousness simply ignores too much evidence from our experience, much of which was known to the ancients and more of which has been established by biology and neuroscience in the last two centuries. Third, the specifically Advaitin conception of personhood, which maintains that the most real thing about us is the thing that is least human, has implications both experiential and socio-moral that give too little importance to the phenomena of individual growth and social change. The "practical Vedānta" of modern Hindu thought is, for the latter reason, much more appealing than the classical mystical variety. All that said, the radicality of the Advaita view performed a vital function in the history of Indian thought, as most radical views which compel a sufficient number of serious thinkers do. It challenged the other schools of Indian thought to their respective cores. Advaita forced every other persuasion of Brāhmiṇical philosopher to think far more carefully than they often previously had about the relationship between our deepest inwardness and the world in which we find ourselves.

2

The Abode of Recognition

Memory and Selfhood in Classical Nyāya Thought[1]

This chapter will attempt to demonstrate that the strongest defense of the continuity of self-consciousness given by classical (*prācīna*) Naiyāyikas against Buddhist critiques can be found in what are effectively phenomenological arguments that connect the capacities of recognition and memory with the notion of *ātman*. In brief, the predominant Buddhist accounts of memory insist that its conditions and influence on experience can be described without recourse to a continuous and unitary self-consciousness, and it will be argued that these accounts are insufficient as explanatory models. What classical Nyāya philosophers call recognition (*pratyabhijñā*) and recollection (*pratisaṃdhāna*) provide us with a much more convincing model of how both epistemic recognition and what is referred to in modern psychology as "autobiographical memory" are made possible. This finding will hardly secure the entire fund of classical Nyāya ontological and soteriological commitments regarding *ātman*. But it will, if successful, buttress the notion that a continuity and unity of the subjective capacities of self-consciousness, whatever its nature and tale of emergence, makes better sense in describing our experience than a Buddhist theory that analytically denies the reality of any such self-consciousness.

Allow me first to briefly locate my position in the context of classical Nyāya-Buddhist debate. The Naiyāyikas offer a variety of arguments attempting to establish their particular conception of the self against various Brāhmiṇical schools as well as contra the denials of Cārvāka (Materialism) on the one hand and Buddhism on the other. Their individual arguments have differing degrees of strength. I think that the more closely Naiyāyikas tended to espouse epistemic and what I am here dubbing "phenomenological" arguments, the better they fared, while more strictly ontological arguments proved to be far weaker. Hence, when classical Nyāya insisted against the Materialists that the presence of *ātman* made the difference between a living and dead body, or when they maintained against the Buddhists that psychological qualities must inhere in selves just as properties inhere in metaphysical substances, I think these defenses of *ātman* were their weakest and the most susceptible to refutation. If the reality of selves can only be established in a substance ontology akin to that of classical Nyāya, then such arguments pointing to a predication regress in relating qualities to substances as were given by the Mādhyamika Candrakīrti or the Advaitin Śrīharṣa will always cast a considerable pall of doubt over that ontology. If the only defenses against the argument that the inherence (*samavāya*) that glues a quality to a substance must inhere in another level of inherence *ad-infinitum* are the ones Gaṅgeśa offers, namely that qualities can be known as self-characterized (*svalakṣana*) before they are located in a substance, and that inherence relations are natural (*svabhāva*), these represent, as Stephen Phillips has pointed out, significant concessions and susceptibilities in relation to the Buddhist arguments (1995: 208). However, the Brāhmiṇical Logicians were on stronger ground when they insisted, rebutting the Materialists, that we are primarily aware that we are having cognitions not just by observing our body but through self-conscious awareness. They are also more secure when they turn back the Buddhist doctrine of the auto-apprehension (*svasaṃvedana*) of awarenesses by pointing to evidence that not all awareness-events are apprehended, and whether such apprehension takes place depends on the dispositions and agency of self-consciousness. I highlight the arguments surrounding memory, recognition and continuity here because I believe they are philosophically the strongest of Nyāya defenses of *ātman* against both the Buddhist critiques and their rival depictions, and my aim here is to demonstrate why this is so.

What I think the Buddhist-Nyāya arguments on this issue point up is what it means for an awareness-event to be experienced as a memory, what sorts of phenomena an experience presents to us in order for us to regard it and treat it as a memory and not some other kind of experience. The ontological status of the self, as well as what is remembered, are, within the confines of this restricted argument, less important than what sorts of experiences memory requires in order for it to be the kind of experience we take it to be. On examination, it will be found that the scholastic Buddhist representations of memory and its relation to self-consciousness, given that the latter has not only no causal role in remembering, but only a quasi-logical and not really any phenomenological status, render their descriptions unsatisfying. On the other hand, Nyāya portrayals insist that self-consciousness can be found to play both phenomenological and causal roles in our experiences of memory. In fact, I take the latter characterization to apply to Nyāya explanations of consciousness in general, namely that they give credence to everyday phenomenological experience, and insist at the same time that there is no such thing as a "qualitative" experience that lacks a causal explanation.[2] Understood in this light, I believe what we will find is that the mainstream Buddhist models simply do not provide us with an adequate description of those experiences we call memories. This is precisely because these accounts lack what the classical Nyāya depiction offers, namely an actual and not just a fictive self that experiences and owns the recollection and an "abode" (*saṃdhāna*) in which a memory lives its life. The latter feature of their theory of memory and its relation to self-consciousness lends, it will be seen, a special vivacity to the Nyāya-Vaiśeṣika portrayal of the embodied and individuated *ātman*.

In the *Ātmavādapratiṣedha* section of his monumental *Abhidharmakośabhāṣya*, Vasubandhu devotes a chapter to refuting the Tirthika (probably Vaiśeṣika) conception of *ātman*, during which he deals with Nyāya objections to the theory he defends. In the Sautrāntika model he advocates in this text, Vasubandhu enumerates the causal conditions necessary to make a mental event (*citta*) a memory. A memory occurs when a mental event is 1.) causally connected to a previously experienced object, 2.) inclined toward a previously experienced object, 3.) found to discern an object similar in form to the previously experienced object, 4.) accompanied by some resolve or habit in relation to the previously experienced object and 5.) not inhibited by any intervening emotion that would change the nature of the psychophysical factors that support it, thus occluding the memory (*Ātmavādapratiṣedha* 4.1 Deurlinger 2003: 96). One of the first notable aspects of this causal itinerary of a memory, and one which Vasubandhu spends a good portion of the chapter defending, is the relative passivity of the process. Memories "occur" (*vartate*) as mental events in a certain causal series, and when we speak as if a mental event exercises some agency in "cognizing" (*vijñānati*) a previous experience, that agency only applies to its own capacity to causally pass some similar (*sādṛṣya*) impression of an originally experienced object onto a succeeding cognition in the stream, like one echo of a bell causing the next or one flame of a fire giving rise to another (*Ātmavādapratiṣedha* 4.3, 5-6; Deurlinger 2003: 97–8, 99–100). Cognitions become distinct from one another because their causal factors are complex and varied. Different formations (*saṃskāra*) are impressed onto each cognition by its specific outer and inner causal antecedents. This explains in a general way why one cognition may be a perception and the next a memory as well as why when a monk remembers a woman, he will feel revulsion while when a layman remembers one, he will be filled with various kinds of delight (*Ātmavādapratiṣedha* 4.7; Deurlinger 2003: 101). So, the subjective variation in qualities of memories depends not merely on the thing initially experienced but on previously accreted personality factors that make their impressions on the memory. The only agency ascribed to a memory on this view is its ability, once made, to affect other successive cognitions. But since each memory is only momentary, that causal influence is at best indirect. The passivity of memories is underlined by Vasubandhu when he argues in detail against the Vaiśeṣika contention that a self must own his memories or be the agent that actively recalls something from his past. Vasubandhu replies that the notion of self as "owner" or "sender" of a cognition can just as well be replaced by the notion of the memory's cognitive cause. Even condition 3.) above, requiring that a previously experienced object be recognized in order to be recalled, is accounted for by the fact that each cognition apprehends its own (*svasaṃvedana*) mode of awareness. But even this recognition is not the owner of the memory, for Vasubandhu. it was that originary cause that "sent" the impression the memory holds, and thus, to wit, "owns" it (*Ātmavādapratiṣedha* 4.3 Deurlinger 2003: 98).

But even metaphorically referring to an initial apprehension of an object as the "owner" or "sender" of a succeeding memory of it, though it is fairly consistent with the notion of mental causality the Buddhist espouses here, strains credulity. Let us track a conscious continuum of a very familiar sort through Vasubandhu's route. A previous temporal state and position of the aggregate "person" that became "me," at a very young age, learned to play a musical piece on a given instrument. In subsequent performances of this piece, the succeeding "persons" in the stream do not experience the exact same tones that resounded when the piece was first played correctly nor the exact way the fingers moved on the instrument on that initial occasion. Instead, similar impressions of those tones produce a mostly latent inclination to play the piece with different instruments. When I might happen to see the same type of instrument I have learned to play in subsequent experiences, this latent inclination is, given the causal history of my collective aggregates, activated. Well, we can see how conditions 1.), to some extent 3.) and 4.) outlined by Vasubandhu have been met. We may also include 5.) to this list if there happen at the present moment to be no experiential factors overwhelming recall of the initial experience, if attention is not occupied or distracted. But what of the Buddhist account of what inclines the current state of the aggregated configuration I label "myself" to recall the original piece? Naiyāyikas too acknowledge the role played by the accretion of mental formations that build our habits and dispositions, but in the Nyāya account, such formations can remain latent in the first place because they are enduring features of an enduring self. In the Buddhist view, the original performance itself, the inclination to replay the piece it created, and the causal power of each episode, according to the "theory of the momentariness" (*kṣanavāda*) of experiences Vasubandhu adheres to, disappear even before the very next mental event occurs. Such momentary and self-enclosed cognitions explain little of how a disposition like the inclination to play previously learned music on an instrument can in fact leave any imprints (*vāsanā*) on any succeeding cognitions. This is because the causal history that is being relied on to explain our experience is for all intents and purposes cancelled at the very instant it arises with each new cognition. But, more problematically, it makes even no metaphorical sense to say that this original moment of performing a learned musical piece "owns" my successive memories or "sends" them to me, for, since that moment is forever gone, it has the capacity neither to possess nor to send anything. Memories may be initiated by first experiences, but the original experience does not in any intelligible sense "own" the memory, the memory is instead owned by the person I am now who remembers it. A more likely scenario of remembering a childhood experience of learning and playing a piece of music must involve some levels of agency and interest in the recollection that have some intentional continuity with the past. In such rememberings, an active effort is made by a consciousness with both a past and a set of accreted interests to retrieve past experiences. The "needs" and "interests" of a person who experiences themselves as the delimited center of a specific narrative history, and not the original event or a set of isolable latent inclinations which are automatically triggered, like lights in a pinball machine, seem behind an effort to actively retrieve past experiences and relate them to the present.[3] The Naiyāyikas were most avid about such examples of active learning, and even understanding the utterances of others, having already learned a language, to illustrate such continuity and agency. Now, pointing this out is not a denial of the fact that memories have their beginnings in originary experiences. Nor does it deny that the Buddhist framework we find in Vasubandhu's arguments do explain certain kinds of memories referred to in contemporary discussions as episodic, or even reflexive memories that allow me to avoid painful sensations like touching hot pans in the kitchen as a child. It is the active retrieval of memories in recollection, and what circumstances "incline" us to retrieve them, that are at issue here. And Vasubandhu's passive architectonic seems ill-equipped as it stands to describe the lives of memories and the agency persons exercise in accessing them.

Now, one possible defence of Vasubandhu's portrayal has been offered by his translator, James Deurlinger. He emphasizes that Vasubandhu's causal model of memory is not meant to serve as means to "translate sentences, without loss of meaning" from the personal level of memory description into an objective causal explanation (Deurlinger 2003: 240–1). Instead the issue is whether some notion of a continuous and unitary metaphysical *ātman* is required for an objective causal description of memory. This approach also permits Vasubandhu, according to Deurlinger, to "explain away" memories in which the Naiyāyikas insist one remembers oneself having an experience and not merely the object content of that experience (2003: 243–4). The problem is that such attempts to reduce self-consciousness by "explaining it away" only end up reducing the putative value of the explanation being offered.

Vasubandhu himself, as Deurlinger admits, does not deny that we construct personal narratives and conceptually relate those narratives to memory experience within our conventional activities (*saṃvṛti*) and daily business (*vyavahāra*). And so Vasubandhu agrees that the phenomenological fact of our experience of memories requires some account. In Deurlinger's interpretation of Vasubandhu, our experience of personhood is a conceptual product. In Deurlinger's formulation, our phenomenological sense of self comes from, or is a product of, our conceptual activity.[4] In Ganeri's representation, Vasubandhu may qualify as something of a "cautious reductionist" insofar as he recognizes that our sense of self is, while surely not any irreducible real, "a structural property of the stream" of consciousness (Ganeri 2012: 67).[5] But what Vasubandhu actually goes about showing is that this finished product of self-conscious narrative is not itself in any way a causal support of the experience of memory. Thus, the self-consciousness we experience ourselves as having in memories does not really play any role in them, but is only a contingent by-product; Vasubandhu's arguments, that is, demonstrate that we can have memories, and explain them, without having self-consciousness.[6] But it is the phenomenological actualities of our experience that the reductive explanation was intended to account for in the first place. That is to say, the Buddhist reductive explanation of memory is parasitic on our actually experiencing ourselves as persons with autobiographically significant memories, and it is precisely this experiencing that should be findable somewhere, in whatever transformed way, in the causal story. That means that the phenomenological experience of memory is only causally explained when all of its attendant features have too been causally explained. Were the debate about the self merely one of when it plays a role in a causal account of memory, either at the beginning or the end of the process, then it would not be the reality of self-consciousness that presented the problem, but only its order of emergence and how it is constituted. But Vasubandhu and the Buddhists go farther by positing that the autobiographical significance of our memories and the self-consciousness for which they seem to be meaningful are false constructions, they are neither the cause nor the effect of the phenomenal or experiential process, and so are not real in any way. But in this event, it is not just the case, as Deurlinger believes, that sentences about our personal memories and experiences suffer "loss of some meaning" when an attempt is made to "translate" them into causal sentences, but rather that narrative memories and self-consciousness don't translate into the causal story at all.

The implication of this would seem to be that the reductive causal explanation of memory we find in Vasubandhu is not in fact an explanation of our experience of memory and putative selfhood. Instead, he renders what we sought at first to explain in our experience, and what indeed first prompted us to seek for an explanation, to be merely illusory. If there is no translatability of causally connected states to those recollective and autobiographical experiences whatsoever, then the causal explanation has lost its very status as an explanation of the latter, and is instead a story unto itself. Even if one wants to argue that autobiographical memory and self-consciousness are "constructions" as the Buddhists do, such arguments do not themselves imply that such constructions are always erroneous. And if Vasubandhu wishes to call self-consciousness an experienced construction, an account of how it is constructed would seem to be in order.[7]

Of course, the Buddhists could and did deny that even the seemingly most familiar of our experiences, even ones with phenomenological currency and the ability to motivate our actions, needed to be acknowledged any existential status so long as they could be subjected to conceptual analysis. In the works of the eleventh century Yogācāra logician Ratnakīrti, we find both an ingeniously argued denial that a purported continuous self can actually exercise any causal efficacy and a refutation of the Nyāya conception of recognition. Ratnakīrti's fascinating *Kṣaṇabhaṅgasiddhiḥ Vyatirekātmikā* operates with the time-honored Buddhist definition of existence as the causal capacity of a thing to bring about an effect (*arthakrīyakāritva*). Its aim is to defend the contrapositive thesis that no non-momentary (*akṣanika*), or permanent, (*sthira*), entity can bring about either successive or non-successive (*kramākrama*) events. That is to say, it is impossible for the permanent *ātman* to be a cause of anything. Nevertheless, it is possible for us to conceive of a permanent *ātman* without thereby giving some tacit acknowledgment to the existence of any such self. The arguments proffered for the first proposition are relatively standard Buddhist fare for Ratnakīrti's time. The supposed causal power of a non-momentary or permanent entity, especially when such causal power can be attributed to that entity's "autonomous essence," cannot itself be temporalized. This leads to the consequence that the causal power of a permanent entity must either continue to produce a single effect at all times without being interrupted or its causal power must always be held in abeyance (*Kṣaṇabhaṅgasiddhiḥ Vyatirekātmikā* 83.20; 84.11; McDermott 1970: 20–1). In the former case, the effects would not be successive but themselves eternal, and in the latter, no effects would be produced, both eventualities proving Ratnakīrti's thesis. To the Naiyāyika rejoinder that the self only produces effects in cooperation with other accompanying factors, Ratnakīrti responds that, since the occurrence of accompanying impermanent factors is required for the permanent *ātman* to be efficacious, this only proves that causal powers really belong to those impermanent factors, rendering the causal power of the self nil (*Kṣaṇabhaṅgasiddhiḥ Vyatirekātmikā* 83.22-29; McDermott 1970: 21).

At this point, in the debate dramatized by Ratnakīrti's text, Nyāya logicians invoke their axiom that, if something is found to be 'non-existent' (*abhāva*), no affirmation or denial of properties in it can be true, since nothing can be asserted or denied of a non-existent entity. That is to say, a non-existent entity cannot even come to awareness (*buddhi*) in order to be negated. My argument about why a sufficient causal explanation has to account for all the phenomenological data in experience in the preceding paragraph very much follows along such lines. Therefore, Ratnakīrti's thesis that "no non-momentary entity produces subsequent or non-subsequent effects" commits the fallacy of *aśrayāsiddhi* or "unestablished support," since an entirely non-existent entity could not causally produce a concept of itself in thought.

From here on, Ratnakīrti spends much logical effort to actually deny that we can conceive of the illusory specter of the self when we attribute actually experienced qualities to it, qualities that are supposedly analytically contrary to the former's nature. When we think, that is, of what causal productivity entails, we realize that, by definition, causal productivity requires change, and this implies that causation cannot be predicated of any unchanging substance, which is precisely what the supposed "self" would be. This means that we can form an imagined awareness (*vikalpabuddha*) of an unreal self, but only under two very restricted conditions, namely when real attributes are denied to inhere in it, or when unreal attributes are affirmed of it. However, as Ratnakīrti insists, an unreal entity like the self cannot serve as the subject term of any sentence that predicates real attributes to it (*Kṣaṇabhaṅgasiddhiḥ Vyatirekātmikā* 81:23; McDermott 1970: 18). This latter, seemingly overly radical, consequence was one Ratnakīrti apparently felt forced into by the textual Nyāya opponent. The Naiyāyika tries to demonstrate in the course of debate that a non-momentary entity must have at least one causal capacity, that of causing awareness of itself by being the *pratiyogin* or object of negation in a proposition denying its reality and causal efficacy (*Kṣaṇabhaṅgasiddhiḥ Vyatirekātmikā* 81.8; McDermott 1970: 18). Ratnakīrti is adamant that permanent entities cannot be objects of knowledge (*pratitiviśaya*) in any logical sense. While they can under the restricted propositional conditions outlined above be conceptualized, they cannot be even the potential loci of real attribution, and so are not even potentially knowable or determinable in that way *Kṣaṇabhaṅgasiddhiḥ Vyatirekātmikā* 81.18; McDermott 1970: 18). Therefore, to propositionally affirm that an unreal entity possesses real attributes would garner for the unreal entity a kind of thinghood and capacity to influence real things (*vastubala*). And, unlike conceptual constructions that do possess such capacities and so might actually be usable, a "non-momentary entity" does not have these (*Kṣaṇabhaṅgasiddhiḥ Vyatirekātmikā* 82.22; McDermott 1970: 19–20). The grovel of all this logical subtlety reveals that we do not even become conceptually aware of self-consciousness by wrongly associating actually experienced attributes or activities to it. We posit selves only by rightly denying their reality or by engaging in manifest sophistry by associating other unreal qualities with them. And so it is here, in one of the great Buddhist treatises meant to establish momentariness and with it the falsity of enduring subjectivity and recollection, that we have actually wandered about as far away from experience as we can possibly get. For what is most presciently to be denied, the self, turns out not to be a misinterpretation of our actual experience in the world, but only a rather elementary logical error.

This obliteration of even our phenomenological sense of selfhood also erases our sense of recognition. Ratnakīrti invokes precisely the very unintelligibility of permanence, or non-momentariness, the two terms being precariously treated by him as equivalent, to reject any relation between the two. In order for there to be recognitive synthesis (*pratyabhijñā*) of a particular cognition by a unitary (*ekatva*) self-consciousness, that self-consciousness must be non-momentary. But Ratnakīrti believes he has both positively and negatively established that permanent entities are incapable of serving as causes and are thus by definition unreal. Therefore, not only is the supposedly permanent, unitary self-consciousness a non-entity, but so is the supposed identity that attaches to the recollected object, the impressions of which actually change through time. Therefore, since the unity and identity of both the self and the recognized object fail the reality test, no such thing as the recognitive synthesis that requires them both in order to take place ever occurs either (*Kṣaṇabhaṅgasiddhiḥ Vyatirekātmikā* 84.3: McDermott 1970: 21). We have now reached a stage of

Buddhist argumentation, far more extreme than what we find in Vasubandhu, in which not only self-consciousness is a fabricated construct, but the recognition and memory we believe ourselves to experience do not correspond to anything that actually happens to us either.

Ratnakīrti's treatment takes up standard Buddhist lines of attack against the most vulnerable feature of the Brāhmiṇical conception of the self, namely the belief that it is permanent and thus itself unchanging. The unchanging nature of permanent entities, and the willingness of a number of Naiyāyikas to defend the isolated casual capacities of an unchanging substance, did provide the Buddhists a legitimate target, and we will return to this issue in our direct discussion of the Nyāya position soon. But even so, there is at least one fairly obvious questionable equivocation in Ratnakīrti's polemic. This equivocation is connected to a fundamental characteristic of the Buddhist's own ontological picture that renders even the reductive explanations they prize highly problematic. As has already been mentioned, Ratnakīrti seems to consistently treat the terms "non-momentary" and "permanent" or "unchangingly stable" as synonymous. But it is far from clear that these terms should be held as such. One can surely attribute some temporal continuity or stasis to phenomena without thereby insisting that such phenomena never change. So reticent were most of the Sautrāntika-influenced schools of Buddhist thought to regard continuity as having any temporal endurance out of fear that it would covertly sneak the notion of *ātman* back into ontological discourse, they too quickly embraced the metaphysics of momentariness without appreciating the kinds of problems momentariness saddled their own views with. As one very powerful Nyāya counterargument would run, even in order to transmit memory traces that bore some features similar to the original experience onto the succeeding moment, a cognition would have to retain qualities sufficiently redolent of the initial experience in order to evoke a memory of the latter. This itself seems to witness to some stasis rather than thoroughgoing momentariness. Furthermore, even if the Buddhists insist on maintaining that memory changes every moment, at least some of their presented content must change in ways so minute as to be phenomenologically indistinguishable from previous cognitions so that a memory trace can be said to "resemble" in any meaningful way an original cognition. Such indistinguishability also calls the utter uniqueness of each moment seriously into question. Now, to some degree, this outcome may be attributed to contingent features in the evolution of Buddhist thought. Alexander von Rospatt has demonstrated that the term *kṣana* in early Buddhist commentaries probably meant at most only "a very short time," as the literal sense of the word suggests. But as it was elaborated upon by Buddhist scholastics, it came to mean more and more "the duration of mental entities" which was thought to be "the briefest conceivable event" (Rospatt 1995: 110). I thus very much agree with Tao Jiang, who, following Paul Griffiths and Lambert Schmithausen, argues that this Sautrāntika-Vaibhāṣika conception of momentariness beset their explanations of experience with a "problem of continuity" (Jiang 2006: 41–6). This problem, at least within the Buddhist context, was only effectively dealt with by the Vijñānavāda notions of the "ego-creating" and "storehouse" consciousnesses (*manonāmavijñāna* and *ālayavijñāna*). These latter models served as a basis wherein a seemingly stable identity could be manufactured and where the seeds of experience could be both stored and transformed. But since, historically, the momentariness-continuity debate was the most prominent one between the Buddhists and Naiyāyikas, it is the contours and details of that debate we take up here. We find the Buddhists' own model on this accord faring rather poorly as a recounting of our experience. Ratnakīrti's pointed critique of the Nyāya depiction of permanent selfhood does not make his own portrayal of momentariness or memory any more credible.

Let us turn at this point to the account of the connection between memory and self-consciousness given by the classical Naiyāyikas. In the *Nyāyasūtra* of Gautama, contact between the organ of internal sensation and the self is said to have six signs or marks, which are states of awareness and disposition, namely desire, aversion, will, pleasure, pain and cognition (*Nyāyasūtra* 3.1.17: Thakur 1967). Vātsyāyana elaborates by pointing out that memory always accompanies desire, aversion and will, since these all are affects referring to an object already cognized, while memory contingently accompanies pleasure, pain and cognition, for these may also be about the present (*Nyāyasūtrabhāṣya* 3.1.17: Thakur 1967). I will return below to the significance of the assertion being made here that psychological states are properties of the self and not the body, as this is most important in ascertaining precisely what kind of self is being presented by the Naiyāyikas. Since, at any rate, it is the case, in the Nyāya view, that cognitions belong to the self, a cognition that we recognize as a memory, whether it is about real experiences or illusory ones, must be some kind of synthesis of experiential content such that both the content and the experiencer exhibit some continuity with the original experience. This, according to Nyāya, is precisely where the early Buddhist conceptions akin to those we find in Vasubandhu fall short. In Vasubandhu's framework, all that appears to be constitutively required for us to call an experience a memory is its reception of the causal capacity (*samārthya*) of an initial cognition, the mediation to it of object content that bears some similar features to the object first encountered, the influence upon it of latent, accreted dispositions to react to the object in some way, and the auto-apprehension of the cognition to identify itself as a memory. But under these limited conditions, the seventh century Naiyāyika Uddyotakāra argues, such a cognition will not be able to ascertain whether the object content to which it refers is similar to the object initially experienced, for which a comparative judgment would be required. Nor could we make the determination that the memory content had been caused by the initial cognition, which would again require an additional act of judgment. Nor could we tell that the self-consciousness that now remembers is the same self-consciousness that underwent the original experience, for which is required an act of self-apprehension (*Nyāyavārttika* 64: Thakur 1967). In other words, in Vasubandhu's framework, a putative memory might be aware of content similar to that of the previous experience, but would not be aware of the originary experience, nor that it was caused by the initial experience, nor that the memory belongs to anyone. For distinct cognitions, such as perceptual and memory cognitions, to simply succeed one another in a causally connected series cannot elucidate how a first-person comparison of originally experienced content with presently remembered content, adducing their similarity, occurs. Nor is an attempt in the Buddhist recounting, according to Vācaspati Miśra, to tell us how self-consciousness is even falsely attributed to both experiences (*Nyāyavārttikatātparyaṭikā* 211: Thakur 1967). Now, I think it can be conceded to the Buddhist that some memories may simply occur to one out of the blue given the right conditions, and therefore an agent is not required to explain their active retrieval. However, even in such cases, the apprehension of the cognition as a memory would seem to require the recognition, however brief, that the content experienced is from the past and that this very content relates to my own experience in a narrative continuity. The virtue of the Nyāya account on this score is in its insistence that if a recognition of the similarity of past experience to present experience and a continuous self-consciousness are part of our experience of memories, then they also must be part of the causal story, however dramatic their retranslation into causal terms may in fact be (*Nyāyavārttikatātparyaṭikā* 213; Thakur 1967). The Buddhist portrayals we get in Vasubandhu, and certainly in Ratnakīrti, write such experiential products out of the causal story entirely, suggesting that the bare-bones causal account is reality and the experiential one is a conspicuously arbitrary logical fiction with no explicable connection to reality.

So then, what sorts of synthetic acts, rather than merely passive receptions, factor into our experiences of memory? Most pertinent for our discussion is what is referred to in the *Nyāyasūtra* as recognition and what Vātsyāyana and other commentators label recollection. There are two factors that enable the recognition that we associate with experiences of memory. The first is the aforementioned recognition that the object first experienced and the object being represented now are similar, or are of the same kind, and that the object now recalled was in fact caused by the original perception of it. The two image-experiences then still need to be, not merely temporally and causally connected, but also recognized or apprehended as being so connected. Thus, whether the two experiences being apprehended here are perceptual or conceptual, their apprehension, as Vātsyāyana points out, requires one witness (*sākṣin*) of the various perceptions (*Nyāyasūtrabhāṣya* 3.1.14: Thakur 1967). And this brings us to the second component of recognition, namely the apprehension that the self that originally experienced something is the same self who now remembers it. Vātsyāyana here uses the locution 'recognition of memory' (*pratyabhijña smṛtasya*) to describe a process through which the distinct cognitions "this was seen" and "I saw this" are synthesized in the present awareness that "what I saw before I am seeing now." And it is only with this second act of synthesis that we have a robust memory, since an unexperienced memory is not what we refer to when we report instances of remembering (*Nyāyasūtrabhāṣya* 3.1.14: Thakur 1967). Structurally speaking, in memories, it is not merely the content of the original experience that is remembered, but also the "I" that was aware of the original experience, and it is that very "I" which is also identified as the one having the memory. Otherwise, the memory itself will remain unconscious. Now, there are memories that remain unattended and of which we may for long spells remain unconscious. Surely there are also perceptual experiences that are not apprehended. But the recognition that we experience in a conscious remembrance requires awareness of the temporally distinct contents of experience and memory and the self-consciousness that undergoes them both. Indeed, Naiyāyikas would eventually insist that the awareness of the self in recollective experiences is itself perceptual, and not just inferred, where the inner sense is in direct contact with the self and its attendant qualities.[8] The examples Nyāya philosophers often use to buttress these characterizations of what is required for robust conscious memories are ones that most directly implicate self-suggested or self-determined acts of remembering, such as ardent study in which a purposeful effort is made to clarify a previous perplexity that a learner now wishes to understand more thoroughly. But such examples do serve a distinct purpose in their debate with the Buddhists, who, as was seen above in Vasubandhu's case, offer a mechanical and passive construal of memory in which agency is merely metaphorical, and oddly metaphorical at that.

Of course, none of this detracts from the fact that the Achilles' heel of the Nyāya position is their insistence that *ātman* is permanent. The Naiyāyikas may be more or less on better footing in defending the unity or numerical identity of the self vis-à-vis memories of originary experiences. But the permanence of the self seems much more vulnerable to the Buddhist critiques. There is something undeniably compelling about the Buddhist's pressing rejection of the idea that we experience in either everyday activities or mystical pursuits anything permanent, including most of all a permanent soul. Ratnakīrti also makes a weighty point about the implications of the Nyāya *ātman* being an eternal and changeless substance in its own right, for it is immensely difficult, at best, to defend the idea that such a self, considered in isolation, plays a causal role in the bodily and experiential life. A self that can be both analytically and substantially separated from the body and assumed to be in itself changeless throughout all its experiences and contingently attendant (*āgantuka*) qualities, does at least raise the specters of dualism and the so-called inner, conscious "homunculus" that rules over the unconscious body. In fact, to me, such a self does not even appear to be consistent with much else in Nyāya's own larger ontology. For example, *ātman* was believed to be akin to other non-material substances like "ether" (*ākāśa*) which pervaded all of space but did not impede material objects within it from contact with one another. Thus, the Nyāya self was said to be pervasive of (*vyāpnuvān*) the entire body of an individual. But this would imply that the space that the self-substance occupies grows as the body grows. Furthermore, although cognitions and dispositions like pleasure, pain, desire, memory and will were asserted to be properties of the self and not the unconscious body, these qualities undergo constant change in the interaction that takes place between the embodied self and the world in which it lives. The fact then that the self's extension and dispositions change in accordance with physical changes of the body render Nyāya's essentially religious conviction that the self is immaterial or non-physical at least questionable even on their own terms. But still, the Buddhist contention that there is no continuity to self-consciousness at all, that the only really-existent phenomena of awareness are causally connected momentary bursts of cognition, veers off in an equally untenable direction. I have always therefore thought that the most defensible position regarding self-consciousness lies somewhere in the middle of these opposites. Self-consciousness on this moderate view would be a biologically, psychologically and socially emergent, but causally explicable, phenomenon of embodied existence, subject to change and cultivation but also, in terms of its capacity for *prakāśatva* or subjective luminosity enduring under favorable circumstances.

However, all these drawbacks having been admitted, the forgoing comments at the same time highlight one of the most important strengths of the Nyāya conception of self. While the Buddhists are presented with a target when Naiyāyikas speak of the permanent, changeless self considered on its own, the fact of the matter is that Naiyāyikas far more often articulate a conception of self in relation to its qualities and situated, embodied experience. Chakravarthi Ram-Prasad observes that the Nyāya arguments regarding the relation of the self to memory, serving as a constitutive condition of the latter, reveals that their notion of *ātman* is decidedly "thin," much like the Kantian "I think" which must possibly attend all my experiences (Ram-Prasad 2012: 34–7). For him, this "thinness" of the self in the Nyāya arguments demonstrates that their conception of self cannot be deployed in any sort of Western analysis of personhood. While I do agree that the references to self in the Nyāya arguments about memory are confined to its constitutive role and are thus thin, I would argue that the Nyāya notion of self is, in the larger context of their philosophy, far more robust, and much closer the Mīmāṃsā views than the Kantian. After all, Kant's self is never known in itself, but only as it appears, and while it is a constitutive condition of the conceivability of experience, we don't know exactly what relation it "really" has to its experiences. The same is true of the self's relation to its acts, for in Kant's ethical thought, the self is the condition for the possibility of freedom, but that same self is not the body that moves or the aspect of the empirical character effected by motives. We are dealing in Nyāya, on the other hand, with not merely a thin conception that involves only formal epistemic subjective unity or pristine spiritual identity. Naiyāyikas surely do deny that the self can be identified with the body, but they also emphatically assert that the self's pleasures, pains, attractions, aversions, desires and cognitions belong to it, are located in it, and not in the physical body. The Nyāya self, that is, is a self-with-cognitions, a self-with-desires, -aversions, -pleasures, -pains and will, a self-with-sensations, a self-with body, indeed a self which cannot be conscious at all but for embodiment. In its correspondingly thick relation to memory, it is the self-consciousness spoken of by the fifth century Vaiśeṣika Praśāstapāda as well as Gautama. In their definitions, memory results from the uniquely occasioned contacts (*saṃyogaviśeṣa*) between self-consciousness and inner sensation which are caused by the perception of associated signs (*liṇgadarśana*) bearing similar features to the originary experience, and in which there is concentration (*pranidhāna*) of the mind on the originally experienced object and its context (*nibandha*). A memory is strengthened by the intensity (*patipratyāya*) of the original experience, the will (*icchā*) to remember and often repetition (*abhyāsa*) which reinforces earlier sedimented impressions (*Nyāyasūtrabhāṣya* 3.2.41: Thakur 1967 and Jha 1963: 656–57). If, that is, self-consciousness is tied to memories, it is tied to them through its dynamic engagement with a rich, varied and living past, present and future. And for their part, memories are not only momentary mental explosions in the ever-flowing causal stream of bundled pieces of personality, but also have lives, and live those lives, in the creatures that are their homes.

Notes

1 This essay first appeared as "The Abode of Recognition: Memory and the Continuity of Selfhood in Classical Nyāya Thought." in *Hindu and Buddhist Ideas in Dialogue: Self and No-Self*. Irina Kuznetsova, Jonardon Ganeri and Chakravarthi Ram-Prasad, eds. (London and New York, Routledge, 2012), 115–28. It has been reprinted here with the permission of Taylor and Francis, Ltd., U.K.

2 I believe that this is one of the most significant contributions Nyāya has to make to modern theories of consciousness. The modern phenomenologist, since Husserl, attempts to envelop causal arguments within phenomenological ones, while the contemporary reductionist philosopher of mind tries to get rid of 1st person qualitative explanations in favor of 3rd person causal ones. Partly because Nyāya thought originated in a philosophical framework quite different from the current one with its lingering Cartesian legacies, Nyāya is one model that, to me, clearly demonstrates the virtues of retaining and interconnecting both phenomenological and causal accounts of consciousness.

3 I have in mind here the work of recent developmental psychologists such as Susan Engle (1999) and earlier observations by Frederic Bartlett (1932), 211–12. Engle's work of course is committed to distributive bodily models of memory combined with environmental and social context, but does require the agency of the self in a robust sense as contributing to recollection.

4 In a pivotal section of *Ātmavādapratiṣedha* 2:1, Deurlinger argues that when Vasubandhu says of the self that it is *prajñaptitas asti*, this means that it is "real by way of a conception" rather than that it is 'real as a conception' (2003: 30). The implication of this for Deurlinger is that our notion of the self, while based on the aggregates, is a real result of conceptual activity and so does play a role in the causal process of producing our experiences of ourselves.

5 It must be noted here that Ganeri blends the account of the *Ātmavādapratiṣedha* with the arguments of the *Triṃśatikā* invoking storehouse consciousness and *manonāmavijñāna* to defend this representation. But the model of consciousness found in the former text cannot, in my view, be used to defend the arguments of the

latter text being considered here. Therefore, when Ganeri argues that Vasubandhu holds an unconscious theory of the ownership of self-consciousness, this is, while a perfectly fair description of the views defended in the *Triṃśatikā*, not what we find being argued about ownership in the relevant parts of the *Ātmavādapratiṣedha*.

6 We see in the larger context of the *Abhidharmakośabhāṣya* 9 how Vasubandhu argues against the Pudgalavādins that the self can be derived neither from a substance (*dravyataḥ*) nor from a concept (*prajñaptitaḥ*). Deurlinger's reconstruction of Vasubandhu turns out to be more defensible than the latter's actual position. In my estimation, for Vasubandhu, in this treatise, self-consciousness is simply a false construction and plays no role in the causal process of cognitions, which makes him, as mentioned, a stricter Sautrāntika. This is especially apparent in the way Vasubandhu argues against the Naiyāyikas.

7 This point is made also in the context of modern discussions by Sue Campbell (2003).

8 Udayana argues for knowledge of the self through direct internal perception. We thus find Udayana positing that our immediate awareness of the self is incontestable (*atiprakṣepa*) since it is not derived by other means of knowledge and bears no relation of a feature to that which it qualifies: see Tripati (1989: 743).

3

How Do We Sense?

Imagination in Buddhist and Nyāya Thought[1]

Ever since at least the rise of Western Orientalist scholarship of Indian thought in the eighteenth century, and perhaps before that, people have often turned to the Indian philosophical tradition for certain kinds of spiritual insight. And one of the supposed hallmarks of such Indian spirituality has often been the notion that the world as a whole, and our own fragile and passing lives, are only the illusory appearances of an eternal spirit. And there is much we can find in the Indian tradition that supports the notion. The ancient *Upaniṣad*s alluded to a unitary *brahman* that was the source of all life, and held the world to be the creation of the gods' permeating magic (*māyā*). Over time, the capacities to extend the space of the world and make distinctions between individuated phenomena within it were increasingly attributed to the mind. Vedāntic philosophers like Vidyāraṇya would interpret this *māyā* of the world to be the result of the powers of consciousness to veil (*āvaraṇaśakti*) the true nature of reality and project (*nirmāṇaśakti*) its own multifarious forms upon it (Gupta 1988: 59–60). The seminal Yogācāra Buddhist philosopher Vasubandhu argued that there are two fundamental proclivities of consciousness that manufacture all the heterogeneity in our awareness. For him, these were its karmically inherited ability to impute "non-material ideations" (*abhūtaparikalpa*) like colors, textures, and flavors into sensuous experiences and its habit of distinguishing between the "grasped" and the "grasper" (*grāhya-grāhakā*), the false self and false objects of our experience (Kochumuttom 1982: 45–57, 136–8). According to these trains of thought, where there is the ability to create and multiply images in our awareness, it is there we can find the roots of all delusion.

On the other side of the Indian philosophical spectrum, we are often told were the realists, such as adherents of the Nyāya, Vaiśeṣika, and Mīmāṃsā schools. While these hard-headed thinkers would of course agree that human beings can have fantasies and erroneous cognitions under certain circumstances, our senses and cognitions in most waking experiences are in sufficiently reliable direct contact with things to give us a sound understanding of and practical orientations in an actual world. What we must do, according to these realists, is to develop an epistemology sophisticated enough to distinguish between genuinely perceptual cognitions and cognitions that are tainted by mis-apprehension, fallacy, and fantasy. For the early Nyāya philosophers and for the first representatives of New Nyāya in the twelfth century, when a thing with certain features causes a sensation of that very thing with those features, we have a genuine perception, uncontaminated by errors that might happen to infuse other cognitions. And so we have, supposedly, a paradigmatic divide in Indian philosophy between thinkers who believe that the illusions created by consciousness represent a transcendental and existential problem that must be overcome by meditative insight and those who hold that illusions are a practical pitfall that can be avoided by a proper ordering of conscious inquiry. But the opposition of these schools entails an often hidden but deep agreement between them. They concur that consciousness deceives us about what is real when it produces and projects images of its own onto our experience.

For the last several centuries in Western thought, the power of consciousness to manufacture and project its own images onto our experience has frequently been construed in more positive terms. For Kant, the power of imagination (*Einbildungskraft*) is responsible for some basic kinds of synthetic perception and forms of judgment without which we could not have cognitive experiences or communicate our ideals to one another. In Husserlian phenomenology, imagination can extend the powers of intuition into the grasping of all that is possible, and so lays the basic groundwork for abstraction. In modern analytic thought, P. F. Stawson invited us to think more precisely about not just the differences between imagination and perceptual recognition, but also about their affinities with one another. At first glance then, compared to the classical Indian tradition, recent Western reflection on the relationship between imagination and sensation has become more subtle and sophisticated than a rough-and-ready dichotomy between them. However, B. K. Matilal has demonstrated, more than thirty years ago, that this is not the case. In fact, he revealed, the idea of imagination (*kalpanā* or *vikalpa*) was given a highly technical sense, first by the fifth- and seventh-century Buddhist Logicians Diṅnāga and Dharmakīrti and then by subsequent Nyāya philosophers, and became a pivotal issue in debates between them about the character of perception (Matilal 1986: 309–30). Indeed, the introduction by Diṅnāga and Dharmakīrti of the distinction between "non-imaginative perception" (*nirvikalpapratyakṣa*) and "imaginative perception" (*savikalpa pratyakṣa*) was accepted by both Mīmāṃsā and Nyāya realists, among whom were Kumārila, Vācaspatimiśra, Śridhāra, Udayana, and Gaṅgeśa, within only a few centuries of its initial thematization (Shastri 1964: 437–42 and Taber 2005: 76–8).

What I wish to accomplish in this brief chapter is twofold. The debate between middle-period Buddhist and Nyāya thinkers over *vikalpa* is well known and rehearsed in both classical commentary and contemporary secondary literature. Though I will recapitulate the most important elements of this debate here, my primary goals are the following. I first wish to demonstrate how the Buddhist Logicians Diṅnāga and Dharmakīrti and then Vācaspatimiśra specifically conceived of *kalpanā* as operating through cognitive synthesis. This is a crucial aspect of the Indian philosophical treatment of "imagination" between the fifth and tenth centuries of the Common Era. In significant contrast to the conceptions of imagination as producing illusory cognition mentioned at the beginning of this chapter, which in a variety of ways forged distinctions between things and persons, the Buddhist and Nyāya debates about imagination depicted it as a cognitive activity that joined features or images to one another. This is an especially important aspect of *kalpanā* or *vikalpa*, centrally pertinent to theories about how these effect specifically perceptual awarenesses. After this aim has been fulfilled, I will move on to argue that the Nyāya account of how imagination informs perception, making it both more robust and often more accurate, is philosophically preferable to the Buddhist narrative. The latter, even in Dharmakīrti's nuanced rendition, creates such a gap between imagination and perception that the latter becomes too impoverished to even be considered either perception or a candidate means of knowing (*pramāṇa*). By contrast, what we get from the Nyāya commentary of Vācaspatimiśra is a compelling depiction of how imagination, aided by memory, can and often does help us to ascertain what is real.

By the very meaning of the word, Diṅnāga tells us perceptions are free of imaginative construction (*pratyakṣaṃ kalpanā poḍhaṃ*) (Hattori 1968: 26–7). This immediately raises the question of what imaginative construction consists in for Diṅnāga. Diṅnāga immediately clarifies by claiming that *kalpanā* or the "structure" of imaginative cognitions attaches words and predicates to the sensuous content which itself is non-linguistic, and so the imagination must be a distinct cognition from the sensuous (Hayes 1988: 134). His commentator Dharmakīrti informs us that what *kalpanā* supplies is the "establishing basis" (*sādhana*) for taking the sensory content to be a determinate thing, by appending the color "blue," for example, to the linguistic locus "pot." In other words, when it takes up the content of a sensory cognition, an imaginative construction provides the equivalent of an inferential mark (*liṅga*) which exhibits enough commonality (*samānya*) with other things to enable us to identify a perceptual object as an instance of a general type. That is to say, whatever commonality we derive from our perceptual experience is not acquired from the perception proper, which is nothing more than the contact of sensed content with the sense organ (*pratyakṣa*) (Hayes 1988: 139). Since perceptual content is restricted to what externally stimulates the sense organs (*nirbhāsa*), which Diṅnāga and Dharmakīrti insist is unique (*svalakṣana*) at every moment, any cognition that is characterized by commonality (*samānyalakṣana*) must be supplied with that commonality by another cognition. Imagination then is a cognitive contribution, a cognitive supplement to perception, which forges commonalities between sensory content that the sensory content doesn't exhibit. For the Buddhist Logicians, then, we do not see commonality, we imagine it.

It is crucial to note here that, despite the seminal distinction they end up making between *nirvikalpa pratyakṣa* (imagination-free perception) and *savikalpa pratyakṣa* (imaginative perception), it is only the former that genuinely counts as a perception (*pratyakṣa*) for them. The imaginative perception is really a kind of perceptual judgment. In *savikalpa pratyakṣa*, a robust identification is made of the object through the attribution to it of general features which are not derived from the *nirvikalpa pratyakṣa*. Syntheses of various kinds are going on in imaginative perception which are all cognitive, because they are manufactured by other cognitions, and linguistic, because inferential marks are linguistic. By contrast, a non-imaginative perception involves no cognitive synthesis; it is merely the contact of a sense organ with external content. Furthermore, the imagination-free and imaginative perceptual cognitions are considered not only numerically distinct by Diṅnāga, but also causally distinct with regard to how they arise. An imagination-free perception, for the Buddhist Logicians, is both the sense-organ contact with external content and the auto-apprehension (*svasaṃvedana*) that the cognition taking place is a *nirvikalpa pratyakṣa*. An imaginative perception, again really a perceptual judgment, is the synthetic identification of a perceptual object brought about by other cognitions and the auto-apprehension that this is a *savikalpa pratyakṣa*. These two cognitions have different epistemic results (*pramāṇaphala*) because they have distinct contents (Hayes 1988: 140–1). The imaginative perception does have as part of its content an indirect and diluted sensory core, but only via the recollection of the initial sensory cognition. That is to say, the sensory core of a *savikalpa pratyakṣa* is not directly the external content, but the remembered sensory cognition that had the external content as its object.

This does not, however, entail for Diṅnāga and Dharmakīrti that *kalpanā*, despite what the word itself may often suggest, are illusory or counterfeit cognitions. The Buddhists here sharply part company with other Indian philosophers who consider cognitive distinctions to be in their entirety the product of fabrications or falsifications that obfuscate reality. Of course, in many cases, the commonalities between things that are projected onto sensory content or are inferentially imputed to concepts might be erroneous for the Buddhist Logicians. But the kind of imaginative constructions that Dharmakīrti has in mind are often entirely free of error (*abhrānta*), particularly when they can lead to successful action (Hayes 1988: 139). For instance, as Dharmakīrti's own exegete Dharmotarra has it, during the night, when in need of warmth, we may see some unique flare off in the distance, and our *kalpanā*, our imaginations that have been sedimented by dispositional habituation (*saṃskāra*) and memory, may lead us to believe it is a fire (Dreyfus 1997: 358). If we approach that flare and are able to warm ourselves by it, imaginative constructions that have been obtained via cognitions other than strictly sensory ones have allowed us to accomplish a needed aim. Imagination, therefore, can give us access to what is real. Indeed, it was vital for Dharmakīrti to maintain this possibility that imaginative constructions may lead us to truth. After all, the Four Noble Truths of Buddhism, on the Buddhist Logicians' model, cannot possibly be sensory cognitions, since they identify general causal links common to many different experiences of suffering, desire, contentment, and practice, and so they must be products of inference. If *vikalpa* could in the right conditions underpin correct inferential cognitions for us, then *kalpanā*, when they create perceptual judgments, could prompt us to respond appropriately to sensuous experience. However, Diṅnāga continued to insist that even scriptural statements supported by correct practical inference had to be confirmed by direct meditative experiences before full faith could be put in them (Hayes 1988: 238–9). It is simply necessary then, in order for us to make good epistemological sense out of our experiences, to draw a clear line of demarcation between sensory cognitions that are uniquely qualified (*nirvikalpa pratyakṣa*), and judgments that have been supplemented by other imaginative cognitions (*savikalpa pratyakṣa*) and thereby exhibit enough commonality for determination, identification, and verbalization.

Dharmakīrti, coming two centuries after Diṅnāga and facing down Nyāya and rival Buddhist objections to the system of the preceptor, did provide some needed nuance to the model. Some additional explanation was required for how perceptions infused with imaginative construction were actually formed, and how it was at all possible for them to trigger successful conduct. Repetition of certain kinds of directly sensory experience, aided by memory, is called upon for this. We have recurrent experiences of events that nature brings about, such as the reliably curative effects of herbal medicines or lightning and thunder being produced by a storm (Dreyfus 1997: 148–9). No two lightning flashes are identical, and so, as Diṅnāga avers, there is no specific commonality (*samānya*) that is discernible from the direct contact of lighting with our eyes or the subsequent thunder with our ears. But the sensation of more than one flash of lightning in a storm and the accreted experience of many lightning storms accumulate in memory. Aided by our collection of previously acquired psychological habits and dispositions, imaginations configure similarities among these memories and impute features that resemble (*sādṛṣya*) one another among these many experiences. The next time we sense lightning and thunder, these are associated in *savikalpa pratyakṣa* with previous encounters with storms, and this enables us to take whatever actions are appropriate in the circumstances. This is an ingenious attempt to create a linkage between our direct sensations and perceptual judgments which allow us to react to our sensory experience correctly. Nonetheless, it is still the case for Dharmakīrti that the reactions we have to our experiences are reactions to the mere resemblances (*sādṛṣya*) between things produced by imaginative perceptual judgment, for there are no real commonalities (*samānya*) between things that can be ascertained from direct sensory cognitions.

The tenth-century philosophical polymath Vācaspatimiśra, in his capacity as a Nyāya exegete, concurred with the basic distinction between cognitions that were merely sensory cognitions and cognitions infused with imaginative construction. However, he did not find the Buddhist Logicians' framework sufficient to account for our perceptual experience itself or for how imaginations could accurately enhance our perceptions. He conceded the Buddhist contention that the initial moment of a perceptual experience often does not produce a recognition of things as qualified by common properties (*viṣeśyaviśeṣanābhāva*). This concession was supported by Vācaspati's admission that the initial sensory cognition is not aided by memory, and memory, as we shall see, will be needed to explain how determinate perceptions arise (Shastri 1964: 451). This did not entail for Vācaspati however that the properly perceptual cognition remains in this nebulous condition. Briefly stated, Vācaspati held that Diṅnāga and Dharmakīrti had created such a gap between direct sensation and sensation-with-imagination that no causal bridge could connect them. For Diṅnāga, the *nirvikalpa pratyakṣa* was direct, always novel and unique, and, because it lacked any predication relations, was in principle insulated from error (Hayes 1988: 138–9). By contrast, *savikalpa pratyakṣa* for the Buddhists was always indirect, always involved a forced imposition of imaginative content on a sensory core imported from another cognition, and, because it projected commonalities into experience, could only be indirectly true at best and may be frequently false at worst. There was, in Vācaspati's view, no real synthesis added to directly perceptual cognition by the Buddhist theorists, but instead they allowed for synthesis only within indirectly perceptual cognition where all commonality was manufactured. A more convincing depiction of our everyday experience, for Vācaspati, had to explain how imagination could help us to directly perceive more sharply and robustly.

Now, Vācaspati was not exclusively aligned with Nyāya thought, as he wrote powerful commentaries on Yoga and Advaita Vedānta as well. He therefore doubtless felt more at liberty to make adjustments to foregoing Nyāya commitments about perception than Naiyāyikas who were more doctrinally committed to principles laid down in Gautama's *Nyāyasūtra* and early commentaries. And in making these adjustments, Vācaspati courted risks that might make devoted adherents of Nyāya reject his views. After all, the standard classical Nyāya position on the commonalities (*samānya*) between things is that they were natural features of these things. There are, as the standard story goes, natural (*jāti*) features of things like extension, color, shape, texture, and other qualities that actually were inherent (*samavāya*) in the makeup of things and made them their natural ingredients (*dravya*). Therefore, for *prācīna* Naiyāyikas, the similarities we perceive among things are actually in those things, and so commonalities can be directly sensed in phenomena without any need of imaginative enhancement. The Nyāya philosopher loyal to the school's principles should presumably have simply defended this standard position, for it is the very bedrock of Nyāya realism (Chakrabarti 2000: 4–5). In fact, for those who would continue to defend the pristine clarity of early Nyāya theory, it is a shame that innovators and Navya-Nyāya thinkers accepted the divide between *nirvikalpa pratyakṣa* and *savikalpa pratyakṣa* at all, as Vācaspati did. That acceptance, after all, eventually led to hyper-abstract systems like that of Gaṅgeśa, which made direct perception so nebulous and "immaculate" that it was incoherent. Still, Vācaspati's analysis of the connections between imagination and perception was ingenious and worth philosophical consideration. This is so precisely because he does not, like the New Nyāya thinkers, veer off into abstractions, but offers appealing concrete examples for his views.

Vācaspati first reformulates the definition of perceptions, characterizing them as brought about not only by direct sense-organ contact but also by whatever comes into the range of a perceptual cognition (*yad eva indriyajasya jñānasya gocaras tat pratyakṣaṃ na tv indriya saṃbaddham*) (Shastri 1964: 452). This expanded definition leaves room for previous cognitions to fill out an initially indefinite sensation. Previous cognitions, memories, have made us familiar with the relational ties between things and their properties. And so, we remember that certain features are always found in certain kinds of things, and these memories can be relied on for the imaginative content that takes features (*dharma*) as "marks" of the things in which they are found (*dharmin*). Thus, as Vācaspati tells it, while the initial sensory contact with a thing makes us aware of a form (*rūpatayā*), the memory bringing the imagined relation between presently sensed features and recalled things mingles with the sensation, while the sensation continues to be experienced, such that the object we finally fully perceive possesses a form (*rūpitayā*) (Shastri 1964: 456). Imagination, on this view, must surely assist, through memory, in the delivery of "marks" or common features through which things are recognized, lest a sensation be only an unnoticed physical interaction between a thing and a sense organ. But, so long as the features or qualities of things in question are in fact seen in the sensory cognition, then imagination helps us to perceptually recognize what a thing is with the aid of things remembered that resemble the present. Imagination lends to perception what Monima Chadha has rendered a "recognitional capacity" (*saṃvid sāmarthya*) (2006: 336).

The examples that are used to demonstrate the Nyāya representation of the perceptual process are instances of our perception of things like sandalwood for the classical thinkers and a jasmine flower for Jayanta. We may, in an initial moment of sensation, see something with a certain shape and a certain color, but still not be sure what it is. We have in this moment a sensory stimulation, to be sure, but nothing that can be called a perception. In an often unapprehensable instant, a memory is triggered of a previous experience in which something with a quite similar shape and color was perceived, alternatively, a fragrant kind of wood or a fragrant flower (Shastri 1964: 464, 467). The contribution of this memory is amended to the sensuous experience of the initial instant, and gives our sensation an anticipation of sweet fragrance. Unlike the presently directly sensed shape and color before us, the sweetness is not directly sensed, but imagined through a memory. All the same, the additionally projected sweetness leads to the perceptual identification of what we see as sandalwood or a jasmine flower. Now, whether this perceptual identification is correct or not may often have to be proven by subsequent action. We may approach the object, pick it up and find that it is something other than we anticipated. All perceptual cognitions, definite or indefinite, could turn out to be erroneous upon attempts at corroboration, a fact that even Dharmakīrti was compelled to admit. However, Vācaspati insists, such initial sensations aided by imagination and memory are also quite often correct. And when they are, we can be justified in claiming that the imagination-equipped memory contributes to, enhances, and verifies our perceptions. Indeed, in many cases, we cannot make an intelligible claim to have perceived something without the help of imagination.

At first glance, Dharmakīrti's example of our ability to rightly respond to medicines or lightning and the Nyāya story of how we can scope in on objects in our environment may seem effectively alike. Both allow for imagination and psychological dispositions to make an indeterminate sensory experience a determinate perceptual experience, as well as to react fittingly to the latter. And, apropos of our first aim in this chapter, both models depict imagination (*kalpanā*) as a synthetic cognitive activity, forging connections between distinct cognitions and yielding from them determinate perceptions. However, this similarity is broken at a crucial point. In the case of the Buddhist theory, the object of a determinate perception is the cognition that sensed something indeterminate, and so the sensory content is not in any way influenced by the determinate perception. All that happens in determinate perception, for Diṅnāga and Dharmakīrti, is that an originally sensory cognition gets associated with general concepts by other cognitions, and so what was originally sensed is not informed or clarified by these processes. In the specific representation we are given by Vācaspatimiśra, it is the content, the sensuous object that is associated with a memory, which in turn is illuminated and determined in an imaginative perception. It is true that later Naiyāyikas would shy away from Vācaspati's explanation, somewhat beguiled as they were by the Buddhist rejection of memory influencing an original sensation. The Buddhists did not think that memory could affect an originary sensation any more than imaginative judgment could, for memory is not involved in the initial sensory contact, and that contact, once completed, is not altered. Naiyāyikas after Vācaspati, deterred by this Buddhist objection, turned to the notion of *pratyabhijñā* or the "recognition" of substance-quality relational ties in previous experiences. "Recognition" in this sense is, for these later Nyāya thinkers, not memory, but a species of apprehension that acknowledges the association of certain features with certain things. It was opponents of Nyāya like the eleventh- and twelfth-century Advaitin Śrī Harṣa who pointed out that *pratyabhijñā* was not in any way functionally distinguishable from memory, and that many of our experiences of things that are present before us (*anubhāva*) involve remembrance (Bhandare 1993: 93). Despite this historical turn against Vācaspati by loyal Naiyāyikas, it seems to me that Vācaspati's depiction has great merit precisely because it does allow for previous memories to have a say in determining what the object of a sensation might be.

Now that it has been shown how these variant Buddhist and Nyāya accounts provided for the synthetic activity of imagination in presenting to us determinate perceptions, we can turn to which of these models is philosophically preferable and why. The Buddhist's systematic distinction between non-imaginative and imaginative perceptions cannot overcome the problem that it deprives the direct sensory experience of any cognitive value. If no feature-placement or association is present in genuinely perceptual experience, then perceptions would seem to be constantly chaotic in ways that we do not recognize as perceptual. The Nyāya model, particularly that of Vācaspati, not only appears to overcome classical Nyāya doctrinal worries, but also offers a portrayal of our sensations as fittingly layered and textured, and the suggestion that other kinds of cognitions mingle with sensations in order to make them more robust should not over-worry us.

In the formulations of Diṅnāga and Dharmakīrti, much emphasis was laid upon the inerrancy of sensory cognitions. Some of this emphasis came from Buddhist doctrinal commitments to the priority placed on direct experience over reason and heresay, as well as the assumed pristine nature of meditative perceptions. Some of it also doubtless was owed to the general Indian philosophical tendency to represent direct perception as the king of all means of knowledge, the most reliable source of our justified beliefs and the origin to which the objects of every other kind of knowledge, inferential or testimonial, could be traced. Still other elements of it were a Buddhist version of a widely accepted acknowledgment that some sensory cognitions were not clear, but vague and amorphous enough to prevent us from identifying their objects. All the same, the borders between *nirvikalpa pratyakṣa* and *savikalpa pratyakṣa* are so starkly drawn by the Buddhists, even taking into account the sophisticated nuance of Dharmakīrti, that it is impossible for our other cognitions to touch or make anything out of our sensations that we could intelligibly speak of or communicate. What the Buddhists do, in fact, is to transform the acknowledgment that some of our sensations are vague into an insistence that all of our sensations are vague. But now, for the Buddhists, vagueness is not a flaw, but is instead the result of the ever-changing and uniquely caused state of reality at any given moment. The ever-changing and uniquely caused state of things is of course Buddhist metaphysical doctrine. But when that conviction is applied to perceptual theory, it turns perceptions into non-perceptions.

This problem resides at two levels. The first is the level of knowledge. As Matilal pointed out long ago, the Buddhist sealing off of non-imaginative perception from every possibility of predication may have insulated it from error, but it also insulated it from truth (1986: 333–9). Sensations which exhibit no determinate features whatsoever might be free from error in the very weak sense that we can say we actually have such experiences and they are direct. But it is hard to identify what is true about them. Direct perceptions do not, in the Buddhists exposition of them, fulfill any truth conditions, and their content, being in principle inaccessible to other cognitions, is epistemologically irrelevant. Inference, in fact, as Diṅnāga and Dharmakīrti have it, seems despite their overt arguments to fare better than perception when it comes to yielding knowledge that matters to us. After all, with inference, it is possible for the marks (*sādhana*) imagination supplies to be free from error (*abhrānta*) and inference can fulfill reliable truth conditions unless they are controverted in the future. On the other level, in the Buddhist portrayal, what is it that we, for instance, see anyway? We "see" indefinables succeeding indefinables in no particular arrangement. Each sensory cognition vanishes the moment it arises, none is ever directly associated with any other cognitions we have, and so their contact with our sense organs remains in toto unconscious. There is also an outright denial of perceptual commonality or continuity in Diṅnāga's and Dharmakīrti's framework, such that we never perceive the same thing from one moment to the next, never perceive anything twice, and so could never, in the strict sense, count experiences like staring, gazing, or even contemplating as perceptual. These kinds of untoward consequences betray the fact that, in conceptualizing the pristine character of "non-imaginative perception" as they have, the Buddhists are defending a doctrine of reality more than they are explaining our everyday experience. Now, the Buddhists may indeed have perfectly good reasons for being skeptical about and critical of the "overcrowded ontology" of systems like classical Nyāya, particularly when the latter claims we can directly see things like the class-types of everything before us (cowness) and the non-presence of everything not before us (absences of elephants in a room). But addressing the threat of metaphysical overpopulation by eliminating the possibility that any continuous creature can stay in any abiding place even for two moments pays too high a price to be able to elucidate our experience.

Now, it is certainly the case that the shortcomings of Diṅnāga's theory were identified perspicaciously and corrected ingeniously by the ninth-century

Mīmāṃsā philosopher Kumārila (Taber 2005: 96–112). However, Kumārila's insistence that the initial perceptual experience could not be in error loosely resembled the Buddhist position, whereas Nyāya's insistence that any perceptual cognition can under certain circumstances be erroneous seems more sensible. And that accounts for the focus in this chapter on Vācaspatimiśra. Vācaspati's innovations on the classical Nyāya notion of perception did, as we have seen, raise some doctrinal specters, but they were hardly insurmountable. In fact, the most basic of early Nyāya commitments about perception may have left fruitful room for sympathetic thinkers to push past the bewildering numbers of nested metaphysical "universals" that loaded down classical texts. Those scholars who are wary of the *nirvikalpa/savikalpa* dichotomy being taken too far by Naiyāyikas may have some warrant for their trepidation too, as it led some Navya giants like Gaṅgeśa to postulate airy definitions of sensation that struggled to cover all cases (Phillips 1995: 135–6, 210–11). Despite Diṅnāga's disingenuous invocation of the Nyāya definition of perception as "non-verbal" (*avyapadeśyam*) in his own definition, all this meant for the first Naiyāyikas was that immediate sensory contact was not verbalized, not that it was non-verbalizable (Chadha 2006: 334). Further, the Nyāya philosophers were not compelled by the classical causal connection between imagination-free and imaginative perception to deny that other cognitions could influence that connection, for the initial sensation was only the main instrumental cause (*kāraṇa*) of the determinate perception and not its only and sufficient cause (Chadha 2006: 335). And besides, who are we to deny new generations of philosophers from reforming classical positions when needed? We should not prevent Buddhist thought or Nyāya thought from learning and growing any more than we should prevent other traditions from doing so.

What is philosophically appealing about Vācaspati's presentation of this issue is that he allows for the possibility that initial sensory cognitions may be either unnoticed or indeterminate and for other cognitions, often unconsciously, to buttress them with associations that have already been learned. And this buttressing enhances our perceptual experience, makes it clearer, and, indeed, structured. And we should feel compelled, even by the most mundane of everyday experiences, to allow for the fact that genuinely perceptual experience exhibits structures. When either an adult or a very young child lifts a cup of cool water to their mouth, the coolness and any flavor that has been added can be sensed in the fluid, and not in any other random locus of which we are also perceptually aware. When either an adult or a very young child looks at the trunk of a tree, they see ridges and patterns that are inlaid into that trunk, and not spread out across the foreground or sky. When a very young child sees an adult plucking at the strings of an instrument and hears the sounds being emitted from it, the child reaches for the strings so they can make the sounds too, rather than looking for some other place in the room for the chords she hears. Now, memories and acquired psychological capacities need to be called upon in many cases to explain all these forms of recognition, but it would be straining credulity to claim that these recognitions are not really perceptual. And such recognition can be evoked without recourse to "concepts," which is one reason I have resisted translating *kalpanā* or *vikalpa* as "concept" in this chapter. Our recognition of these "arrangements" or "configurations" (much more literal senses of *kalpanā*) in initial perceptual encounters can be stored in memory and recruited in later experiences to help us anticipate and identify initially vague objects in later experiences. Vācaspati's model may even profitably be put into dialogue with modern brain studies, which strongly support the proposition that initial visual stimulations are identified very differently by us depending on which neural pathways—which other cognitions—the first stimulation is associated with. The greatest advantage, then, that Vācaspati's narrative of imaginative perception has over Diṅnāga's and Dharmakīrti's is that it demonstrates how imagination does not always and only obfuscate or distort our sensory experience, but instead often helps us to rightly sense.

Note

1 Early versions of the arguments presented here were posted by me on "The Indian Philosophy Blog" on May 17, 2014 http://indianphilosophyblog.org/2014/05/17/imagination-in-perception/

The version of the essay found in this chapter is original.

Part II

Madhyamaka Buddhism

4

What Kind of Designation Is "Emptiness"?

Reconsidering Nāgārjuna's MMK 24:18

Ancient Texts and Modern Hermeneutics

The plethora of interpretations that the second- and third-century founder of Madhyamaka Buddhism, Nāgārjuna, has been the focus of over the past seventy-five years of Anglophone scholarship has been, to say the least, breathtaking. In the 1950s, T. R. V. Murti (1960) likened the philosophical project of Nāgārjuna to that of Hegel, refuting wayward, partial metaphysical systems in order to develop a comprehensive conception of the absolute. Shortly thereafter, Richard Robinson (1964) portrayed Nāgārjuna, along with the following Mādhyamika commentators in India and China, as proto-analytic philosophers, who exposed the logical flaws in all metaphysical systems without positing another metaphysical system of their own. Mervyn Sprung (1979) fundamentally agreed with the anti-metaphysical depiction of Nāgārjuna, but thought it could best be understood through comparison with the later Wittgenstein than with early analytics. In a combination of deepened scholarship on the debates current with Nāgārjuna in Indian Buddhist circles and a subtle consideration of belief and language, David Kalupahana (1986) envisioned Nāgārjuna through Jamesean pragmatism. At this point, somewhat suddenly, a series of readings emerged that aligned Nāgārjuna's presumably thoroughgoing anti-metaphysical perspective with Western Derridian or deconstructionist social critiques, readings such as those found in Harold Coward (1990), G. T. Martin (1995), and B. S. Yadav (1992). Since then, a wide range of literature has proliferated which casts the second-century monk-philosopher in a number of contested but related shapes, as for example a classical skeptic (B. K. Matilal 1986), an anti-realist (Mark Siderits 1980), and an anti-essentialist (Jay Garfield 1995).

There is of course a straightforward sense in which all of this modern re-interpretation is quite expectable. It is after all something of a hermeneutical truism that every thinker, being rooted in their environing cultural and historical contexts, will be drawn in the first place toward ancient and classical texts that the modern can somehow see as speaking to those contexts, and will read the ancients into the more familiar modern frameworks. However, as Andrew Tuck (1990) noticed even as early as three decades ago, when these various Anglophone receptions of Nāgārjuna become so widely variant, the question arises as to whether modern readers were being too dismissive of Nāgārjuna's own context and too loosely importing his thought into forms of philosophical significance quite different from his own. In this chapter, I would like to emphasize this very point by focusing on a verse from Nāgārjuna's *Mūlamadhyamikakārikā* (hereafter abbreviated MMK) that a number of important commentators have strongly fixated on for the last five decades.

I believe there is always a need in intercultural philosophical scholarship to go as far as one can in determining the meanings and significant contexts within which ideas arose and were discussed, and only then reflecting on our own evaluations of those ideas. It is not so much a matter of pretending that we are not in the hermeneutic situations that we are in, or pretending that we can escape our own cultural environments and dawn the cloaks of the ancients. After all, recovering the ancient meanings of terms and reconstructing the contexts in which those ideas flourished is often beyond our capability, given the somewhat limited textual and historical materials that are at our disposal. It is rather more of an effort to temporarily resist the temptation to affect an unmediated translation of ancient thought into the coils of contemporary philosophical problematics, to momentarily set aside our own assumptions and expectations, and listen and read before we speak and write. This seems to me an important imperative of the intercultural philosopher, and more than that, an opportunity to learn from and reflect on unanticipated directions and possibilities of thought.

The MMK verse that will be the focus of our efforts will be the acclaimed 24:18.[1] The text of the verse reads:

yaḥ pratītyasamutpādaḥ śūnyatāṃ tāṃ pracakṣmahe /
sā prajñaptir upādāya pratipat saiva madhyamā //

This stanza has been taken by modern interpreters to be the preeminent verse in Nāgārjuna's entire philosophical corpus, precisely because it offers a succinct and clear definition of *śūnyatā* or "emptiness," and emptiness indeed appears to be the most important concept of Nāgārjuna's major works. Robinson (1964: 49) identifies "emptiness" to be the "key term" in the entire "expressional system" or "symbolic system" of language, which at once linguistically identifies the non-systematic nature of referential language but is itself no referent. Sprung (1979: 18) saw both Nāgārjuna's original verse and Candrakīrti's commentary on it as establishing that "emptiness" is the supreme "non-cognitive" notion, and also pointing to the general underlying "nominalist" character of Madhyamaka philosophy of language. Kalupahana (1986: 340), in certain respects drawing on Sprung's view of "nominalist" expressions being "everyday language" but in others departing strongly from it, takes 24:18 to be mainly declaring that the term "emptiness" is a mere "convention" describing Buddhist praxis. Garfield (1995: 304–5), translating the text from Tibetan and pressing for a powerfully "anti-essentialist" understanding of the entirety of Nāgārjuna's thought, also follows Candrakīrti closely in coming to the conclusion that "emptiness" should be considered a "social convention" rather than a referential term. According to David Burton (1999: 90), who critiques the fundamental principles and approaches of Nāgārjuna's philosophy, this verse equates "emptiness" with a mere "conceptual construction" (*prajñapti-sat*), and the full implications of this compel us to conclude that Nāgārjuna, in rejecting even any substantive reality to the most basic of Buddhist ideas, is himself a kind of pan-illusionist. Despite the striking variety of these readings, one conviction they share is that, because MMK 24:18 annunciates a definition of "emptiness," and because the very nature of Nāgārjuna's entire philosophical stance is found in his thematization of "emptiness," the proper interpretation of this stanza will provide one with the guiding concept of Nāgārjuna's thought. MMK 24:18 has then become, so to speak, the "central verse" of the "central philosophy" (Madhyamaka). However, I will argue in this chapter that the modern readings of this stanza, and Candrakīrti's exegesis on which they are based, are for a number of reasons, flawed.

Before I proceed to identify the problems I have with one classical and many of the modern readings of MMK 24:18 and suggest a solution for them, I will take a moment for a brief disclaimer. The arguments I will make in this chapter, though they ultimately will reflect my own conclusions, are not all original. Though I part company with him on a few important issues, I am heavily influenced by the scholarship of Joseph Walser on this matter. With regard to some components of the relevant evidence and analysis, I will spend less time than Walser does discussing them, and with respect to other components of the case, I will devote more time than he did. I reiterate some arguments that he has made here, but also contribute a number of my own insights. The final conclusions of the investigation are my own, and on the most central interpretive question, my position differs from Walser's. But I have found that, in the thirteen years that have elapsed between the publication of Walser's study *Nāgārjuna in Context* and the writing of this version of my essay, the Anglophone philosophical scholarship on Nāgārjuna has not taken nearly enough note of Walser's historical and textual findings. By adding my own reflections, emphases, and conclusions to Walser's, I hope to bring the philosophical implications of the perspective I will defend here into the light.

The Puzzles and Readings of MMK 24:18

The first line of MMK 24:18 is grammatically and conceptually straightforward and unproblematic.

yaḥ pratītyasamutpādaḥ śūnyatāṃ tāṃ pracakṣmahe /

Whatever is conditionally co-arisen, we proclaim that to be emptiness.

Here, emptiness (*śūnyatā*) is declared by all Mādhyamika Buddhists (*pracakṣmahe*) to be a synonym for, to have the same meaning as, the fundamental principle of causality, explained in the Buddha's own *Discourses*, of "causally conditioned co-arising" (*pratītyasamutpāda*). In the larger scope of the entire *parikṣa* of MMK 24, to which we shall later return, the Mādhyamika finds himself in the position of needing to clarify what is meant by the term "emptiness" because his opponent (the text's *pūrvapakṣin*) believes the idiomatic meaning of the word to be "non-existence" or "absence" (*abhāva*). If, the *pūrvapakṣin* complains, the fundamental causal principle of the universe is "non-existence" understood as "emptiness," then no entity in the world, no person, and not even the Four Noble Truths themselves have any existence, and this would reduce Buddhism in total into a kind of metaphysical and practical "nihilism." Nāgārjuna, in the first line of 24:18, prepares to turn the tables on his textual Buddhist opponent by insisting that, when he deploys the term "emptiness," it should be understood to mean nothing more than that fundamental principle of causal relation that all Buddhists, Mādhyamikas included, resoundingly accept, namely *pratītyasamutpāda*. Now, this declaration of the synonymous relationship between the expressions "emptiness" and "causally conditioned co-arising" does not completely resolve matters, because, by this time, different schools of Buddhism had markedly variant models of the process and components of *pratītyasamutpāda*. However, for the time being, we can accept the sense of this first line of 24:18 as clear, with Nāgārjuna averring that the expressions "emptiness" and "causally conditioned co-arising" should be taken to mean the same thing.

The difficulty in determining the meaning of the verse is presented by its second line.

sā prajñaptir upādāya pratipat saiva madhyamā //

While the line certainly tells us something emphatically (*saiva*) about the "middle path" (*madhyamā pratipad*), it also appears to be articulating something about what sort of a "notion" or "designation" (*prajñapti*) "emptiness" is.[2] The variety of existing translations of this entire verse exemplifies the philosophical frameworks within which the respective modern readers see "emptiness" as most relevant.

> We declare that whatever is relational origination is *śūnyatā*. It is a provisional name (i.e. thought construction) for the mutuality (of being) and, indeed, it is the middle path. (Inada 1970: 148)
>
> We interpret the dependent arising of all things as the absence of being in them. Absence of being is a guiding, not a cognitive notion, presupposing the everyday. It is itself the middle way. (Sprung 1979: 238)
>
> We state that whatever is dependent arising, that is emptiness. That is dependent upon convention. That itself is the middle path. (Kalupahana 1986: 339)
>
> Whatever is dependently co-arisen, that is explained to be emptiness. That, being a dependent designation, is itself the middle way. (Garfield 1995: 304)
>
> Dependent Origination we declare to be emptiness. It (emptiness) is a dependent concept; just that is the middle path. (Siderits and Katsura 2013: 280?)

K. K. Inada's reading, commendably enough, does not tread much on the ground of modern Western philosophical issues, and instead takes the MMK as a kind of negotiation between what had become the new Buddhist scholastic "extremes." These extremes view *karma* in terms of either its "continuity" (*śāśvata*) through time and lives or its "interruption" (*ucceda*), its preclusion of a continuous self (Inada 1970: 104–5). For Inada, the twin concepts of "relational origination" (*pratītyasamutpadā*) and *śūnyatā* do not create an alternative philosophical "view" of how *karma* operates, but instead reject these views without its own "conceptual content." For him, conditioned co-arising and emptiness are just "provisional names" for the immediate experience of what comes to be (Inada 1970: 148). This use of language to reject reifying views constructed by language is a tendency of Madhyamaka that makes it so congenial, for Inada, to Zen thought.

However, for the remainder of the previous translators, a very great deal seems to be read into the compound in the second line of MMK 24:18, *prajñaptir upādāya*. We see this more in Sprung's "guiding, not a cognitive notion, presupposing the everyday" and Kalupahana's "dependent on convention" than Garfield's and Siderits's/Katsura's more literal attempts "dependent designation" and "dependent concept," respectively. But their interpretive approaches to this verse, and particularly in the degree to which they take this verse to be a key to Nāgārjuna's whole thought, betray predominantly Western philosophical concerns. Sprung, as we have seen, is convinced that Nāgārjuna is an anti-metaphysical thinker in the Wittgensteinian mold, and so his translation of *prajñaptir upādāya* takes the form of an explanation of what "non-cognitive" and "everyday" language is supposed to be. Kalupahana believes Nāgārjuna is making of emptiness a kind of Jamesean "convention," which does not in the strict sense refer to anything that can be metaphysically reified but is yet locatable within human experience and can be made into a consequential life practice. Garfield and Siderits, in distinct ways, see Nāgārjuna involved in a philosophical battle that resists somewhat perennially recurrent forms of "essentialism" and "realism." Their translations of *prajñaptir upādāya* therefore emphasize the idea that "emptiness" cannot possibly be a referring term, but must be a term dependent on the interconnected web of meanings firmly embedded within the network of language. The persisting trend to understand "emptiness" and "causally conditioned co-arising" as designations with merely conventional rather than metaphysical resonance then makes "emptiness" a powerful tool that can be deployed in contemporary academic philosophical debates. This way of comprehending MMK 24:18 has given rise to a provocatively new approach to seeing the relationship between Nāgārjuna's formulation of the "two truths" for both Garfield and Siderits. Even though MMK 25:8–10 appears to emphasize that the Buddhist practitioner wishing to attain to *nirvāṇa* must recognize the distinction (*vibhāga*) between "paramount truth" (*paramārtha satya*) and the "truth of conventional transaction" (*vyavahāra satya*), both Garfield (2010: 23–38) and Siderits (2003: 9–23) have argued that the MMK actually reduces all truths to "conventional" ones. This move seems to demonstrate that MMK 24:18 and the rest of Nāgārjuna's thought has, at least to a notable degree, been extracted from the realm of Buddhist practice, because the importance of understanding the distinction between the two truths in MMK 24:8–10 is to attain liberation. In the modern recension, the verse is employed in the service of a "semantic interpretation" instructive for modern Western philosophy of language.

This chapter certainly does not take the view that all that Nāgārjuna has to say about emptiness, causality, and language is irrelevant to modern philosophical concerns. That is surely not the case. Indeed, all of these translators and scholars have furnished abundant and important reasons for why contemporary thinkers concerned with issues of metaphysics, ethics, and the philosophy of language and logic should regard Nāgārjuna with great seriousness. However, for one thing, there can be found on occasion in some of their works, most notably Sprung (1979: 18) and Burton (1999: 95), a grudging admission that their large-scale representations of Nāgārjuna's claims cannot be found to be overtly thematized in any writing reliably attributed to the Madhyamaka founder. For the other translators and commentators here, Kalupahana excepted, there is a rather pronounced and overt reliance on the commentary of Candrakīrti, and further extended into the Tibetan tradition on Tsongkapa, in disambiguating MMK 24:18 as well as the rest of the entire treatise. Indeed, Candrakīrti's reading has become the standard and generally accepted explication of the precise meaning of Nāgārjuna's works, favored over Bhāvaviveka as well as subsequent Chinese commentators. There are understandable reasons for this preference. Candrakīrti, as we will see, provides the most thoroughgoing and detailed elucidation of MMK 24:18, and does so with a focused grammatical analysis and standard Buddhist concepts. Candrakīrti's case lends itself rather easily to modern "nominalist" and "conventionalist" positions with regard to views of metaphysics and philosophy of language as well. So the preference for Candrakīrti's representation of the MMK can be understood as a kind of modernist hermeneutical preference, and not just a preference for a particular classical commentator.

Candrakīrti and the "Standard" Reading

Nonetheless, as I have done in part elsewhere but will expand on presently, I will proceed to identify five arguments detailing why Candrakīrti's reading of MMK 24:18, as well as the modern exegesis that relies so heavily on that reading to produce the most prevalent intercultural representation of Nāgārjuna, are not, on close examination, particularly convincing. Candrakīrti's reading is, no doubt, a possible one, and one from which Indian, Tibetan, and Western enthusiasts have drawn much of great interest. However, as I intend to demonstrate, what Nāgārjuna proclaims on behalf of Mādhyamika Buddhists in MMK 24:18 is actually much more straightforward, much more consistent with the entirety of his argument in the twenty-fourth *parikṣa* of the work, and much more like similar things he says in his other works, than the balance of his modern readers have tended to think.

Let us begin with the seventh-century exegesis of MMK 24:18 found in Candrakīrti's *Prasannapadā*. After he lays out a fairly obvious explanation of the stanza's first fairly obvious line, Candrakīrti sets out to disambiguate the verse's second line.

> And on to the nature of emptiness, to that "designation depending upon" (*prajñaptir upādāya*). That very emptiness is established as a "depending designation" (*upādāya prajñaptir iti*). A chariot is designated (*prajñapyate*) as depending upon the wheels (*cakrādīny-upādāya*) and the (other) parts of the chariot. Thus, a designation depending on (a thing's) own parts (*svāṅgānyupādāya prajñapti*) does not exist in the condition of autonomy (*svabhāva*). And emptiness is whatever does not exist in the condition of autonomy. Truly, the definition of emptiness is established as that which is not in the condition of autonomy, (and is in turn) called "the middle path." That which is not in the condition of autonomy surely does not exist. Neither is there a non-existence of that which is not in the condition of autonomy, for that does not cease to exist. Thus, avoiding the two dogmas of existence and non-existence, emptiness is defined as that which is not in the condition of autonomy and is designated (*prajñapyate*) as "the middle path" or "middle way." Thus, the identifying terms (*viśeṣasaṃjñā*) of the nature of causally conditioned co-arising are "emptiness," "depending designation" (*upādāyaprajñapti*) and "the middle path." *(Prasannapadā* 24:18)[3]

Candrakīrti's first task here is to clarify the expression *sā prajñaptir upādāya* that begins the second sentence of the stanza. As Mattia Salvini (2011: 235), following the classical grammarian Candragomin, has recently pointed out, *upādāya* is a *lyabanta* verbal form, or "absolutive," meaning that its action of "depending" must have been completed, either chronologically or logically, prior to the "designation" (*prajñapti*) mentioned in the sentence. "Emptiness" then is a designation that can only be made after it has been derived from (*upādāya*) something else. However, this presents a difficulty in the syntax of the statement *sā prajñaptir upādāya* in line 2 of MMK 24:18 because, though *upādāya* is a transitive verb, its object is found nowhere in the line (Walser 2006: 258). Salvini (2011: 239) does not think that this omission of a transitive object in the line presents any particular problems, as he provides examples of other texts where *lyabanta* forms lack transitive objects, but their reference to something else should be understood from context. However, since no transitive object is available from the context either, Candrakīrti is compelled to explain what is going on. Fortunately for him, there is plenty of precedent specifically in early and foundational Buddhist works such as the *Milindapañha* and *Kathāvattu*, where the meanings of terms like "chariot" or "person," while not referring to fundamental realities, are "dependent on" or "derived from" (*upādāya*) their parts. Candrakīrti makes full use of the former example, maintaining that "emptiness," like the term "chariot," is an *upādāya prajñapti*, a designation that does not itself refer to anything, but derives its meaning from parts. But what, in that case, are the "parts" of "emptiness?" To this, Candrakīrti has recourse to the fact that "emptiness" has just been declared a synonym for "causally conditioned co-arising" (*pratītya samutpāda*), and this too has its "parts" or "limbs" (*aṅga*), namely the twelve-limbed wheel of incomprehension, birth, attachment, becoming, death, and so on. In like manner, the "middle path" (*madhyamā pratipad*) has its "limbs" too, right view, right speech, right livelihood, right concentration, and so forth. Therefore, all these terms, "emptiness," "depending designation," and "middle path" can be understood as "identifying terms" (*viśeṣasaṃjñā*) for "causally conditioned co-arising." "Emptiness" derives its meaning from the limbs of causally conditioned co-arising, and that is why it should be understood as an *upādāya prajñapti*.[4]

To say that "emptiness" is nothing but a "depending," or in modern translational parlance a "constructed," "non-cognitive," or "conventional" designation is a monumentally important decision in how we understand Madhyamaka Buddhism as a whole. If this reading is correct, the expressions "causally conditioned co-arising" and "emptiness" are not metaphysically or ontologically referring expressions; they are not preferable or more accurate descriptions of reality or the natural order than alternative expressions, even expressions like *svabhāva* or *ātman*, which the very notion of *pratītya samutpāda* seems to be pitted against. If "conditioned co-arising" and "emptiness" are in any respect better than other expressions that appeal to *svabhāva*, on this account, it is because the former notion better facilitates Buddhist practice, and better mediates the ultimate aims of that practice, than do other possible linguistic constructions. Or, on some modern readings like Robinson's or Sprung's, it may be better to the degree that the terminological equivalent of *pratītya samutpāda*, namely "emptiness," is a linguistic symbol which communicates something, but in an "anti-logical" or "non-cognitive" fashion. An interpretation of Nāgārjuna that renders even the Buddha's central teachings as mere "conceptual constructions" plants the roots of Madhamaka Buddhism firmly and deeply in the soil of a kind of nominalism, conventionalism, or even deconstructionism that modern readers, from their various perspectives, are strongly invested in.

The Need for a Reappraisal

Despite its grammatical complexity and the building of its case not from the surrounding verses of MMK 24 but from earlier Buddhist treatises, Candrakīrti's exegesis here makes an initially compelling impression. The appeal of the reading can be ascertained from the sheer numbers of Tibetan and well-versed Western commentators who have been firmly convinced by it.[5] However, a number of crucial considerations call this extrapolation into serious question as a reconstruction of Nāgārjuna's intended point in MMK 24:18. I will begin by summarizing these considerations and then detail each in turn.

First, Candrakīrti would have us believe that the kind of "designation" under discussion in MMK 24:18 is a foundational Buddhist technical term, a "depending designation" (*upādāya prajñapti*) akin to those that derive their meanings from parts, like "chariot" does from its "parts" and "person" does from its *skandha*-s. However, Nāgārjuna's other uses of the word "*prajñapti*" in the MMK almost all lack an overly technical sense, instead referring to terms that, in different cases, may or may not make something known to us. There is, however, one occasion where Nāgārjuna explicitly evokes the technical sense of *upādāya prajñapti* as designations for personhood that derive their meaning from the *skandha*-s. But in this instance, significantly, Nāgārjuna flatly denies that *upādāya prajñapti*, as descriptions depending on the *skandha*-s, can serve as explanatory models for the "empty" *Tathāgata* or liberated Buddha. If in MMK 24:18, we take Nāgārjuna to be affirming that "emptiness" is a "depending designation," it is very difficult to square this with another clear instance in which he forthrightly denies that such "depending designations" which reduce persons to *skandha*-s can give an accurate description of the "empty" Buddha. Either he is contradicting himself in an unfortunately flagrant way here, or, if not, we must understand MMK 24:18 differently from Candrakīrti.

Second, there are several verses in other works that are regularly attributed to Nāgārjuna that appear to be direct echoes of MMK 24:18. These verses announce conspicuously that the expressions "causally conditioned co-arising," "emptiness," and "the middle path" should be understood as carrying the same meaning and implications, and their equivalence is attributed to the Buddha himself. However, the expression *upādāya prajñapti* is found in none of these other verses. If Candrakīrti, and those readers who follow him, insist as they do that MMK 24:18 fixes a signature philosophical principle of Nāgārjuna's, namely that "emptiness," like "causally conditioned co-arising" and "the middle path" should be comprehended as "depending designations" that derive their meanings from their constituent parts, then they should have a good answer to the question of why Nāgārjuna does not even hint at this point when proclaiming the synonymy of the former three expressions in his other works. This again raises the suspicion that "depending designations," as Candrakīrti understands them, do not figure in Nāgārjuna's conception of "emptiness."

Third, commentators who come before Candrakīrti, in the four centuries intervening between the MMK and *Prasannapadā*, either do not feel the need to comment at all on the meaning of 24:18 in the context of the *parikṣa*'s extended argument or their comments do not necessarily imply there is anything significant about the verse other than its equation of conditioned co-arising with emptiness. In each case, the commentators Buddhapālita, Kumārajīva, and Bhāvaviveka either make no attempt to explain the content of MMK 24:18 or provide glosses that are uninformative or merely reinforcing of the stanza's first line. As we shall see, it is possible to read Kumārajīva's and Bhāvaviveka's brief glosses as in elusive ways agreeing with Candrakīrti's explication. But their respective interpretations could be claiming something far more straightforward and, if you will, "anti-climactic" than Candrakīrti's account. Indeed, the fact that Candrakīrti, unlike other early commentators, devotes so much exegetical effort to MMK 24:18 may indicate that he was attempting to establish a reading of it that other scholars and translators did not see. In any event, the ambiguity of the earlier commentators suggests at least that, before Candrakīrti, there may have existed either no unanimous view of the meaning of this verse within Buddhist circles or a consensus that its meaning was so self-evident that it required no explanation.

Fourth, and here I take my cue from the work of Walser, Nāgārjuna's second- to third-century Buddhist monastic audience was not only immersed in very different debates from those in which the seventh-century Candrakīrti involved himself, but the former, in attempting to stake out new ground in ongoing scholastic debates, had to formulate his positions with great care. Indeed, misunderstanding and large degrees of radical innovation could easily draw charges of creating schisms in the monastic orders of Nāgārjuna's time, and this in turn could lead a perceived inducer of schism to being expelled from the monastic community, thus making it impossible to have their works read and discussed. These dangers are readily perceivable in

Nāgārjuna's works, of misunderstanding "emptiness" (*śūnyatā*) as "non-existence" (*abhāva*), and by implication understanding him to be claiming that the Four Noble Truths do not exist. Nāgārjuna thus had to keep the notion of "emptiness" as he understood it closely allied with principles his fellow monastic scholars were more likely to readily accept. Candrakīrti, on the other hand, is operating in robustly subsidized and safe monastic historical circumstance in which the meaning of "emptiness" has been debated among several major schools for a few hundred years, and so lies well within the bounds of legitimate speculation. These historical and doctrinal differences should make us wary of thinking that the seventh-century Candrakīrti is doing nothing more than mediating the unvarnished thought of the third-century Nāgārjuna.

Finally, I would argue that the very dangers Nāgārjuna was facing as we have mentioned them in the preceding paragraph make it philosophically, and not just socially, unlikely that he understood *śūnyatā* to be an expression like "chariot" or "person," that is, as an *upādāya prajñapti* in the Abhidharma sense. After all, the words "chariot" and "person," ultimately, are false expressions; they directly refer to entities that, metaphysically speaking, do not exist for most Buddhists. In a way, Abhidharma Buddhists who foreground this sense of *upādāya prajñapti* can forgive people for using such expressions in conventional discourse, for the expressions help people undertake and fulfill important social tasks. On top of that, the expressions can be "bailed out" of philosophical trouble through the acknowledgment that they "derive" (*upādāya*) their senses from the parts of which they are constituted, which are real. Nonetheless, to use the words "chariot" or "person" as referring terms, to assume they direct our attention to reality, is simply not justifiable for Buddhists; it epitomizes philosophical falsehood. Now, if Nāgārjuna believes, as he says in MMK 24:18 and elsewhere, that "emptiness" is a synonym for "causally conditioned co-arising" and "the middle path," then also claiming that these expressions are "depending designations" makes their assertion just as false as the assertions of Brāhmiṇical mendicants when they teach about *ātman*. Since the idea of "causally conditioned co-arising" and the practices of "the middle path" were constantly on the Buddha's own lips in the *Discourses*, it simply strains philosophical credulity to suppose that Nāgārjuna, in attempting to legitimize his introduction of "emptiness" by equating it with "conditioned co-arising" and "the middle path," also believed all these terms were ultimately falsehoods on a par with ideas like *ātman*.

After having shown that Candrakīrti's reading, and by extension the predominant trends of elucidating MMK 24:18 are problematic, I will suggest two alternative approaches to understanding the verse, both grammatically and in the context of the immediately environing arguments of *parikṣa* 24. The first approach employs a strategy of parsing the second line differently than the standard reading, which would divest the use of *prajñapti* in the stanza of any technical baggage and render the verse equivalent to other verses in Nāgārjuna's corpus that invoke the identity of "conditioned co-arising," "emptiness," and the "middle path." However, the second approach, which I find decidedly more plausible, will treat the expression *upādāya prajñapti* in MMK 24:18 as a technical compound, but one which is much more in line with how Prajñaptivāda Buddhists of the period used it, rather than how it was employed by either the Pudgalavādins contemporary with Nāgārjuna or the Prāsaṅgikas who followed him. I believe this second approach avoids all the difficulties that Candrakīrti's reading saddles us with, and will resolve much of the confusion that has arisen from this pivotal but enigmatic verse.

Nāgārjuna on Types of Designation

There are four verses in the MMK in which Nāgārjuna employs either the nominal *prajñapti* or the verbal *prajñapyate*, but in none of these instances is the term used with a specific technical sense intended. Instead, the expression applies to circumstances in which a "designation" assigned to something either can make it known or fail to make it known.

> Through seeing and hearing, through feeling and the others, how would a particular entity, prior to being singled out, be designated (*prajñapyate*)? (MMK 9.3)

> (There is) the designation (*prajñapitam*) of "self" and the teaching of "no-self." The Buddha's teaching is of no particular "self" or "no-self." (MMK 18.6)

> Time without duration is not grasped, a duration of time is not acknowledged; even were time ungraspable to be grasped, how would it be designated (*prajñapyate*)? (MMK 19.5)

> There is no evident perfection without imperfection, we reveal (*prajñapayemahi*); thus perfection cannot follow except on condition of imperfection. There is no evident imperfection without perfection, we reveal (*prajñapayemahi*); thus imperfection is not acknowledged except on condition of perfection. (MMK 23:10–11)

The first verse is meant to show, through the raising of a question, that a phenomenon (*bhāva*), before it is singled out (*prāg vyavasthito*) by the process of sensation, cannot be given a name, or designation (*prajñapti*). The second stanza calls the notion of "self" a mere "designation" (*prajñapti*) as opposed to the formulation of "no-self," which is said to be a "teaching" (*deśita*). But in 18:7 it then denies that the Buddha's teaching is of any "particular" (*kaścid*) self or non-self, for if a definitive notion of a particular "self" or "no-self" to be posited, then some account would have to be given of its negation, and that misses the point of the Buddha's teaching. The verse from MMK 19 once again debunks the possibility, with a question, that time is either without duration or that a definitive duration of time can be identified or made known (*prajñapyate*). MMK 23:10 portrays the Mādhyamika as revealing (*prajñapayemahi*) the interdependence of all states of affairs through their proclamations. In all of these verses, the nominal *prajñapti* and its verbal counterparts carry quite generic senses, specifically the act of putting something into words for the putative purpose of making it known. No technical reading of the vocabulary is called for.

However, we find in MMK 22:1–10, toward the opening of the *Tathāgataparikṣa*, an extended discussion of precisely the Abhidharma conception of *upādāya prajñapti* that is operative in early texts like the *Milindapañha* and *Kathāvattu*, which is appropriated by Candrakīrti. The question that is taken up by this collection of stanzas is whether the released, or liberated, Buddha (*Tathāgata*) could be known through a method of reduction to the *skandha*-s. And, once we have the answer to that question, what are we to make of the relation between the released Buddha and "emptiness" (*śūnyatā*) as it is articulated in the rest of the MMK? The passage addresses both of these questions.

> Seeking an idea (of him) in the fivefold approach (*pañcadhā*),
> he does not exist by means of another existing thing,
> so how can the *tathāgata* be made known (*prajñapyate*)
> by means of depending (*upādānena*)?
> That which is depended upon and that which depends
> are empty in every respect.
> How can an empty *tathāgata* be made known
> by means of the empty?
> "Empty" and "not empty" are not to be an account *(vaktavyam);*
> "both" and "neither" are designations (*prajñapty*)
> only narrating (*tu kathyate*) a meaning (*artham*). (MMK 22:8–11)

In one respect, it is not surprising that the analysis of *Tathāgata* is distinguished in this *parikṣa* from the analysis of every other Abhidharma category, since the liberated nature of the released Buddha made the notion unique with respect to all other phenomena for the Ābhidharmikas. However, because of the invocation of "emptiness," this chapter is still quite pertinent to our inquiry. Nāgārjuna rejects here quite clearly the notion that the *Tathāgata* can be understood, like other putative persons, through reduction to the five *skandha*-s via "depending designations" (*upādāya prajñapti*) . However, he also distinguishes the kind of philosophical account (*vaktavya*) that *upādāya prajñapti*-s give from the discursive function of the term "emptiness." While it may fairly be said that terms like "empty" and "not empty" are "designations" (*prajñapti*), instead of reducing things to their constituent parts, the designation of "emptiness" only "narrates" (*kathyate*) a meaning (*artha*). That is to say that, while *upādāya prajñapti*-s of the reductive sort might be felicitous for analyzing how compounded phenomena can be broken down into their constituent parts, they cannot, for Nāgārjuna, give a philosophical account of emptiness, for they cannot explain the "empty" nature of the *Tathāgata*. Here, then, we have quite a conspicuously clear instance of Nāgārjuna denying the ability of "depending designations" which reduce things to their constituent parts to account for any "empty" phenomenon, since in the present case both the *Tathāgata* and the *skandha*-s themselves are said to be empty.[6] The question then becomes the following; if Nāgārjuna argues, as he clearly does in MMK 23:1–10, that "depending designations" which reduce composite phenomena to their parts cannot provide a philosophical explanation for "emptiness," then how could he claim in 24:18, if we follow Candrakīrti's understanding, that the term "emptiness" itself is a "depending designation," reducible to its parts? We seem to be left with two alternatives. Either Nāgārjuna has baldly contradicted himself or Candrakīrti's understanding of MMK 24:18 is not justifiable.

And there is another conceptual problem here, pinpointed long ago by Burton, but about which I will add my own perspective. Nāgārjuna, on Candrakīrti's reading of MMK 24:18, in claiming that both "emptiness" and "causally conditioned co-arising" are "depending designations" of the Abhidharma variety, just fails to understand the Abhidharma distinction between "depending designations" and "causally conditioned co-arising." For the Ābhidharmikas, the distinction between *prajñaptisat* ("merely" designated, compound entities) and *dravyasat* (substantial, uncompounded *dharma*-s) does not entail that the former are conditionally co-arisen and the latter are not. While uncompounded *dharma*-s, like fire-*dharma*-s or water-*dharma*-s, were not subject to causally conditioned co-arising in the respect that they could be reduced to parts, they did participate in the causal order of *pratītya samutpāda* by regularly giving rise to certain phenomena rather than others and constituting composite phenomena that were themselves causally and notionally interdependent (Burton 1999: 90).[7] This entailed, for the Ābhidharmikas, that a *dharma* could possess *svabhāva*, or have causal "autonomy" over what sort of phenomena it was independently of other phenomena, but it still conformed to the other conditions of *pratītya samutpāda*. Thus, Nāgārjuna and by extension Candrakīrti, in claiming that the ideas of *svabhāva* and *pratītyasamutpāda* are simply mutually exclusive, that a phenomenon can either only be substantially autonomous or conditionally co-arisen, have utterly failed to comprehend the Abhidharma position and have subtly shifted the meaning of *pratītya samutpāda* to suit their own purposes (Burton 1999: 93). Indeed, for Burton, Madhyamaka Buddhists, in creating a false, categorical equivalence between lack of substantial autonomy (*niḥsvabhāva*) and causally conditioned co-arising, have erected a pan-conceptualism or pan-illusionism (*prajñaptivāda*) on entirely false Buddhist philosophical grounds. I think Burton's objection and the latter charge that comes along with it might be more pertinent if the only available conception of *upādāya prajñapti* were of the reductive variety under discussion here. I think that Candrakīrti's insistence that this reductive type of *upādāya prajñapti* explains the term "emptiness" implicates Candrakīrti for making precisely the errors identified by Burton. However, as we will see in more detail later, Leonard Priestley and Joseph Walser have ably shown that there were several other conceptions of *upādāya prajñapti* common to two different schools of Buddhist thought which were probably operative in Nāgārjuna's lifetime. Identifying which one of those alternative conceptions Nāgārjuna was invoking in MMK 24:18 will be crucial to understanding the far more likely intended meaning of this enigmatic verse.

A Twofold, Threefold, or Fourfold Equivalence?

As we have seen earlier, in his commentary on MMK 24:18, Candrakīrti argues that there are three "identifying terms" (*viśeṣasaṃjñā*) which are equated by Nāgārjuna with "causally conditioned co-arising," namely "emptiness," "depending designation," and "the middle path." In short, Candrakīrti has Nāgārjuna insisting that we should comprehend that (1) "conditioned co-arising" and "emptiness" are synonyms, (2) "emptiness" (and so "conditioned co-arising" too) is a "depending designation," itself non-referring but reducible to its parts, and (3) rightly apprehending all this is itself "the middle path." In his own unpacking of this verse, Garfield (1995: 304–5) emphasizes the "critical three-way relation" that MMK 24:18 establishes between these alternate terms for "conditioned co-arising," and in so doing argues that "emptiness" should be taken as a conventionally referring and not absolutely referring term significant for communication and practice. This then is the standard Prāsaṅga reading as well as the generally preferred reading of the modern commentators who rely on Candrakīrti.

However, if we take the text of MMK 24:18

yaḥ pratītyasamutpādaḥ śūnyatāṃ tāṃ pracakṣmahe /
sā prajñaptir upādāya pratipat saiva madhyamā //

as fixing this "fourfold" relation between causally conditioned co-arising, emptiness, depending designations, and the middle path, and assume that this fourfold relation is at the very core of Nāgārjuna's thought, we find ourselves confronted with another textual conundrum. There are at least three other instances in the generally accepted corpus of Nāgārjuna which otherwise seem to conspicuously emphasize the relation between conditioned co-arising, emptiness, and the middle path, and so strongly echo MMK 24:18. But in all of these instances, no mention whatsoever is made of "depending designations." These instances are the following:

yaśca śūnyatāṃ pratītyasamutpadāṃ madhyāmam pratipadam ca /
ekārthām nijagāda praṇamāni tamapratimabuddham // Vigrahavyāvartanī 70
I venerate the incomparable Buddha, who has taught that
emptiness, conditioned co-arising and the middle path have one meaning!

yaḥ pratītyasamutpādam śūnyatām saiva te matte /
bhāva svatantro nāstiti siṃhanādas tvātulaḥ // Lokātītastava 22
What is conditioned co-arising, that is exactly what you think is emptiness.
"No independent thing exists"; that is your supreme lion's roar!

yaḥ pratītyasamutpādam śūnyatām saiva te matte /
tathāvidaśca saddharmas tat samaśca tathāgatha // Acintyastava 40
What is conditioned co-arising, that is exactly what you think is emptiness.
Of that kind is the true teaching and such is *tathāgata*.

The first verse, the concluding one of *Vigrahavyāvartanī*, is especially telling, given the virtually unanimous consensus that the core text, if not the autocommentary, is from the same hand as Nāgārjuna's MMK. Here, *śūnyatā*, *pratītyasamutpāda* and *madhyāma pratipada* are said in the teachings of the

Buddha to have "one meaning" (*ekārtha*). The other two texts, the *Lokātītastava* and *Acintyastava*, affirm the equivalence of causally conditioned co-arising and emptiness in exactly the same diction, and then simply identify that equivalence as the "true teaching" and attribute that equivalence to the Buddha himself, without explicitly mentioning "the middle path."

Where Nāgārjuna is consistent in the combination of these four respective verses is in the insistence that "conditioned co-arising" and "emptiness" are synonymous expressions. If we take this minimal literal agreement to most surely represent his unwavering and core position, then there is at least a two-way or reciprocal relation between the expressions *pratītya samutpāda* and *śūnyatā*. However, if we permit ourselves to consider the possibility that the "middle path" mentioned in the MMK, the "lion's roar" of the *Lokātītastava*, and the "true teaching" of the *Acintyastava* are more or less equal kinds of endorsement, which seems plausible, then we could consider conditioned co-arising, emptiness, and the middle path of MMK 24:18 to make up a threefold relation. The odd-term-out, so to speak of MMK 24:18, is *upādāya prajñapti*, which appears in only one of the four verses considered here. It is then the presence of this term in the MMK, and not the absence of the term in the remaining three texts, that requires explanation. And whatever this explanation may be, it seems unlikely that we will be justified in supposing that the Prāsaṅgika "fourfold relation" between these terms which includes *upādāya prajñapti* must be fundamental to Nāgārjuna's philosophy. If it were, why would Nāgārjuna fail to invoke *upādāya prajñapti* in all of these other stanzas which, in all other respects, agree with MMK 24:18?

Walser hypothesizes that the absence of *upādāya prajñapti* in the texts *Vigrahavyāvartanī*, *Lokātītastava*, and *Acintyastava*, all composed in a later period than the MMK, may reflect a doctrinal shift of emphasis on Nāgārjuna's part. This doctrinal shift, according to Walser, is explained by Nāgārjuna in making accommodations to the Pudgalavādins in his early work but not needing to do so in his later treatises (Walser 2006: 261–2, 267). While in many other respects I agree with Walser's analysis, for reasons I will explain later, I don't think this precise reconstruction is correct. Both philosophically and doctrinally, I believe it is unlikely that Nāgārjuna is employing a Pudgalavādin application of *upādāya prajñapti* in MMK 24:18. Most basically, however, Walser accurately assesses the challenge facing us when confronted with this textual problem. We must explain the apparently idiosyncratic, rather than paradigmatic, appearance of *upādāya prajñapti* in Nāgārjuna's equation of conditioned co-arising and emptiness in the special instance of MMK 24:18.

Later, I will offer two candidate explanations for this, but make a stronger case for the second explanation.

Commentarial Ambiguity

As we have exhaustively detailed, Candrakīrti's exegesis of MMK 24:18 is rich, both grammatically and conceptually. It explains in thick and robust detail why he believes Nāgārjuna holds that the expressions "conditioned co-arising" and "emptiness" should be read as "depending designations" that, like the words "chariot" or "self," can be reduced to their constituent "parts" or "limbs" (*aṅga*). It is, once again, at the very least understandable that this interpretation gained such popularity among classical and modern readers, as it is such a detailed elucidation.

In fact, however, in the collection of the earliest commentaries on the MMK, it is the only detailed interpretation available to us. The four commentaries that pre-date Candrakīrti's seventh-century *Prasannapadā* do not offer clear disambiguations of MMK 24:18. The vocabulary that two of these commentaries employ could be taken as suggestive of the comprehensive explanation of Candrakīrti, if one is permitted to assume that this vocabulary is being used in a univocal way. But the texts in question do not, of their own accord, support that assumption even nearly to the extent of being dispositive. The examination of these four commentaries will not require overmuch space. The first, the *Akutobhyā*, a supposed autocommentary on the MMK by Nāgārjuna himself but probably done by a later author, makes no comment on the verse at all, and that dispenses with the first source.

Because the next historical recension we have on the MMK appears in the form of a translation, the fourth- and fifth-century *Zhong Lun* (中論) of Kumārajīva, accompanied by the commentary of Qingmu, we must pay special attention to what degree of conceptual overlap or conceptual transformation attends the diction of MMK 25:18. Kumārajīva translates the verse as follows:

> 眾因緣生法 我說即是無.
> 亦為是假名 亦是中道義. (*Zhonglun*, *Taisho* 1564 XXX)

Here, "causally conditioned co-arising" is equated by the first line with 無 *wu*, "nothing," which is Kumārajīva's direct rendition of *śūnyatā*. The second line proffers that "this: (the closest antecedent for "this" in the text is 無 *wu*) is also "called" (為 *wei*) a 假名 *jia ming*. In the Chinese context, the expression 假名

jia ming does not overtly carry the reductive, analytical overtones of *upādāya prajñapti* as the latter has so far been discussed. Instead, the question that a 假名 *jia ming*, as a certain species of "name" or "word" (名 *ming*) brings to mind is what relationship it bears to other kinds of 名 *ming*. It is possible, certainly, to understand 假 *jia* as meaning "artificial" or "fake," and so the expression 假名 *jia ming* could refer, in a strong sense, to a word or a term that is not or does not denote anything real. The early Han Dynasty lexicon, the *Shouwen Jiezi*, for example, defines *jia* as the opposite of 真 *zhen*, "genuine" or "real," and other early philosophical texts, such as the *Xunzi*, seem to employ this usage. Such an understanding could at first glance be seen as resonant with Candrakīrti's commentary. However, this is hardly the only possible sense, nor even the one most consonant with the Kumārajīva/Qingmu complex. The expression 假名 *jia ming* is quite frequently used with a different sense in classical Chinese philosophical literature. Frequently, a 假名 *jia ming* is simply another name or alternative designation for something or someone usually known by a more familiar name. In the Disputation Chapters of the *Mozi*, a defense of expressions that are 假 *jia* is formulated by illustrating that animals such as dogs are often known through the creation of "surnames" (猶氏 *you shi*) for them, and this gives 假名 *jia ming* the sense of names that are "borrowed" to refer to things otherwise named (*Mozi Jing* B 10/12B 3,4; see: Graham 1964: 14). Near the close of the *Zeyang* chapter of the *Zhuangzi*, we find the assertion "道之為名，所假而行," meaning "the name '*dao*,' though borrowed (假 *jia*), yet proceeds" (*Zhuangzi* 25:12). This seems to accord with the rest of the text as well as with passages in the *Dao De Jing* which aver that, while that which gave rise to and shapes the unfolding of the cosmos cannot be given an adequate name, *dao* may be the most fitting name for it, and so *dao*, as a "borrowed name," will have to do. In the *Zuozhuan* commentary on the sixth year of Duke Huan's reign, it is reported that a certain Shi came to Duke Huan's realm. Some Song Dynasty commentators apparently believed that this Shi was also known as "the Duke of Zhou," a 假名 *jia ming* or "borrowed name" for Shi.[8] Kumārajīva does not comment further on MMK 24:18 and, even more tellingly, he does not employ the expression 假名 *jia ming* in his translation of MMK 23:1–10 where the Sanskrit text refers to reductionist forms of *upādāya prajñapti*. In his commentary on Kumārajīva's translation, Qingmu does extrapolate on the meaning of "emptiness" (空 *kong*) which in his commentary becomes yet another term for "nothing" (無 *wu*). But what he has to say about *jia ming* only reinforces the impression that it is meant as an "alternative name."

是物屬眾因緣故無自性。
無自性故空。
空亦復空。
但為引眾生故。
以假名說。(*Zhonglun*, *Taisho* 1564, XXX, 0033b15)

The causally conditioned existence of things thus lacks *svabhāva*.
The lack of *svabhāva* is thus empty (空 *kong*).
"Empty" is also empty.
But it is used to guide worldly beings.
It is therefore said to be a borrowed name (假名 *jia ming*).

Qingmu adds the term "empty" to the diction of the verse, and immediately warns that the term "empty" should not itself be taken to refer to something that has *svabhāva*, in contrast to all those things that are conditionally co-arisen. But for the benefit of worldly beings, the word "empty" can stand as yet another term for "causally conditioned co-arising." Notice that the term "empty," employed for worldly beings, is designed to "lead" (引 *yin*) and "guide" (導 *dao*) them, not to mislead them. This role of the term "empty" will thus be properly served not by its being a "fake name," but by its being an "alternative name." Here, then, we should not understand the operative sense of 假名 *jia ming* as a "pseudonym," but as a "synonym." Qingmu's note then supplies more weight to the likelihood that Kumārajīva simply considers "nothing" or "emptiness" to be alternative expressions or synonyms for "conditioned co-arising." Nothing here requires 假名 *jia ming* to be the reductive Abhidharma variety of an *upādāya prajñapti*, a "designation depending on parts."[9]

The sixth-century *Buddhapālitavṛtti* likewise does not comment on this verse. That in itself is not insignificant. The *Buddhapālitavṛtti* is often taken as the precursor of Candrakīrti's commentary and is doxographically considered the forerunner of Prāsaṅgika commentarial literature.[10] The lack of any direct explication of this verse in the *Vṛtti* could be taken to imply either that the meaning of the verse was so obvious that it required no elucidation or that there was no "standard" reading of the verse among the Buddhist philosophers of the period. The fact that Candrakīrti delves into such detail about the verse in the seventh century does not speak favorably for the first alternative. Why would a verse whose meaning was so evident to all in a like-minded Buddhist tradition need such a suddenly detailed treatment?

The fourth commentary belongs to the seventh-century Bhāvaviveka. His only gloss on the second line of MMK 24:18 deals with *upādāya prajñapti* by saying it means *upādānam upādāya prajñaptiḥ* (Nagao 1991: 192–3). There are perhaps two ways, quite different from one another, that *upādā*, in its accusative nominal and absolutive senses, could be taken here. Were we to take *upādānam* in the accusative nominal form to refer to the "grasped" *skandha*-s, as is certainly widespread enough in Buddhist usage, then Bhāvaviveka would mean by this clarification, quite straightforwardly, that the designations MMK 24:18 is identifying are "designations depending on the *skandha*-s." That would put Bhāvaviveka shoulder-to-shoulder with Candrakīrti on the meaning of this verse. While this is possible, it is hardly certain. That is because, as most classical and modern scholars recognize, Bhāvaviveka and Candrakīrti seem to noticeably part company on the very notion of "conventional truth" (*samvṛti satya*). Stating the matter somewhat dogmatically for the purposes of brevity, while Bhāvaviveka devotes his entire commentary to what he believes a most fruitful analytical project of distinguishing conventional truths from conventional falsehoods, a distinction which speaks in favor of Buddhist conventions as opposed to Brāhmiṇical conventions, Candrakīrti considers conventions to be more or less on par with one another, insofar as they are all analyzable into other merely conceptual components. (Siderits 1997: 69–92). If that distinction between the two philosophers carries through, they may not have been inclined to read MMK 24:18 in the same way. The other way to read Bhāvaviveka's gloss *upādānam upādāya prajñaptiḥ* could be as a mere grammatical clarification. Since, in the original verse, *upādāya* lacks an accusative object, Bhāvaviveka assigns it one, even if it is uninformative. In this vein, Bhāvaviveka unpacks *upādāya prajñapti* as a "designation depending on what it depends on" or a "designation based on a basis." That seems perhaps an even less likely reading than the first given that in this case the gloss explains nothing at all. Why would Bhāvaviveka, a normally methodical and verbose commentator, insert an explanatory comment to a verse which did not even attempt to explain the verse's content? However, since Bhāvaviveka extends no more help to the reader on this issue, we have no way of divining his intent.

Where does this leave us? In the first four centuries of commentary on the MMK, five extant commentaries are available. With reference to MMK 24:18, two of those commentaries, the *Akutobhyā* and the *Buddhapālitavṛtti*, make no attempt whatsoever to explain the verse's meaning. One commentary, Candrakīrti's, offers a fine-grained grammatical and conceptual analysis which concludes that the expressions "conditioned co-arising" and "emptiness" are, akin to words like "chariot" or "person," reliant on their constituent concepts and processes, and are therefore "depending designations" of the Abhidharma variety. The remaining two commentaries, one a Chinese translation of the MMK by Kumārajīva and the other a supposedly Sanskrit original of Bhāvaviveka, despite their glaring want of detail, could be interpreted as in accord with the explanation Candrakīrti eventually supplies, but they could just as easily be read as repeating the vocabulary of the root verse without making much effort at disambiguation. At best, then, for the advocates of Candrakīrti's reading, these five commentaries exhibit a lack of corroborated unanimity, where Candrakīrti's eventual explanation is tacitly affirmed by the majority, but about which there is no especially strong support. At worst, Candrakīrti is quite alone in his view of MMK 24:18, with the remaining exegetes finding nothing in the stanza requiring any particular philosophical analysis beyond the obvious equation of conditioned co-arising with emptiness the stanza declares on its own. Either way, if we are looking to the commentarial literature before Candrakīrti for evidence that his view was the standard one of the verse, the evidence we have is not dispositive. I would argue that, combined with the other evidence and considerations being presented here, it is more likely that Candrakīrti's formulation of MMK 24:18 was unique to him. He is the one commentator we know of in the four centuries that have elapsed since Nāgārjuna's career who goes out of his way to plead for a certain specific explication in which crucial Buddhist technical terminology, the terminology closest to the heart of the Buddha's teaching, should be taken as reductive "depending designations." His could well be a case of protesting too much.

Historical and Hermeneutical Considerations

In interpreting the classical Indian philosophical tradition as a whole, not to mention one of its specific *darśana*-s, it is quite natural and in many cases entirely desirable to simply defer to the clearest cases made in any given commentarial tradition. After all, each of those traditions represents a heritage of thought, debate, and interpretation. Thus, if we find some texts that appear in need of clarification, we turn to the nearest commentators who provide the most informative explanations. It is those explanations that, we presume, were not only passed on from one generation to the next inside of a community of thought, but were especially cherished as sure guides to liberating praxis. As a general matter, I would count myself among those readers who are inclined to prefer classical commentarial illuminations to modern ones, and in part, that very conviction underlies what I am attempting to accomplish in this chapter. We have every good reason to consult the ancients and go as far as we can in ascertaining their most probable intentions before we engage in flights of fancy that speak to our more immediately environing philosophical puzzles. So, then, since Candrakīrti does, there is no question, give us the most robust account of Nāgārjuna's MMK 24:18 in the centuries that elapsed between the two, and since Candrakīrti was both an heir to and advocate of Nāgārjuna's Buddhist intellectual and practical enterprise, then what excuse do we have to question his commentarial explanations?

The answer is this. Four to five hundred years, even four to five hundred years of a period that is immensely difficult to reconstruct with great historical precision, is a long time. During any five hundred-year period, much can and, we should fully expect, does undergo significant change. If it is indeed a hermeneutical truism that interpreters are of necessity partly shaped by present historical circumstances rather than being pure conduits of an original meaning, then this truism also applies to interpreters within a tradition of thought, not only to ones outside of it. So, in order to discern how a commentator might be embellishing, extending, or transforming the meaning of a root text, we should also attend to the historical particularities of the commentary and how they may importantly differ from the root text. This attention need not by any means be directed at the goal of undermining the commentator's interpretation, but should always, at least, be focused on articulating the commentator's creative contributions to or unique reception of the root text rather than just the commentator's devoted fidelity to it. And sometimes commentators do offer dubious readings; that happens.

Are there then some basic probable facts we can glean about Candrakīrti's hermeneutic circumstances, and how did they differed from Nāgārjuna's? Little can be known about Candrakīrti's life from subsequent but historically proximal reconstructions. The Tibetan doxographical classification of Buddhapālita and Candrakīrti as advocates of a definitive Prāsaṅgika school over against the definitive Svatāntra school of Bhāvaviveka is almost certainly a retroactive one, as this scholastic distinction is unknown in Buddhist Sanskrit works. So, to begin with, Candrakīrti was not aware he was defending a Prāsaṅgika reading of Nāgārjuna against a Svatāntra reading, but merely thought he and Buddhapālita understood Nāgārjuna correctly while Bhāvaviveka did not, and so he was involved in a debate internal to Madhyamaka. Candrakīrti probably lived in the first half of the seventh century CE and was associated with the Nālandā Mahāvihāra monastery, which at the time according to Xuanzang enjoyed ample patronage under Harśa of Kannauj and was a bastion of the full range of thriving Mahāyāna schools. We can tell far more about Candrakīrti's overt commitments from his own textual corpus, and the still-surviving Sanskrit original of his *Prasannapadā Madhyamakavṛtti*, a direct commentary on the MMK, in particular. In this work, he addresses extensive criticism to three particular targets. One line of critique is directed to Bhāvaviveka for censuring Buddhapālita's resistance of commitment to any philosophical view (*dṛṣṭi*), a resistance that Candrakīrti believes is fully supported by Nāgārjuna's *Vigrahavyāvartanī*. This first critical evaluation is most consequential for Candrakīrti because Bhāvaviveka claims to be an exponent of Mādhyamika, but according to Candrakīrti departs dramatically from evidently genuine Mādhyamika fundamentals. Another strand of polemic is aimed at the Diṅnāga school of Buddhist thought, which makes what Candrakīrti judges to be wholly unwarranted distinctions between the self-characterized (*svalakṣana*) and generally characterized (*samānyalakṣana*) objects of cognitions. Diṅnāga builds from that the kind of epistemology that is again ruled out by Nāgārjuna's *Vigrahavyāvartanī*, the main argument of which is that objects and means of knowing cannot be distinct ontological categories (Siderits 1981). Finally, Candrakīrti assails Vijñānavāda Buddhists for formulating the thesis that all experience emanates from "mere cognition" (*vijñaptimātra*), as this stance fails to appreciate the core of Nāgārjuna's teaching that all things, not only the objects of consciousness but consciousness itself, are empty.

Without delving into the details of these critiques and the degree to which Nāgārjuna's MMK can be suitably marshaled against Candrakīrti's rivals, we can envision a number of basic yet important facts regarding Candrakīrti's hermeneutical situation. By Candrakīrti's career, to begin with, Mahāyāna itself was a recognizable movement of thought and practice contrasted with other communities such as the Staviras. Further, for Candrakīrti, the school of Madhyamaka is also a distinct bulwark of resistance to other Mahāyāna metaphysical systems such as the Diṅnāga school and Vijñānavāda. In addition, Candrakīrti himself considers Madhyamaka to have fallen prey to internal distortion, thanks to the contemporary Bhāvaviveka's attacks on Buddhapālita's faithful adherence. What Candrakīrti considers a genuine representation of Madhyamaka views is therefore urgently called for, and the aim of the *Prasannapadā* is precisely to reflect that genuine representation. We can say then without controversy that Candrakīrti was self-consciously crafting his commentary on the MMK to defend an institutionally and intellectually demarcated Madhyamaka stance, and that commentary is meant to rebut internally deviant Madhyamaka views and externally errant Mahāyāna doctrines. Surely, as the outstanding scholar he was, Candrakīrti is fully aware that the original purveyor of Madhyamaka, Nāgārjuna, was primarily in combat with his own distinct set of opponents, and Candrakīrti draws from sources that render the positions of those opponents visible. But Candrakīrti's commentary on the MMK is throughout overtly directed at his own explicitly identified foes, most of whom were his contemporaries.

The most probable historical and philosophical circumstances of Nāgārjuna himself were likely dramatically different, to say the least, from Candrakīrti's. And these differences are important in appreciating the relationship between the MMK and the *Prasannapadā*. To begin with, to cite a general scholarly consensus that dates back at least a century, in Nāgārjuna's lifetime, during the rough period of 150–250 CE, there was no such thing as a separately recognized monastic tradition (*nikāya*) that was labeled by the term "Mahāyāna." The precise geographical, cultural, and practical origins of what was to become Mahāyāna Buddhism remain disputed among historians. Still, everything from the general dearth of monasteries bearing Mahāyāna inscriptions to the absence of direct textual references to Mahāyana to the end of the third century make its existence marginal at best. Moreover, according to the testimony of Faxian and Xuanzang, while Mahāyāna was increasingly recognized as a *vāda* or a broad-ranging philosophical view of Buddhist teaching and practice, Mahāyāna monks lived in communities with non-Mahāyāna monks well into the middle of the first millennium CE (Schopen 2000: 20). And whether we are inclined toward Schopen's theory of the twin origins of Mahāyāna among doctrinally embattled monks and forest meditation communities or Hirakawa's hypothesis that Mahāyāna sprang from lay donations and worship or Lamotte's insistence that Mahāyāna was to a considerable degree a legacy of the Kuṣāṇa states, there is something of an agreement among them that Mahāyāna does not really predominate in the northern and middle regions of India until the fifth century (Schopen 2000: 20ff; and Lamotte 1954: 392).[11] If we are to take the sixth-century Paramārtha and the seventh-century Avalokitavrata at face value and place the early origins of Mahāyāna texts sometime around the splits among the various factions of second-century BCE Mahāsāṃghikas, even though it was not then identified as one of the "eighteen sects," and combine this with the historical evidence and the development of textual materials, we are led to a modest early pedigree for early Mahāyāna. By Nāgārjuna's lifetime, Mahāyāna was, if anything, a fledgling and diffuse set of views about Buddhist doctrine, and not Buddhist *vināya* rules, which literally bumped elbows as a minority community with more dominant Buddhist schools within mixed monasteries. According to Walser's extensive study, this would most likely place Nāgārjuna in a position in which, while he wanted to make a case for a Mahāyāna notion of emptiness (*śūnyatā*) that differed from prevailing Sarvāstivāda, Pudgalavāda, Saṃmitīya, and Prajñaptivāda ideas, his approach would have had to envision possible accommodations with all these perspectives (see, for example, Walser 2006: 239, 248–9). This would have been an especially crucial approach for Nāgārjuna, according to Walser, because the minority Mahāyānists were vulnerable to charges of splitting the order (*saṅghabheda*) with provocative views, the penalties for which could be destruction of their literature and exile from the monastic community, penalties which were sometimes exacted in the early centuries of the movement (Walser 2006: 89–147). These accommodationist strategies, Walser argues, can be seen in everything from Nāgārjuna's frequent attempts to locate signature Mahāyāna teachings in the "words of the Buddha" (*buddhavācana*) to pleading that, so long as the notion of "emptiness" is rightly understood, it supports rather than undermines already-existing scholastic categories and frameworks.

It is not necessary here to affirm all of the details of Walser's account of Nāgārjuna's most likely historical places of residence and patrons nor the shifting philosophical loyalties he suggests are betrayed between Nāgārjuna's composition of the early MMK and the late *Ratnāvali*. I agree with some of Walser's conclusions on this matter and disagree with others, as I will argue further later. I take the general characterizations Walser outlines with regard to Nāgārjuna's hermeneutic circumstances to be plausible. And if they are, then the environing conditions of the philosophies of the second- to third-century Nāgārjuna and the seventh-century Candrakīrti sharply diverge in some quite significant respects. Nāgārjuna is forging a specific Mahāyāna vision of "emptiness" that mostly apposes Sarvāstivāda but that he is convinced fundamentally agrees with the Buddha's teachings and most accurately explains much existing scholastic doctrines. He is not even aware that he is founding anything like a Madhyamaka school of thought. Instead, he wishes to vindicate his conception of emptiness by positively associating it with widely accepted Buddhist ideas, though he does seem to feel safe in targeting mostly Sarvāstivāda positions. Nāgārjuna's strategy of vindicating Mahāyāna thought is mostly accommodationist and associative. By contrast, for Candrakīrti, what passes for a wide spectrum of scholastic Mahāyāna views is fraught with error, delusion, and misunderstanding, particularly among two of the most popular schools of the time, Vijñānavāda and Diṅnāga's *pramāṇavāda*. And even more urgently, for Candrakīrti, there was a Mādhyamika tradition, centuries old, originated and nurtured in the works of Nāgārjuna himself, Āryadeva and Buddhapālita, that needed to be defended from monumental distortion at the hands of Bhāvaviveka.

Against these dangers, for Candrakīrti, Nāgārjuna's MMK along with his other works must be recruited and mined for arguments the original author could not have anticipated, directed against views that had no real precursors in his time.

Envisioning this relationship between the two great personages of Nāgārjuna and Candrakīrti, we should be neither surprised nor scandalized by instances in which Candrakīrti creatively extrapolates an argument from the MMK that might not exactly be in the root text's stanzas themselves. Nor should we begrudge Candrakīrti the hermeneutic right to do this, as an advocate of a living tradition which must face novel challenges through the ages. Nor even, I would say, should we begrudge modern interpreters the hermeneutic right to creatively riff on the writings of both Nāgārjuna and Candrakīrti in order to marshal philosophical resources to address the challenges of their own era. That is how the philosophies of the ancients have remained relevant to vastly different cultures of readers and practitioners of different eons. However, as I am arguing in this chapter, that does not mean we should not be attentive to occasionally forced readings by the commentators, and reflect on the implications for how to understand distinct views we may discover in the root text compared to the exegete. That is, it seems to me, quite normal scholarly and philosophical business. Candrakīrti's reading of MMK 24:18, is, I believe there are abundant and good reasons to suspect, just such an instance of a forced reading that required of Candrakīrti some special pleading that is not, in the end, especially convincing. And that conclusion in turn has implications for understanding and evaluating the widespread dependence of modern interpreters on Candrakīrti's recension of Nāgārjuna.

Philosophical Problems

I will now move to the fifth reason I have cited for my doubts about Candrakīrti's reading of MMK 24:18. Candrakīrti, by calling "emptiness" a reductive variety of "depending designation" that dissolves the reality of composite concepts by breaking them into their parts, makes "emptiness" vulnerable to the very dangers from which Nāgārjuna was trying to insulate it. Fundamentally, if Candrakīrti is right, if "emptiness" and "causally conditioned co-arising" are, like the words "chariot" and "person," non-referring terms, then their direct meanings are fictive. Granted, surely, Candrakīrti allows for the "conventional" utility of the expressions "conditioned co-arising" and "emptiness," as they can facilitate practice. He also notes that there is some genuine philosophical advantage to these terms, given that, since they are "depending designations," while they may not invoke realities that are self-established or ontologically autonomous (*svabhāva*), neither are they completely "non-existent," for their constituents are experienced by us. However, in the strict sense, the purportedly direct reference of "causally conditioned co-arising" and "emptiness" should be granted no more purchase on reality than terms like "chariot" or "self."

Let us recall once again Candrakīrti's own explanation of the second line of MMK 24:18.

> That very emptiness is established as a "depending designation" (*upādāya prajñaptir iti*). A chariot is designated (*prajñapyate*) as depending upon the wheels (*cakrādiny-upādāya*) and the (other) parts of the chariot. Thus, a designation depending on (a thing's) own parts (*svāṅgānupādāya prajñapti*) does not exist in the condition of autonomy (*svabhāva*). And emptiness is whatever does not exist in the condition of autonomy. Truly, the definition of emptiness is established as that which is not in the condition of autonomy, (and is in turn) called "the middle path . . ." Thus, the identifying terms (*viśeṣasaṃjñā*) of the nature of causally conditioned co-arising are "emptiness," "depending designation" (*upādāyaprajñapti*) and "the middle path." *Prasannapadā* 24:18

The case Candrakīrti makes seems innocuous enough. Since Candrakīrti's avowed overt position is that, while conventional terms are conventionally useful but not philosophically viable, the "middle path" should consist in continuing to use conventional language while ever resisting the attachment-driven temptation to construct yet another inadequate metaphysical vision of them. We had best not, in Candrakīrti's ideal Madhyamaka, make metaphysical reifications of even the pronouncements of the Buddha, for the whole aim of Buddhism is to overcome all reifications and attachments. So far, Candrakīrti's effort to make Buddhist praxis proceed from "all convention and no theory" looks promising.

But the promise carries with it an enormous peril. The peril is that the *upādāya prajñapti*-s of "chariot" and "self," when subjected to proper analytical scrutiny, are false notions. The idea that there are real composite things in the world that are accurately referred to by the expression "chariots" is, on the Ābhidharmika understanding which Candrakīrti actively adopts, false. And by extension, the idea that there are real composite things in the world that are accurately referred to by the expression "selves" is most certainly, on the Buddhist view Candrakīrti embraces, false. By extension, if conditioned co-arising and emptiness are "depending designations," then by parity of treatment, they are also false ideas.

And Candrakīrti hardly shies away from this very implication. In his exegesis of MMK 24:8 which focuses on the "truth of common conduct" or "conventional truth" (*samvṛti satya*), Candrakīrti offers two etymological extrapolations of *samvṛti*, one deriving it from the root *vṛt* and another from the root *vṛtt*. These two alternative derivations result in three possible meanings for the word, the first being "total concealment" (*samantād varaṇa*), the second "mutual existence" (*paraspara saṃbhavana*), and the third the "agreement of worldly, customary transaction" (*saṃketo lokavyavahāra*). The expression *samvṛti satya* for Candrakīrti then encompasses all three meanings, dependent existence, daily communication (*vyavahāra*), which he explicitly notes is the relation between the "designator and the designated, the cognition and the cognized" (*abhidhānābhidheyajñājñeyādi lakṣaṇa*), and total concealment (*samantād varaṇa*). His explanation of how conventional truth conceals is quite striking. Candrakīrti takes special note of the fact that Nāgārjuna's complete phrase in MMK 24:8 is "worldly conventional truth" (*lokasamvṛti satya*) and explains the expression by saying that a "*skandha*-constituted self" (*skhandātma*) is a "mental designation depending on the aggregates" (*skandānupādāya prajñāpyamāna*), and as such, it is its own world (*loka*). In his treatment of the very next verse, MMK 24:9, Candrakīrti gives voice to an incredulous textual opponent who worries that, if ultimate truth is to be strictly distinguished from conventional truth, then what have become Buddhist conventional truths, the *skandha*-s, the elements, the sense bases, as well as the Noble Truths and conditioned co-arising themselves would be rendered false. Before defending the persisting practical utility of the *skandha*-s, the Noble Truths and conditioned co-arising, Candrakīrti concedes the point of the objection by responding: "this is indeed true" (*satyametadeva*). Candrakīrti embraces a Madhyamaka that is boldly radical, not hesitant to assert that even the Buddha's own teaching of "causally conditioned co-arising" is, in one distinctly identifiable respect, a noble lie.

As we have seen, however, all this is of a piece with Candrakīrti's avowed project. Denouncing followers of the Buddha, especially those who rely on Abhidharma concepts, is at the very top of his agenda. Moreover, Candrakīrti invests a great deal in verses such as MMK 25:24 as well as *Vigrahavyāvartanī* 29, where Nāgārjuna seems to deny that either the Buddha or he teaches any positive truths that can be put into language.

sarvopalambhapaśamaḥ prapañcopaśamaḥ śivaḥ /
na kvacit kasyacit kaścid dharmo buddhena deśitaḥ // (MMK 25:24)

The pacification of all ascertainment,
the pacification of (conceptual) proliferation,
the auspicious!
No particular *dharma* was taught by the Buddha
anywhere to anyone.

yadi kācana pratijñā syānme tata eṣa bhaved doṣaḥ /
nāsti ca mama pratijñā tasmān naivāsti me doṣaḥ // Vigrahavyāvartanī 29

If I had a particular thesis (*pratijñā*),
then this error would obtain.
But I have no thesis,
and thus the error is not mine.

There is much in these verses and others redolent of them in Nāgārjuna's corpus that requires careful interpretation, the opportunities for which are beyond the scope of this chapter. For example, MMK 25:24 concludes a *parikṣa* that attacks a number of "views" (*dṛṣṭi*) and concludes that the Buddha taught no views and even no *dharma*. But it is quite debatable whether the *dharma* invoked in the verse refers to truth in total, or whether it refers to a "particular (*kaścid*) *dharma*" that is identifiable with only one school. Wilhelm Halbfass (1988) persuasively argued long ago that Nāgārjuna may well be using the term "*dṛṣṭi*" in an exclusively pejorative sense to castigate "mere views" which he rejects, but these are regularly contrasted with the *dharma* that was taught by the Buddha, and especially that *dharma* mediated by the teaching of the two truths in MMK 24:8–10. It is also highly likely that the *Vigrahavyāvartanī* was written in the genre of *vāda vitaṇḍā*, wherein the task was to refute Nyāya-Vaiśeṣika theories of knowledge without positing a counter-theory overtly or by implication, rather than a treatise proscribing the formulation of any theory whatsoever (Matilal 1986: 49–56, 65–8). But even without entering these interpretive weeds, Candrakīrti, in his representation of Nāgārjuna's thought, seems to be making a basic conflation. It is one thing to say that the Buddha taught no truths, and quite another to say that the Buddha taught falsehoods. Candrakīrti seems to make this conflation without any fear of the implications of the second option. He is in a position, hermeneutically and institutionally, to take this bold step. He is a seventh-century advocate of a recognized *vāda*, Madhyamaka, whose very existence is not really imperiled but well-subsidized, and which insulates itself from error by disassociating itself from other schools which make forthright metaphysical and epistemological claims. Given the discussion of the previous section of this paper, we should ask ourselves whether Nāgārjuna was in a similar position. Would Nāgārjuna, whose promotion of a slowly and obscurely emerging Mahāyāna, which had to face the risks of being obliterated from the intellectual record and ejected from monastic orders as a vulnerable minority, have saluted his philosophical rivals with the announcement that the Buddha taught falsehoods? That is unlikely in the extreme.

And there is yet another major philosophical problem confronting Candrakīrti's depiction of Nāgārjuna's thought. To make the point with general reference to the MMK, Nāgārjuna appears not to have philosophically bought in to the assumptions according to which the Abhidharma conception of *upādāya prajñapti* functioned as a reductive analytical device. In MMK 4, Nāgārjuna adjures the possibility that the *skandha*-s can exist or operate independently of one another. In MMK 6, he parts from the view that phenomena (*bhāva*) can either be eternally fixed by characteristics or free from characteristics. MMK 13 avers that the *saṃskāra*-s should not be appealed to as a final term of reduction. MMK 20 attacks the very conception of a combination (*sāmagryā*) as a contained and unitary bundle of causal conditions. And, as we have seen, MMK 22 denies that either the concepts of the *Tathāgata* or emptiness can be accounted for by depending designations (*upādāya prajñapti*). If at the very foundation of the Ābhidharmika formulation of "depending designations" is their function of dissolving composite entities into their constituent but real parts, then it would seem a poor tool indeed for a philosopher who spends protracted efforts to show that combinations are not a coherent topic of analysis, parts are artificially hypostasized putative entities and that "depending designations" themselves cannot be descriptions of emptiness. Therefore, for Nāgārjuna to have undermined the targets, the analytical function and the efficacy of Abhidharma "depending designations," and then to claim that "emptiness" itself is a "depending designation" would, as above, implicate him in a glaring incoherence.

Our critical examination of these five issues, Nāgārjuna's overt treatment of *prajñapti* and *upādāya prajñapti*, the majority of other statements in his corpus that do not associate *upādāya prajñapti* with emptiness, the ambiguous but wanting confirmation of "emptiness" as an *upādāya prajñapti* by other early commentators, the hermeneutic differences between Nāgārjuna and Candrakīrti, and the serious philosophical challenges of taking *śūnyatā* as a "depending designation," compel us to face a new challenge. If this examination has rendered Candrakīrti's reading of MMK 24:18 problematic, then how should this pivotal stanza of Nāgārjuna's *caturāryasatyaparikṣa* be understood? I will now attempt to address this challenge, and proffer two possible explanations of Nāgārjuna's MMK 24:18 that render it consistent with its immediate context, with the rest of Nāgārjuna's works, with the bulk of the early commentarial literature and as philosophically cogent. After presenting these two possible explanations, I will make the case that the second is more likely. I will then close this chapter with brief reflections on some implications of the result of this project for contemporary scholarship.

The Case for Simple Synonymy

The verses which open the twenty-fourth chapter of the MMK articulate the exasperated objections of a Buddhist opponent of Nāgārjuna's who takes "emptiness" to be a dire threat to the very existence and practice of Buddhism. This exasperation has its cause in the opponent's belief that, by the expression "emptiness" (*śūnyatā*), Nāgārjuna colloquially means "non-existence" (*abhāva*).

> *yadi śūnyam idaṃ sarvam udayo nāsti na vyayaḥ /*
> *caturṇām āryasatyānām abhāvas te prasajyate //*
> *parijñā ca prahāṇaṃ ca bhāvanā sākṣikarma ca /*
> *caturṇām āryasatyānām abhāvān nopapadyate //*
> *tadabhāvān na vidyante catvāry āryaphalāni ca /*
> *phalābhāve phalasthā no na santi pratipannakāḥ //*
> *saṃgho nāsti na cet santi te 'ṣṭau puruṣapudgalāḥ /*
> *abhāvāc cāryasatyānāṃ saddharmo 'pi na vidyate //*
> *dharme cāsati saṃghe ca kathaṃ buddho bhaviṣyati /*
> *evaṃ trīṇy api ratnāni bruvāṇaḥ pratibādhase //*
> *śūnyatāṃ phalasadbhāvam adharmaṃ dharmam eva ca /*
> *sarvasaṃvyavahārāṃś ca laukikān pratibādhase //* (MMK 24:1–6)

> If all of this were empty, there would be no arising nor perishing.
> There would follow the non-existence of the four noble truths.
> Wisdom, relinquishing, meditative cultivation and realizing
> would not follow from the non-existence of the four noble truths.
> No acknowledgment of the four noble truths
> would come from non-existence,
> there would be no cultivation or abiding in the fruits,
> and no experiences of them either.
> There would be no monastic order,
> nor any persons belonging to it.
> From the non-existence of the noble truths,
> there would also be no acknowledgment of the true *dharma*.

In the non-existence of *dharma* and the monastic order,
how could awakening arise?
Your discourse abandons the three jewels themselves.
From emptiness, even the existence of *dharma* and *adharma*
and all the collective common practices of the world are abandoned.

The core of the chapter addresses this worry. It does not do so by embracing a denial of true doctrine (*saddharma*). Instead, it affirms that a proper understanding of "emptiness," not as "non-existence" but as "causally conditioned co-arising," leaves all of the cherished Buddhist ideals firmly in place. It is only by disassociating the meaning of "emptiness" from "causally conditioned co-arising" that one, according to Nāgārjuna, courts the danger of losing the Buddhist path. For the moment, I will leave the initial phrase of MMK 24:18's second line ambiguously translated for the purposes of clarifying it in the following presentation.

svabhāvād yadi bhāvanāṃ sadbhāvam anupaśyasi /
ahetu pratyayān bhāvaṃs tvam evaṃ sati paśyasi //
kāryaṃ ca kāraṇaṃ caiva kartāraṃ karaṇam kriyām /
utpādaṃ ca nirodhaṃ ca phalaṃ ca pratibādhase //
yaḥ pratītyasamutpādaḥ śūnyatāṃ tāṃ pracakṣmahe /
sā prajñaptir upādāya pratipat saiva madhyamā //
apratītya samutpanno dharmaḥ kaścin na vidyate /
yasmāt tasmād aśūnyo hi dharmaḥ kaścin na vidyate //
yady aśūnyam idaṃ sarvam udayo nāsti na vyayaḥ /
caturnāṃ āryasatyānām abhāvas te prasajyate // (MMK 24:16–20)

If you perceive these phenomena as entities that are self-produced (*svabhāva*),
you will perceive these very phenomena as uncaused and unconditioned.
You will contradict the cause, effect, the agent itself,
the instrument, act, arising, ceasing and fruit.
Whatever is conditionally co-arisen, we proclaim that to be emptiness.
That ("emptiness") is a *prajñaptir upādyāya*.
This is precisely the middle path.
Any particular thing that is not conditionally co-arisen is not acknowledged.
For this reason, any particular thing that is not empty is not acknowledged either.
If all this is not empty, there exists no arising nor extinction,
(and) this would imply the non-existence of the four noble truths.

The resounding and unequivocal point of this collection of verses is that, when Nāgārjuna refers to the "emptiness" of all phenomena, he means nothing but the "causally conditioned co-arising" of all phenomena. Since all practitioners accept, as they should, the Buddha's teaching of causally conditioned co-arising as the correct account of how things and persons in the world arise, interact, and perish, as well as their possibilities of rebirth or release, there is nothing at all about "emptiness" that threatens the Buddhist worldview or practice. "Emptiness" is but a reaffirmation of the causally conditioned, co-arisen nature of all things, and not at all, as the opponent had feared when the *parikṣa* commenced, a denial of phenomena, persons, the order, or practice. There is something else that must be noticed here. Absolutely nothing in this block of verses, and in fact nothing in the entirety of MMK 24, warrants the mention of *upādāya prajñapti* as the Abhidharma analytic method for reducing composite terms to their parts. The discussion is simply not about the Ābhidharmika notion of an *upādāya prajñapti*, a "depending designation." It is far less of a surprise that no other early Mādhyamika commentator explicitly, or even at all, brings up the Abhidharma *upādāya prajñapti* here, and far more jarring that Candrakīrti does.

It is, even in view of this, undeniable that the diction of the first half of MMK 24:18's line 2 is *sā prajñaptir upādāya*. If Candrakīrti's attempt to resolve the puzzle of this diction's abrupt appearance does not clarify it, and the other early commenters are of little help as well, then how should we understand it? I would argue that the disambiguation of this phrase would make the most sense of it contributed to, rather than detracted from, the overall point of the environing context of verses, which is evidently the synonymy of "conditioned co-arising" and "emptiness." In this respect, the translation of Kumārajīva and the notes of his commentator Qingmu put us on the right track. They make the case that "emptiness" is just an alternative name or "borrowed name" (假名 *jia ming*) for conditioned co-arising. But how could this depiction be applied to the original Sanskrit vocabulary of *prajñaptir upādyāya* as it appears in the stanza? There are two ways of doing this.

The first of these strategies is sheerly grammatical.[12] We must notice an important detail in the second line of MMK 24:18.

sā prajñaptir upādāya pratipat saiva madhyamā

The line consists of two separate sentences, or at the very least two independent clauses. Were the entire line only one sentence, the *sā* that begins the line would be followed by the coordinating conjunction *ca* after the second *sa*. Instead of this, the second *sa* is qualified by the emphatic adverb *eva*, and this demands that we understand the second *sa* of the line to refer to a distinct subject from the first *sā*. The frequent absence of indicative verbs in Sanskrit as well as the common omission of implied accusative objects from transitive verb forms would permit us several options in identifying where they lie here. One of those options would have the line read:

sā prajñaptir (tāṃ) upādāya (asti) / pratipat saiva madhyamā (asti) /

But this would put us right back where we began with the puzzle that opened this paper, namely why *upādāya* still lacks a transitive object. Indeed, this rendition is precisely how Candrakīrti and apparently Bhāvaviveka read the line in the first place. But the other option would be to parse the line like this:

sā prajñaptir (asti) / (tāṃ) upādāya pratipat saiva madhyamā (asti) /

This formulation would enable Nāgārjuna to do several things that appear consistent with all the instant purposes. Omitting the two explicit mentions of *asti* and omitting the accusative object of *upādāya* in this fashion would permit him to emphasize the equivalence in meaning of "conditioned co-arising" and "emptiness" and assert that correctly understanding this is the key to Buddhist practice. Parsing the line this way would also allow him to retain the metrical integrity of the *śloka*. It would make optimal sense if the first *sā* in the line, having feminine grammatical gender, not only modified *prajñapti* but corresponded to the feminine gender of *śūnyatā* in the first line. The second line of MMK 24:18, on this construal, would literally read:

This is the designation ("emptiness").
Once that (*tāṃ*, designation) has been grasped (*upādāya*),
this is the middle path.

This grammatical resolution of the interpretive problem of MMK 24:18's diction does have the virtue of affirming the synonymous extension of "conditioned co-arising" and "emptiness" equated by the first line, and thus cementing the tie between the verse on the context of the *parikṣa*.

But I must admit that this is, at best, a highly counter-intuitive and inelegant remedy. Nāgārjuna's verses are, as a rule, composed with a coherent flow and felicity of expression. Solving this particular textual difficulty in such a clunky manner, one which admittedly seems to be even more ad hoc and forced than I am arguing Candrakīrti's exegesis is, is just not convincing. A more natural reading of the line, and one that coheres with Buddhist philosophical vocabulary in broad scope, does strongly suggest that, with *prajñaptir upādyāya*, Nāgārjuna is recruiting technical terminology into the service of his argument.

It is here that the recent scholarship of Leonard Priestley and Joseph Walser comes to our aid. It does so, I will ultimately maintain, not quite as they specifically intended, but it makes available what I believe to be the correct resolution of this most thorny issue. Priestly and Walser both provide extensive textual evidence to demonstrate that the Abhidharma reductive conception of "depending designations" that we have heretofore been wrestling with was only one of several formulations of *upādāya prajñapti* available in Buddhist philosophical circles. Since we have found ample reasons to doubt Candrakīrti's essentially Ābhidharmika formulation of "depending designations," it falls to us to see whether one of the other available frameworks of *upādāya prajñapti* may yield interpretive fruit.

The first of these other notions of *upādāya prajñapti* was put forth by the Pudgalavādins. Priestley (1999: 138–41) demonstrates that, between the Theravāda, Sarvāstivāda, Sautrāntikas, and Pudgalavāda camps, there were a number of variations on this particular conception of *prajñapti*, with some designations classified as non-referring but reducible to real entities, others enabling the understanding of a term or idea and still others referring as general terms to the particularized *svabhāva* of *dharma*-s. Priestley (1999: 145–51), consulting various commentaries on the *Abhidharmakośa* as well as Buddhaghoṣa, then distinguishes between concepts produced by a combination of designations, meditative practices, and internal imagination which, while they are mental phenomena and not *dharma*-s themselves, reveal the nature of *dharma*-s and allow one to transform them. Priestley then recounts that the commentary on the *Puggalapaññati* refers to words for mental images that have generalized mental forms as their objects also as *upādāya prajñapti*, as these too are concepts "based on" some content (1999: 151). This means that any "designation," including the "depending designation," has two components: the "name" (*nāma*) component, through which the *prajñapti* reduces the composite phenomena to the *dharma*-s that make it up, and the *artha* or "meaning" component, which refers to a simple idea or image (1999: 152–3). All this entails for the Pudgalavādins that, in referring to a "person" (*pudgala*) as a real phenomenon, the *upādāya prajñapti* of a "person" in its naming function is reducible to the *skandha*-s out of which the person is made, but in its "meaning" function refers to a person as a simple idea that is not dependent on the *skandha*-s. It is this latter idea of a "person," who enjoys continuity through time that makes all the other Buddhist assertions about *karma*, rebirth, practice, and release true assertions. Walser (2006: 200–3, 242–3) adds to these observations additional citations from the *Puggalapaññatti Aṭṭhakathā* and some Saṃmitīya elucidations of the Pudgalavādin doctrines wherein, according to the latter, *upādāya prajñapti*, in addition to reducing things to their parts, can also facilitate an understanding of things that have "indeterminate" (*avācya*) relations. Other relations that are known through the "meaning" functions of *upādāya prajñapti* on this account are exampled as those between a shadow and a tree, fire and fuel, the sun and moon in measuring time and an external and internal meditative image. As Walser emphasizes, the relationship between a shadow and a tree, the sun and moon in measuring time and meditative images cannot be analyzed in terms of part-whole relations. And so, for the Pudgalavādins, the *upādāya prajñapti* of the "person" may reduce the person to their *skanda*-s in one respect, but also identify an "inarticulable" (*avācya*) relation between the person and the *skandha*-s which maintains the notion of "person" irreducibly.

For reasons we need not dive into here, Walser believes that Nāgārjuna made various efforts to accommodate Pudgalavāda views in the early phases of his career during which he composed the MMK. This is reflected in how Walser concludes Nāgārjuna is making Pudgalavāda-inclined arguments about action and fruits in MMK 17 as well as other places. Thus, in his analysis of MMK 24:18, Walser (2006: 258–60) thinks it likely that the notion of *upādāya prajñapti* invoked is of the Pudgalavādin variety. Though his explanation of this determination is brief, Walser reasons that, in MMK 24:18, Nāgārjuna may be referring with *upādāya prajñapti* to designations that do denote the interdependence of things on one another in fashions that are non-reductive but inarticulable.

I do not see, unfortunately, how this Pudgalavādin take on *upādāya prajñapti* in any way clarifies MMK 24:18. In this light, the verse would have to be read in this fashion.

> *yaḥ pratītyasamutpādaḥ śūnyatāṃ tāṃ pracakṣmahe /*
> *sā prajñaptir upādyāya pratipat saiva madhyamā //*
>
> Whatever is conditionally co-arisen, we proclaim that to be emptiness.
> That is a designation depending on (indeterminate, irreducible relations).
> This is precisely the middle path.

It is not at all clear, in this reconstruction, how the Pudgalavāda analysis of tress and their shadows, fire and fuel, or external and internal meditative images can shed any light on what Nāgārjuna means to say about the relation between "conditioned co-arising" and "emptiness" here. If Nāgārjuna believes emptiness is in one way reducible to conditioned co-arising but in another way not reducible to it, he offers no explanation for that view anywhere in the MMK or anywhere else in his corpus. In addition to that, the Pudgalavāda conception of the person's relation to the *skandha*-s is dealt with in MMK 18 in a way that, to some extent, does affirm the interdependence of the *ātman* on *skandha*-s, but ultimately shrugs off the whole problem as a "conceptual proliferation" (*prapañca*) to be given up in 18.9. This seems not to be an endorsement of Pudgalavāda teaching. So, I don't think a Pudgalavāda framework for *upādāya prajñapti* aids us in understanding MMK 24:18.

In fairness to Walser (2006: 260), he also concedes in his discussion that the other major formulation of *upādāya prajñapti*, this one proffered by the Prajñaptivādins, may also be what Nāgārjuna had in mind in this verse. In the Prajñaptivāda framework, there are certain pairs of concepts for which the meaning of each concept of the pair is unintelligible without its partner. Each concept in this pair would therefore be a "reciprocal designation" (*anyonya prajñapti*) for the other. This can be seen in several pivotal claims made by the Prajñaptivādins. Both Xuanzang and Diṅnāga retrospectively summarize the basic principles of the Prajñaptivādins in their respective translations of the *Sannayabhedaparacantacakra*. The Prajñaptivāda view of the *skanda*-s represents them not as irreducible targets of analysis, but as causally interdependent on one another, making their respective designations interdependent on one another (*anyonya prajñapti,* 施設 *shi she*) (2006: 218–21). As Walser (2006: 237–8) sees it, there are definite instances in the MMK when Nāgārjuna himself makes use of this conception of *anyonya prajñapti*, as for example in MMK 4.1–2, where he writes that form (*rūpa*) cannot be conceived of in the absence of the cause (*kāraṇa*) of material form, and in 4.4–6 where he continues that "what is to be caused" (*kārya*) cannot be conceived of in the absence of the cause (*kāraṇa*). These mutually entailing conceptual pairs do not exhibit a relationship between a whole and its parts as in Abhidharma representations of an *upādāya prajñapti*, and in fact their relationship is irreducible because one cannot be thought without its counterpart. But, for the Prajñaptivādins, *anyonya prajñapti* is nonetheless a variety of *upādāya prajñapti* because each term in these kinds of conceptual pairs depends (*upādāya*) on the meaning of the other term in the pair.

As noted earlier, Walser does in a most cursory way allow for the possibility that Nāgārjuna deployed the notion of *anyonya prajñāpti* to explain the relationship between conditioned co-arising and emptiness in MMK 24:18. But he thinks the *upādāya prajñapti* that makes its appearance in the verse is more likely of the Pudgalavādin sort. The reason Walser has for this hedge, it appears, is that while Nāgārjuna does initially resort to reciprocal designations to explain various phenomena in the opening stanzas of MMK 4, by its close, from MMK 4:9–11, Nāgārjuna goes on the offensive against other forms of reciprocal conceptual interdependence (Walser 2006: 244). For my part, as we have just seen, a Pudgalavāda framework for "depending designations" does not seem to shed much light on MMK 24:18. I think that the Prajñaptivāda thematization of *upādāya prajñapti* as *anyonya prajñapti* or "reciprocal designations," on the other hand, allows the verse to fit in seamlessly with its immediate argumentative context. If we are permitted to understand *upādāya* as *anyonya* in 24:18 and leave the rest of the passage (MMK 24:16–20) translated as it was laid out several pages ago, we have the following:

> If you perceive these phenomena as entities that are self-produced (*svabhāva*),
> you will perceive these very phenomena as uncaused and unconditioned.
> You will contradict the cause, effect, the agent itself,
> the instrument, act, arising, ceasing, and fruit.
> Whatever is conditionally co-arisen, we proclaim that to be emptiness.
> That ("emptiness") is a reciprocal designation
> (reciprocal with "conditionally co-arisen")
> This is precisely the middle path.
> Any particular thing that is not conditionally co-arisen is not acknowledged.
> For this reason, any particular thing that is not empty is not acknowledged either.
> If all this is not empty, there exists no arising nor extinction,
> (and) this would imply the non-existence of the four noble truths.

In this light, MMK 24:18 only underlines the point that is explicitly argued for in the stanzas that precede and follow it, namely that Nāgārjuna's use of "emptiness" entails nothing more than "conditioned co-arising," and these mutually entailing concepts explain the orders of nature, *karma*, and practice. Understood in this way, MMK 24:18 would be precisely echoed in the three other similar verses of Nāgārjuna's corpus, *Vigrahavyāvartanī* 70, *Lokātītastava* 22, and *Acintyastava* 40, all of which merely equate the meaning of these terms with no relevant need to add *upādāya prajñapti* into the mix. This would also explain the relative silence or curt treatment of the balance of Nāgārjuna's first five hundred years of commentators, who either felt that there is no need to explain the already obvious point of MMK 24:18 or, like Kumārajīva and Qingmu, merely note that "emptiness" is just an alternative term for "conditioned co-arising." This reading would allow Nāgārjuna to explain to non-Mahāyāna Buddhists in his own historical context that nothing about his notion of "emptiness" represented the slightest threat to Buddhist doctrine and practice. On the contrary, "emptiness" should be considered synonymous with the "causally conditioned co-arising" that we find in Buddha's own teaching. This employment of "emptiness," according to which it should be taken as a term whose meaning depends on "emptiness" and vice-versa, rather than throwing up a host of difficult philosophical problems, resolves problems. In short, if Nāgārjuna is in MMK

24:18 using mutual dependence to explain the relationship between conditioned co-arising and emptiness, this choice avoids all the exegetical and philosophical problems that Candrakīrti's resorting to the Ābhidharmika *upādāya prajñapti* lays at our feet.

Brief Reflections on Hermeneutics

As was pointed out earlier in this chapter, it is certainly understandable why Candrakīrti's reading of MMK 24:18 gained such traction among modern commentators, as well as among classical Tibetan ones. After all, Candrakīrti offers the lengthiest and most robust explanation of the meaning of the stanza of all the early exegetes, and he does so in a way that is consistent both with some foregoing and well-known Buddhist ideas and with his own overarching philosophical aims. Beyond that, most of the contemporary readers and interpreters of Nāgārjuna in Anglophone scholarship have self-consciously and purposely adopted Candrakīrti's perspective because these modern commentators are convinced that Candrakīrti's Nāgārjuna can be recruited, with formidable philosophical firepower, into their own pitched battles against essentialism, realism, and a referential perspective on language. And, despite everything I have written here, the modern interpreters may continue to be inspired, informed, and motivated by Candrakīrti's Nāgārjuna, as this is fully their hermeneutic and philosophical prerogative.

Based on my own examination of the issue and the available evidence, I believe there are a number of serious textual, historical, hermeneutical, and philosophical problems with Candrakīrti's reading of MMK 24:18 which render it forced, incoherent, and not compelling. Instead of reverting to modern ideas or arguments in order to resolve the puzzles of the stanza, I have looked back to classical sources, where it seems to me a perfectly lucid and sound resolution can be found for these puzzles. When dealing with ancient philosophers, it is always most hermeneutically prudent to look first to the ancients in order to see how they addressed such conundrums before reaching into our own modern philosophical toolbags. This is especially the case in the context of intercultural philosophical reflection, impacted as heavily as it has been by seven preceding centuries of Western colonialism.

I would like to make my final point in as precise and charitable fashion as I am able, because I think the case warrants maximum charity. I am not, in this chapter, accusing the bulk of contemporary interpreters of covert philosophical colonialism. As noted, it is a hermeneutic truism that any interpreter in any age will be largely driven by the historical, social, and in this case philosophical concerns of his or her own age. That is just as true of me as it is for modern interpreters as it is for Candrakīrti as it is for Nāgārjuna himself. I take nothing about finite human hermeneutical circumstances to be scandalous; they follow from our finite and limited natures. But neither are they completely immutable. We can struggle against them and expand our own vision by, as is also envisioned in the hermeneutic encounter, being open to and transformed by the texts and frameworks of the past. The modern interpreters of Nāgārjuna, all of them, have done precisely this. They have turned to a classical commentator to help them understand Nāgārjuna's intent and significance, and their efforts have thus far been laudable and have done a palpable service to intercultural philosophy. My aim in this chapter has not been to reject the work of modern Nāgārjuna exegetes nor to reject the wisdom of Candrakīrti. My aim, instead, has been to show that there are times when the classical commentarial tradition that is preferred is not necessarily the one that makes the most sense of a text in its own setting, but a commentarial tradition that empowers moderns to face down whatever they perceive to be the philosophical nemeses of our own times. In the case of MMK 24:18, I think we see this phenomenon at work. Our interpretive vigilance and hermeneutic alertness must always be functioning as we continue the debate about what our predecessors were trying to achieve. That is the best way for us to both fully inhabit our own era and acknowledge the ancients with genuine philosophical honor.

Notes

1 This chapter is a continuation of a discussion I, at least in part, initiated a decade or so ago with my 2010 essay "Acquiring Emptiness: Interpreting Nāgārjuna's MMK 24:18" (Berger 2010). This paper prompted an initial critique and response that can be found in J. L. Garfield and J. Westerhoff (2011) and my response (Berger 2011). A further critical evaluation of my initial essay can be found in M. Salvini (2011). This essay will continue that discussion, in part by correcting some initial errors in my reading identified by Salvini, but nonetheless persisting in the larger interpretation I first offered. It would however be remiss of me not to mention that my own views of Nāgārjuna's thought, which depart in some ways sharply from the balance of modern construals, were strongly influenced by, though do not always agree with, the historical treatment of the philosopher found in the work of Joseph

Walser. My evaluation of the genuine importance of Walser's work will be discussed here.

2 The connection between "emptiness" and the "designation" or "notion" mentioned in this second line seems to be indicated by the fact that both are feminine nouns.

3 Translations of Sanskrit and Chinese terms and texts in this chapter, unless otherwise indicated, are my own.

4 Salvini (2011: 237) even speculates that, because the *pratītya* in *pratītya samutpāda* is also a *lyabanta* or "absolutive" form, its identical syntax with *upādāya* may suggest that Candrakīrti takes "causally conditioned co-arising" and "depending designation" to be synonyms as well, and so he feels at liberty to basically equate the meaning of all four terms in the stanza. Burton however, as we will see shortly, thinks that understanding the "parts" of a chariot or the *skandha*-s of a person to be analogous to a proper understanding of the "limbs" of conditioned co-arising is an errant move. That "ignorance," "birth," "desire," "grasping," and the rest are constituent processes of conditioned co-arising as a whole is certainly fundamental to all Buddhist thought, but to see these processes as "parts" of conditioned co-arising in the way that axles and wheels are parts of chariots or *skandha*-s are parts of persons is something that the Ābhidharmikas, according to Burton, did not countenance.

5 I would argue, and assume that the argument would be reasonably uncontroversial, that the appeal of Candrakīrti's representation of Nāgārjuna's ideas lies primarily in the possibilities that this reading opened for a synthesis between Madhyamaka and Yogācāra thoughts. The bridge of that synthesis would seem most likely to be built from the resources of a mere "conceptualism" (*prajñaptivāda*). Otherwise, it is, to say the least, difficult to reconcile the outright Madhyamaka rejection of *svabhāva* with the complex Yogācāra artifice of three kinds of *svabhāva*.

6 This is also consistent with the entire thrust of MMK 4, where the *skandha*-s, owing to their interdependence, are to be considered empty.

7 These points had been made much earlier in Anglophone scholarship on Abhidharma; see Warder (1971), and Williams (1981).

8 See Hu Anguo's commentary (*Qunqiu Hu Shi Chuan*) on the events of Duke Huan's sixth year as reported in the *Qunqiu Zuozhuan*.

9 It will doubtless be noticed that I am not including Sengzhao or Jizang in my rehearsal of early Chinese commentaries on the MMK here. These figures were developing a distinctive tradition of *Sanlun* in China that, in the case of the former, drew heavily on Daoist ideas and emphasized the existential dimensions of emptiness. In the case of Jizang, his interpretation of 空 *kong* or "emptiness" is so tightly bound up with his systematic insistence that it should exclusively be understood as the relinquishing of obsessions with metaphysical views that he is not much concerned about its terminological relationship to "conditioned

co-arising" in MMK 24:18. It might be argued, I admit, that Jizang's view could be considered as agreeing with a certain interpretation of Candrakīrti, but that would need to be dealt with in an entirely separate work. Indeed, modern readings of Madhyamaka as a thoroughly anti-metaphysical perspective might be closer to Jizang's recension than to Candrakīrti's. In any case, the emphasis that Jizang places on the requirement that Mādhyamika Buddhists are not to embrace doctrines of existence or non-existence, where 空 *kong* is often wrongly understood as "non-existence," is not a controversial position in the school. Further, the word "空 *kong*" even for Jizang is not a falsehood, but a "remedy" that is adopted for its heuristic value in discouraging attachment to views, whereas the "ultimate truth" of reality is inexpressible and unthinkable for him (Rogacz 2015: 134).

10 In their reply to my initial essay on this topic, Garfield and Westerhoff recruit Buddhapālita's work in a general way against my arguments that Candrakīrti's reading should not be considered normative. They conclude their critical review of my work that the supposed unanimity of Buddhapālita and Candrakīrti against the views I am explaiņing here show that this is clearly a case of "Berger verses all the sages" (2011: 268). However, a rehearsal of the early commentarial literature here, which can also be found briefly in Walser 2006: 258–9, would seem to show that not even all the sages agreed about the meaning of this stanza.

11 Even the earliest mention of Mahāyāna in Buddhist inscriptions, specifically at the Abhayagiri monastery in Sri Lanka, are not found until the third century, and even then is identified by a different name, *Vetullaba* (see Holt: 63–4). Faxian, in his early fifth-century visit to Sri Lanka, recognizes no Mahāyāna movements there.

12 In my first essay devoted exclusively to this topic in 2010, I also argued for a grammatical solution to the problem, but there I tried to show that this passage and other Pāli texts allowed for a passive sense of *upādāya*. I have been persuaded by Salvini's excellent 2011 piece in the *Journal of Indian Philosophy* that this detail of my original proposal was errant. I therefore abandon that argument here. However, as I will show, the two solutions I detail later allow the overarching claims of my original argument to stand.

5

"The Social Meaning of the Middle Way"

B. S. Yadav and the Madhyamaka Critique of Indian Ontologies[1]

Introduction

The essays of Bibhuti Singh Yadav (1943-1999) represent Buddhism as a social invective against various Indian ontologies that either directly underwrote caste society or did nothing to upset the status quo.[2] Specifically, Madhyamaka Buddhism, of Nāgārjuna's and Candrakīrti's variety, rejects both the hierarchical essentialism of caste society and the escapism of a reclusive, renunciate and metasocial *nirvāṇa*, leaving the individual to demand social equality on religious grounds (Yadav 1992: 162).[3] The real significance of dissolving the boundaries between *saṃsāra* and *nirvāṇa* in Madhyamaka lies in its opening the way for Buddhists to return from the forests to their homes and speak to society in its own language, but speak as reformers, so that the call to social justice could re-enter the Indian life-world on Indian terms.[4]

It is Yadav's social vision of Madhyamaka Buddhism that I wish to emphasize in this expository essay, as I believe if offers a significant contribution to English-language studies of Indian Buddhism and its implications. It has become common in English scholarship to view Prāsaṅgika Madhyamaka as a Buddhist school devoted only to the refutation of philosophical theorizing as such, the adherents dedicating themselves to the undoing of Hindu and Buddhist metaphysical and epistemological theses while cunningly avoiding any implications of holding their own positions, since theory is a sign of attachment. Yadav was quick to add to this view that there were no such things as socially or politically innocent metaphysical or epistemological theories (*prameya-pramāṇaśāstra*) in the Indian philosophical context. The builders of ontological systems, including for Yadav the Hindu Naiyāyikas and Pūrva and Uttara Mīmāṃsakas as well as the

Buddhist Mādhyamika Svātantrikas, Sarvāstivādins and Yogācāra-Sautrāntikas, constituted different "group thinks" of a socio-ideological conservative "circle."[5] Behind all the technical objections this "circle" had to *vāda-vaitaṇḍikas* like Nāgārjuna and Candrakīrti, namely that they can neither refute their opponents nor establish their own aims with "empty terms" (*śūnyavāda*) but must submit to propositional and referential assertions or denials,[6] lies according to Yadav a more fundamental social concern.

> Happy with the status quo, the circle excludes the middle.
> It finds comfort in ontological commitments, shying away
> from the ego-centric concerns that get refleshed in
> categories like being and non-being. The circle calls for
> a world where identity has privilege over difference,
> the one over the many, the whole over the part, the caste
> over the individual. Positive posture, which at bottom is
> a form of self-assertion, determines the form and content
> of negation; the conditions that make saying "yes" possible
> also determine the means and limit of saying "no." The circle
> likes unity and coherence; fearful of inner contradiction, it
> regulates deviation and dissent. It does not deny difference or
> plurality, but it relegates them to attributes of identity. No wonder
> the circle insists upon methodological consensus. It talks
> of inside and outside, the law-abiding "I" and the liminal
> "other." It recognizes the other in contrast to itself, in its own
> image and on its own terms, Inside the border there is
> syllogistic coherence, traditions of ontological commitment and
> the harmony of hierarchical society. (Yadav 1992: 153–4)

Ontologically, Indian realists believe that differences between things are possible by virtue of distinct particulars possessing an identity (*tādātmya*) of substance and attributes (*dharma*) in a locus (*dharmin*). Vedāntins hold the inmost "self" (*ātman*) to be free of all internal differentiation, and relegate difference to an ultimately illusory status. Sarvāstivāda Buddhists take up the cause of difference, namely the difference between *Tathāgata* and *saṃsāra* through a doctrine of "self-nature" (*svabhāva*). All these groups, regardless of their seeming philosophical oppositions, are nonetheless using logic and epistemology to buttress theories of the world that justify various socio-political agendas. In the case of Hindu realists, the mission is to support caste distinctions through a doctrine of essences. The Vedāntins, both of the classical and "neo" persuasions, equate Indian national identity with Brahminical tradition. The Sarvāstivādins eschew social participation with the distinction of being the disciples of "the One who has come and gone" (*Tathāgata*). Mādhyamika Buddhists like Nāgārjuna and Candrakīrti reject caste society, but not the social responsibilities that are of a piece with the *bodhisattva* ideal. It is for this reason that they must shun the patterns of thought and language that create the ontologies of identity and difference, which in their turn underwrite social inequality.

> The *bodhisattva* is not interested in going to *nirvāṇa*, let alone in proving the existence of *nirvāṇa* as a positive or negative entity. Existence is relational, and it is in such relationship, in society itself, that salvation is to be found. A *bodhisattva* cannot exit the world, and in the world he demands social equality in the name of *Tathāgata*. Such commitment enjoins that no Buddhist shall ever concede the world to an epistemology of (the) static present. Neither can a Buddhist concede meaning to the logocentric discourse, which insists that all speech is entitative...The point, according to Mahāyāna, is not to do more epistemology, however corrective, and replace the metaphysics of eternal entities with that of static moments. Doing so would be to succumb to the Hindu ideology of the status quo. The point is that Buddhism is about changing the world not knowing things as they are in themselves. (Yadav 1994: 117)

This essay will be an examination of Yadav's representations of Madhyamaka's critiques of the social implications of Hindu realism, Vedāntic "ātmology" and Buddhist essentialism. Through this examination, a greater appreciation can be gleaned of why Yadav believed that the Prāsaṅgika Madhyamaka of Nāgārjuna and Candrakīrti served as a corrective to these implications. It was Yadav's conviction that rendering unsupportable the classical Indian ontologies of identity and difference offers a way to break the stranglehold "the circle" has had on Indian intellectual and social life. Some critical assessment of these arguments will be footnoted along the way, but for the most part this chapter aims to add to current scholarship Yadav's emphasis on the social dimensions of critical Buddhist thought.

The Social Essentialism of the Hindu Realists

Yadav singles out two primary targets for his attack on Indian realism, the thought of the Bhaṭṭa Mīmāṃsaka Kumārila and the system of classical Nyāya. They are also respectively representatives of the two basic ontological orientations in the

Indian philosophical tradition, those of difference and identity. Kumārila's brand of realism is instrumental; it verifies the realities of objects through our ability to use them for practical ends (*pravṛttisāmarthya*). By extension, Kumārila's denigration of Buddhism is based on the suspicion that its lack of realist commitment is indicative of its lack of respect for "common sense" and thus the assumptions that make a harmonious society possible. Buddhism does not acknowledge difference, and difference for Kumārila is the necessary condition for successful practical actions, distinctions between castes, and successful social functioning. The Naiyāyikas, on the other hand, are philosophers of identity, and they are so in two senses, one metaphysical and the other methodological. They believe that objects are wholes (*avayavin*), that is to say, particular instantiations of universal substance-quality relations. Things are identified based on a correct apprehension of essences in which certain qualities inhere. This holds true whether one is attempting to properly locate a tree or a *brahmin*, since both are examples of natural kinds (*jāti*) and not constructed kinds (*upādhi*). This metaphysical essentialism, which serves as a support to the traditional social structure, is backed up by the Naiyāyikas with a methodological bias, which assumes that realistically grounded forms of reference are the only valid forms of discourse and debate. Buddhism on this view is not only disingenuous in its attempt to "refute by saying nothing,"[7] but is also unfit for admission into dialogue, given its "refusal to play the language game" (Matilal 1990: 155). Despite their various ontological prioritizations of difference and identity then, Kumārila and Nyāya close a logical and methodological "circle" around things as they are in themselves, society as it is in itself, and how one intelligibly speaks about both.

Kumārila's picture of the self is that of an agent, a practical being who uses objects different from himself to attain practical goals. More specifically, for the Mīmāṃsakas, *brahmins* use the Vedic texts as their "instrumental reason (*sādhana*)" in order to realize "material and moral ends (*abhyudaya*)" (Yadav and Allen 1995: 156) Yadav therefore identified the "three keys to Kumārila's system of thought" as "common sense, epistemology and scriptural authority" (Yadav and Allen 1995: 159). Indeed all of these elements hang together for the Bhaṭṭas, as the everyday perceptions of "common folks" are enabled in the first place by sensations that owe their input to distinct objects among which there are real differences (Yadav and Allen 1995: 160). Success in worldly matters is thus dependent on the sharpness and accurateness of a person's perceptions, and these perceptions are themselves apprehensions of differences between things.[8] The Vedic texts are a scriptural corpus which contains the instructions for success for all of society, because they reveal things, that is, elucidate differences, as they are in themselves, and therefore can give consequent guidance for human conduct. Yadav and Allen (Yadav and Allen 1995: 165) observed:

> Kumārila was a convinced man. He believed that a good form of life was a prerequisite for a clear and convincing form of thought. Category mistakes, misleading analogies, incomplete or incoherent argument, defiance of common sense—such anomalies ensue from moral failure. There is a causative relation between *dharma* and *śāstra*, being good and the ability to see things as they are in themselves (*dharmaja*)...In Kumārila's view, Vedic texts are the key to the good life; loss of faith in the texts entails confused and deceptive forms of discourse (*adharmaja*)...As long as the Vedas are present, people can differentiate the unpleasantly true form the pleasantly false, *dharma* from *adharma*, truthful speech from the politically correct speech.

The Vedas are the ultimate *pramāṇa* for those who desire heaven (*svarga-kāma*), for heaven cannot be attained by the mere worldly pursuit of *artha* and *kāma*, but must be procured through "eternal deeds" (*nitya-karma*) enjoined by the only texts that are infallible on issues of *dharma* and *adharma*.[9] These eternal duties include observance of one's *varṇāśramadharma*.

While Kumārila holds Gautama Śākyamuni in high esteem for his stern warnings against a superficial and egoistic materialism (Yadav and Allen 1995: 162), he believes that the Mahāyāna Buddhists, who have proclaimed themselves his followers, have erred in their rejection of practical common-sense knowledge, its ultimate extension in the Vedas, and therewith comes their refusal to answer the call to social responsibility. In a poignant passage, Yadav recounts how this dilemma, and Kumārila's attempt to overcome it, led to the great exegete's tragic suicide.

> Kumārila lived in an era when conflicts about the world and (the) worth of human work had hit home, generating much reflection on the nature of family and the relations it entails. The deeds of Siddhārtha Gautama still dominated the forms of life and thought. Ought an individual exit the family—and civil society—to discover the meaning of being in time? Kumārila had a first-hand experience of the divide. His nephew, Dharmakīrti, left the Vedic fold; like most great Buddhist *ācāryas*, he studied Vedic thought and found it wanting. Dharmakīrti became a monk and later turned

> out to be the greatest logician in the history of Buddhist thought. Kumārila was a family man. In his view the father was a father, the son a son, and the former had power over the latter by virtue of sheer difference... He saw no good in a renunciate form of life which he believed the philosophers justified through a theory of metasocial consciousness. Human relations are commanded by the transcendent Vedas...Kumārila takes an objectivist stance in defense of Hindu society, the *sanāntana dharma*. He sees meaning in social stability, in the ideology that a *Brahmin* is a *Brahmin*, a *Shudra* a *Shudra*. (Yadav and Allen 1995: 157–8).

The legend has it that, in order to undermine the unsocial Buddhist doctrines, Kumārila pretended to become a monk, learned the Mahāyāna philosophy inside and out, and then emerged from his mask to defeat his teachers in debate, "a sin in Sanskrit discourse" (Yadav and Allen 1995: 158). Kumārila was so vexed by the resulting pangs of conscience that, instead of accepting Śaṅkara's invitation to him to write commentaries on Advaita, Kumārila immolated himself near Prayag. Kumārila's philosophy and life were a systematic attempt to keep the utilitarian possibilities of difference circumscribed within Brāhmiṇical society.

The Naiyāyikas approved of this vision of the rational life, which had the individual pragmatically oriented based on a true knowledge of things and their relationships in the real world (Yadav 1994: 115). Indeed, Vātsyāyana had appropriated for Hindu logic the role of *anvīkṣikī* as it was defined in Kauṭilya's *Arthaśāstra*, the analytical reflection that was the ultimate ground of all other sciences, including agriculture, politics and, going beyond the Mīmāṃsakas, even *dharma* itself. This raised realistic epistemology to the level of meta-method for all social and political life.

> Such is the enlightened *cogito* of Nyāya philosophy. It does epistemology in the name of constituting a rational order of things, equating meaningful speech with entitative speech. Its discourse is replete with signs and signifiers, its world thick with definite and indubitable referents (*vācya-vācaka*). Epistemology constitutes a world of certitudes, methodically determining the existence and non-existence of things. Epistemology is the foundation, the mind and eye of all other sciences such as ethics and economics, politics and law,

> religion and rituals. Such disciplines are practical, as they are interested in doing things with things, rather than the means of determining their existence or nonexistence. Epistemology offers tools for political management of the world, including the religious world. It grants benefits to practical sciences in the same way a king affirms his sovereignty by doing beneficial things for his servants. Epistemology is the key to all discourse, ranging from the affairs of kings to those of (Gods). (Yadav 1994: 116–17)

In accord with the social and political ascendancy of epistemology, anyone wishing monetary gain and communal influence should acquire them through obeying the rules of discovery and language which the theory of knowledge reveals. (Yadav 1992: 138). These rules entail on the one hand an ontology of identity, in which particulars can be identified as the hosts of qualities, and subjects as the apprehenders of these particulars. They also entail on the other hand a practice of identity, in which logical problems are to be thematized and decided in formalized and regulated ways that will affirm and reaffirm the legitimacy of "the circle." In short, Nyāya theory and method provide an essentialist foundation for hierarchical society.

The Naiyāyikas define knowledge as a cognition which conforms to reality faithfully.[10] Error consists in mistakenly seeing or attributing a quality in a substance that doesn't belong there (*anyathākhyāti*), as when for example a rope is taken to be a snake because of its length, or conch is taken to be silver because it shines in the sun. But a perception is knowledge when a thing is apprehended as a snake because it is seen to have snakeness; an inference is knowledge when a substance is fire because smoke indicates its presence; verbal testimony is knowledge when a trustworthy authority witnesses to the truth of his assertions. Truth is correct and determinate qualification, where substances possess, or are the loci of, their attributes. Some substances are accidentally or contingently qualified (*upādhi*), as when for instance I say that a person is a cook; for that person does not cook all the time, and not all persons can cook. But some substances are naturally qualified (*jāti*), as leaves and tallness are of a tree. In deciding on what it is that actually stands before me in any given case, I must follow certain procedures that will identify for me the unvarying natural inherence relations of substances and their qualities. But just as with objects in the natural environment, people have certain inherent qualities (*guṇa*) that naturally equip them for membership in a caste (*varṇa*, *jāti*). Intelligence and goodness reside in *brahmins*, passion in warriors, and laziness in *śudras*. These qualities in their turn serve as social qualifications and disqualifications; the *brāhmins* must on account of their magnanimity and wit educate the society in religion and values, while the *śudras*, owing to their sloth, can be taken to be suffering *karmic* retribution, and must because of their ignorance serve society without polluting its sacred texts by learning how to read and study them. For Nyāya philosophy, logic becomes hierarchy, ontological essences solidify into fixed social structures.

> Existence is a matter of law and order. The world is a place where people follow their station in life, where unity is more important than equality, where the particular makes sense by virtue of bearing the universal and where individuals are ritually ranked in relation to the social whole. There is a determinable relation between cause and effect, agent and act, knowing and doing, being and social existence. The circle justifies inequality in the name of *karmic* coherence: to each according to the ethical quality of his *karmic* will; from each according to the social worth of that very will. The game of life is played according to rules. There is no rupture in human relations, no gap in what one does and what happens to be, and therefore no room for revolution in the name of social justice. Ontologically speaking, X is Y because of Z; socially speaking, life is as smooth as syllogistic reasoning. "Logic," said the founder of Nyāya, "is the ground of all thinking, the tool of all successful actions, even moral actions."...Ontology...encloses the meaning of the world in scriptural texts, and restricts access to the texts only to those who do *yajna* by virtue of their moral superiority. Hermeneutical reflection is not a natural or fundamental right. It is a matter of morally acquired rights, and it is confined to an ethical aristocracy for the good of society. (Yadav 1992: 143)

In addition to this philosophy of identity which amounts to an ontological essentialism, Nyāya is also the practice of identity. The purpose of philosophical debate, where logic or "inference for others" (*parārtha-anumāna*) is employed, is to dispel doubt (*saṃśaya*). Doubt for Nyāya consists in seeing or considering an amorphous object and, through corrective perception or inference based on a special mark or characteristic, doubt can be eliminated.[11] What formal logic in debate does is to establish truth among competing objective theses (*pratijñā*). Debate is a place, as Yadav puts it, where doubt is "staged," and it is staged in order for philosophers to "make questionable what they themselves believe to be true, and where they dramatize the indubitability of the ego by showing that it is presupposed in the methodic dubitability of all thought" (Yadav 1992: 145). Doubt is in the end useful for philosophers, for it establishes the identity of the doubting subject.[12]

> The ego is appetitive to the core. It posits a "this" as a locus on which to affirm its "I." The relation of "I" and "this" is fundamental; it gets formalized in subject-predicate discourse. The ego incarnates its alterity in the epistemological field where the holding of "I am this" is the ground for beholding the truth of "This is a jar," and where the *cogito* is believed to present things as they are in themselves (*svabhāva vāstu nibandanam*)…Space is a recognitive medium through which the ego confers knowness to an object in order to infer its own existence as the knowing subject. It is a sphere where man hears echoes of the words of which he himself is the speaker. The ego posits space to ascertain its existence through staged referents, to disperse its deceptions in propositional assertions and confessions of faith.[13] (Yadav 1992: 144–5)

Debate becomes in this way for the Naiyāyikas a self-affirming activity, for the same subject of knowledge is both the doubter and the knower. Now, Nāgārjuna and Candrakīrti have proposed to enter the field of debate, but they have done so without believing in the two fundamental assumptions of debate the logicians hold most essential. The first is that language is referential and signifies real objects that in any instant case are either being affirmed or denied. The second is that a debater must have a position which he believes to be true, and on the basis of that truth he assents or objects to contrasting positions. The name of the game in Indian logic, on this view, is commitment. The problem with *vāda-vaitaṇḍika*s like the Prāsaṅgika Mādhyamikas is that they want to debate without committing, either to the objective realism that grounds the Hindu theory of language or a definite position that they themselves wish to establish; the Buddhists wish to use the rules of the game without believing in the rules (Yadav 1992: 144). But, the Buddhists are represented as responding, that is the whole problem. It is really the Naiyāyikas, and not the Buddhists, who debate in bad faith, for despite their insistence that philosophical argument is about truth, what is really important to them is commitment, and that means commitment to rules that have been agreed upon in advance, not that have been proven in debate. This insistence on commitment to the assumptions of the rules rather than merely playing by the rules is a symptom, according to the Mādhyamikas, of the social anxiety of the Hindu logicians about the identity of their community memberships, as logicians and as *brāmana*-s.

> The ego uses space to collectivize itself in a group-think. It carves a cognitive boundary, places its identity inside the boundary and then looks for a competing "other" across the border. Competing collectivities defend their identity in the face of difference, none recognizing the other for what it is, and each requiring all others to witness the superiority of its own claims. Space thus becomes a dialectical stage, a forum for identity play and inter-ontological discourse. Chandrakīrti thematizes the discourse. He wants to look at the psycho-social reasons that force philosophers to formalize the status quo. The need is to return philosophy to the everyday world; the *cogito* to the *ego*; *logos* to *eros*; Being to the desire for immortal identity; singularity of the first cause to sociality of causes and conditions…His strategy is to do immanent criticism, to deconstruct ontological discourse in terms of the rules of that very discourse. (Yadav 1992: 146)

By using logic to dismantle the conclusions of the logicians, the Buddhist seeks to uncover the craving (*taṇhā*) that parches the throat of the Nyāya "group-think." That craving is a craving for their professional identity and the superiority of their social status.

The Conservative Traditionalism of Advaitic "Ātmalogy"

In his final, but in the author's opinion most brilliant, essay, Yadav unravels the central doctrines of Śaṅkarācārya's Advaita Vedānta and relates them to the political agenda of "Neo-Hindu" thought. Advaita represents in the Indian tradition the philosophical and cultural culmination of the ontology of identity. Advaita is after all the search for the eternal, undifferentiated "self" (*ātman*). It seeks to show, through its philosophical elaboration of the *Upaniṣads*, that reality is at bottom utterly free of difference, and that the unitary self is the basis of all consciousness, experience and worldly life. These contentions are supported by Śaṅkara in his much analyzed *Adhyāsabhāṣyam*, which opens his obligatory commentary on the *Brahmasūtra*. *Adhyāsa*, "misplacement," or as Yadav translates it, "mispredication," is Śaṅkara's explanation for how human beings mistake the eternal self for the finite, changing physical body, and so it reveals to us how on the one hand difference is unreal and identity is real, while on the other how human beings live in their self-created world of difference. Human experience requires that there be at least two elements in cognition which are distinct, the self, or "this" (*idam*) and the not-self or "not-this" (*anidam*). However, in everyday experience, these two become confused through a projection of the properties of the one on the other, such that when what qualifies objects becomes attributed to the self, the *ātman* assumes the form of an ego-consciousness (*ahaṃkāra*), that is, it becomes wrongly objectified. This process of mispredication is evidenced by language. In common expressions such as "I know" (*jāñāmi*), the act of perceiving (*upalabdhi*), which takes place by virtue of the psycho-physical apparatus, becomes imposed upon or attributed to *ātman*, which does not act; while the perception (*dṛṣṭi*, *avabodha*) of *ātman* becomes attributed to the empirically individuated mind (*buddhi*).[14] In expressions like "I do" (*karomi*), the activities of the body are projected upon the changeless (*kūtastha*) self, and that self is just as wrongly said be the agent (*kartṛ*) of the acts. Still other sentences like "I am a man" attribute qualities of the bodily substance to the self, or fabricate changing internal states of feeling to the self which is changeless (*nitya*) as in "I am happy." All transcendental error then rests upon the mistaken identification of the self as in one way or another an empirical "I" (*ahaṃ*) rather than *ātman*, which for Advaitins is eternal and unchanging. But we cannot do this, for as Śaṅkara famously states at the beginning of his commentary, the notions of self (*asmadpratyaya*) and not-self (*yuṣmadpratyaya*) are opposed to one another like light and darkness. They cannot be identified without committing logical error. But then again, it is precisely this ongoing logical error that makes life in the world possible, for that is how the self becomes incarnated as a distinct individual with a body, will and aims. It is of course one thing to attack this doctrine on logical and epistemological grounds,[15] but it is much more illuminating, Yadav believed, to see into the very utilitarian opportunities of the doctrine of *adhyāsa*. He wrote:

> "S is P" is a case of *adhyāsa* if P signifies properties that are alien to S, and which nevertheless ought to be imposed on S, if it is to be a site of material and moral interest. "S is S" is true, but it is also a tautology and meaningless. *Adhyāsa* means discovering meaning through mispredicated identity, which necessitates replacing "S is S" with "S is P." Logically speaking, S and P are altogether different (sorts) of entities; the presence of one entails (the) absence of the other in the same place. Difference is the truth, but in it there is no material and moral

> good. Therefore truth must make room for the false, difference for the imagined identity. Being must be altered into Being-as, self into self-as. There is no material or moral good in self-in-itself; it must be construed as something else. Imagined identity is logically odd, but it is also the condition for our being in the world. Life, after all, is larger than logic. (Yadav 2000: 86)

The strange thing about the implications of the doctrine of *adhyāsa* as it expounds on the relation between self and world is not merely what Daya Krishna has noticed, namely that ultimately for Śaṅkara, the absolute difference or dualism between the two is the truth, *a la* Sāṃkhya, and their false identification is the mistake (Krishna 1991: 156–8). It is rather that Śaṅkara posits that the identity of the self can only be reclaimed when the falsity of the useful has served its purpose. "The efficacy of *adhyāsa*," Yadav asserts, "is total. Śaṅkara's agenda is clear. Being in the world…means letting the self be defined in terms of the alien, especially a beneficent alien, that helps promote material and moral interests…The self must first live through non-otherness with the other before it reclaims immediacy with itself in silence" (Krishna 1991: 87). Advaita not only has a spiritual strategy of release, but also a political means of liberation, and subsequent identity-founded domination.

And this means we have seen played out in the history of the independence and concurrent conservative nationalism of the nineteenth and twentieth centuries. For the nationalistic *brāhmins* who headed the Independence Movement, from Roy and Aurobindo to Gandhi and Nehru, India was India and not the West, but India could take to itself the language, thought, religious values and material profits of the West, only to reclaim national identity under the banner of the Brāhmiṇical heritage, which means among other things a nation of privileged and underprivileged castes. The Colonial Period represented an eerie convergence between the externally colonial West and the internally colonial *bhadraloka*.

> The Indian postcolonial discourse, like the Euro-Christian consciousness, is a case of mis-predicated identity…
> Like the colonial West, the self-colonizing subjectivity must find salvation in the discovery and end of difference, be it Buddhist, Islamic or Euro-Christian. The irony is that such elite self-alienation does not truly alienate; it only reinforces the political and social hegemony of elite Brahmanism, lately known as *bhadraloka*. There was, in the nineteenth century, a remarkable coincidence of interests between the colonial West and the self-colonizing agency of the *bhadraloka*.

> The convergence produced national heroes like Rammohan Roy, Keshab Chandra Sen, Swami Vivekananda, Shri Aurobindo, Sarvepalli Radhakrishnan, the Tagores and the Nehrus. Always post-colonial, one step ahead of the rest of society, the *bhadraloka* embraced the colonial knowledge. With active support from Orientalists like Max Mueller and William Jones, they also rediscovered the old Shaṅkarāchārya, elevated the *Upanishads* to texts of salvation, and instituted the neo-Vedantic discourse of India as a spiritual civilization. (Krishna 1991: 81–2)

Yadav's essay traces this history, showing how these "national heroes" used in the most subtle and invisible ways *adhyāsa*, for they were the class that "understood the relation between language and power," taking on Western forms of culture and values and even identifying them with their own heritage, in order to procure their own material and moral interests as cultural elites (Krishna 1991: 111). Yadav protests bitterly against Ashis Nandy's (1983: 107) representation of the "unheroic *Brahmin*," who was forced to appropriate the colonial will in order to survive and protect his nation." "History shows that this was not the case," Yadav retorted, for not only did the *brāhmins* "inherit the legacy of pre-modern India," but they were "the greatest beneficiaries of the *raj*," and their self-conscious imitation of the West assured them political and cultural leadership (Yadav 1983: 123).

The fruits of independence meant that the *bhadraloka* inherited political power. *Brāhmins* are the head of society, and their call for national identity turned out, after all of their dissembling to the contrary, to be all along the reassertion of the Vedic order in which the *śudras* and Dalits were its feet. Now what is required, according to Yadav (1983: 83), is not more blaming of the removed colonists, more "psychopathology of victimized self-hood," but to return the critical gaze on the old order of Brahminical society itself.

> What matters in the Indian postcolonialist discourse is national identity, not social justice. The immense rural population of India, the poor and the subaltern remain as voiceless as ever. It is not surprising that the neo-Vedantic postcolonialis(s) now demand a return to the old Brahminical social order, making India a Hindu nation. And it is no small irony that the poor millions see more good in modernity, the Enlightenment type of modernity, which at least afforded them the right to political self-representation in postcolonial India. They can now have a tryst with their own destinies. (1983: 84)

Alarmed with the political ramifications of Indian nationalism, criticism should now be directed inward; "it is time to recognize that the enemy is within India herself" (1983:, 125), so that social justice and not national identity becomes the order of the day.

> If Orientalism means production of knowledge as an instrument of power, then it was Sanskrit discourse that invented it. There certainly is an oriental Orientalism, a precolonial colonialism, and this too is as systematically oppressive as any. Did not Manu and Shaṅkarāchārya say that the hands and throats of the untouchable are to be cut if they cite the scripture?...The postcolonial discourse has to return home. It has to be a discourse about authentic identity, not the mispredicated one. (1983: 125)

An authentic sense of identity here does not dismiss difference, but instead decries the predilection of the Brāhmiṇical tradition to identify the *sanātana dharma* with caste society, and then disown the results of that identification with "the politics of *karmayoga*." (1983: 117)

The Antisocial Essentialism of Indian Buddhists

Madhyamaka emerged as a result of events which took place inside the Buddhist tradition. It has been interpreted as a response to the appearance of metaphysical theories propounded by various Buddhist schools wrestling with such notions as causation, movement, time, personhood and the relationship between the world, *nirvāṇa* and *Tathāgata*. Nāgārjuna, the great logician and founder of the school, is said to have gone to the bottom of the ocean to rescue the *Prajñāpāramitā* texts from the serpents dwelling there, and thereafter devoted himself to saving the great doctrine of *pratītyasamutpāda* from ontological corruption.[16] Yadav believed that, by emphasizing the relativity of all causes and conditions, Buddhism over time became obsessed with the ontology of difference, an ontology that reified the existence and ontically singular natures of *saṃsāra* and *nirvāṇa*. This process did not merely have intellectual implications, but as with all ontological conundrums, wreaked social confusion as well. The difference between *saṃsāra* and *nirvāṇa* justified the difference between a Buddhist's search for enlightenment and social responsibilities, the demands of the latter being sacrificed to the urgency of the former. The "middle way" is not only non-commitment to all ontological claims, including ones about *Tathāgata*, and the conceptual means (*prapañca*) used to establish them, but also a course between the essentialism of caste society and the essentialism that justified social separatism.

Nāgārjuna's *Mūlamadhyamakakārikā* is a prolonged argument against the doctrines of the Sarvāstivāda and Sautrāntika schools, with special emphasis on the former's doctrine of substance (*dravya*). Specifically, the Sarvāstivāda philosopher Dharmatrāta felt the need to account for the continuity of things given the Sautrāntika principle of "momentariness" (*kṣaṇikavāda*). If *dharmas* could only be said to exist for a mere moment each, then how should we account for the stability of objects, the continuity of persons and their *karma* or even the semantic senses of sentences through the passage of time? Dharmatrāta's answer was that, while the phenomenal being (*bhāva*) of a thing changes constantly, all *dharmas* have an "intrinsic nature" (*svabhāva*) that exists in all three times, the past, present and future, and this intrinsic nature was also thought to be the foundation of all causality, the central principle and concern of Indian Buddhist philosophy (Kalupahana 1992: 162). Nāgārjuna's *Kārikā* responded to the metaphysical tensions between these schools with *śūnyavāda*, which was in many respects a non-substantialist theory of causality, or better, a non-theoretical acknowledgement of the causal dependence of all phenomena.

There is a special reason, on Yadav's view, that causality was so central to the project of Nāgārjuna and Candrakīrti. In the Indian tradition, all ontologies, whether they were extrapolated in terms of identity or difference, were built upon the foundation of making theoretical inquiries into causality. *Pramāṇaprameyaśāstra* consisted in asking what things were and how one can know them to be so. But more than this, to ask what a thing is in Indian philosophy is to ask where it came from, how it came about, just as inquiring into the nature of knowledge means asking questions about how one's awareness is brought about and through what means certainty about each awareness results. This fundamental connection of the questions of Being and causality in Indian thought has deep-seated religious roots, for even the *Nāsadīya* hymn of the *Rigveda* (x, 129) fused, even with all of its skeptical texture, the issues of how the world came to be and who knows how the world came to be. And the creation story of the *Bṛhadāraṇyakopaniṣad* carried this logic a step further, witnessing that the world owed its existence to *brahman*'s urge to have his own identity reflected in the world's plurality, to create all Being merely to be able to look at it and say, "this am I." The philosophical and the religious meet at the inevitable dependence of the desire for ontological knowledge on the compulsion to affirm one's own existence (Yadav 1992: 135).

This means that to ask about Being is to ask about causality, and to ask about causality is to ask about where I came from and where I am going. Hence Yadav's contention that philosophy is undertaken for "ātmological" or "egological reasons;" "to mediate an immediate truth and to reiterate identity through ontological questions, I must ask 'What is Being?' because I cannot stop asking 'Who am I?'" (Yadav 1992: 139). And this is precisely where the Buddhist philosophers, according to Yadav's interpretation of Nāgārjuna, have gone astray. Buddhism was conceived by Gautama Siddhārtha precisely as a means of extinguishing (*nirvāṇa*) the untenable notion of selfhood and the anxious and desirous roots from which that notion arises and for which it is constructed. The Sautrāntikas and Sarvāstivādins have committed the grave error of continencing the attachment to selfhood, indeed legitimating it as consistent with Buddhist discourse, by formulating philosophical systems that reified substances, persons, and even *nirvāṇa* and *Tathāgata* themselves.[17] Nāgārjuna and Candrakīrti take upon themselves the task of uncovering this infectious ontological disease that has covertly found its way into a tradition that was based on a flat rejection of ontology.

> Methodic deconstruction…discerns the "I" as an empty term, a signifier without any referent. No "I," no "this," no subject, no object. So too is the case with "*Tathāgata*" and "*dharma*," if they are used as terms in propositional assertions. Deconstruction draws attention to the mutuality of *ego* and *cogito*, being in the world and doing. In a chapter in his *Prasannapadā*, entitled "Examination of the Noble Truths," Chandrakīrti faces the accusations squarely, raising fundamental issues. Must Buddhism be bound to things about which one can say either that they exist or do not? Should not Buddhism in fidelity to *Tathāgata*, liberate itself from the status quo that either/or logic entails? What happened to the claim that existence is function, that to exist is to change, and that knowledge is born out of emancipitory praxis? Should the Mādhyamika be accused of stealing the Buddha from Buddhists merely because he shows how the metaphysical independence of *Tathāgata* is no more than a cover for the possessive anxiety of the Buddhists themselves? (Yadav 1992: 132–3)

And so Nāgārjuna sets to work on the whole table of Abhidharma categories; *skandhas*, *dhātus*, *karma-karaka*, *Tathāgata*, *nirvāṇa*, the Noble Truths and above all *svabhāva* are emptied of theoretical plausibility by the *catuṣkoṭi*.

Then, in order to bury the tools with which metaphysical systems are built, he writes the *Vigrahavyvārtanī* to show that all the putative "means of knowledge" (*pramāṇa*-s) as theoretically explicated by the Naiyāyikas could be shown to be either argumentatively circular, vacuous, or leading to infinite regress.[18] Five hundred years later, his commentator Candrakīrti takes up arms against the Yogācāra-Sautrāntikas for attempting to improve on Hindu logic, as well as against the rival Madhyamaka school of Svātantra, whose most prominent exponent was Bhāvaviveka. Bhāvaviveka had made the case that, while not true in the "ultimate" sense (*paramārthasatya*)), the agent-action, subject-predicate assumptions that abound in our common language made the most conventional sense as an explanatory model of the structure of the world.[19] This would mean that categories like *Tathāgata*, *nirvāṇa* and *saṃsāra* would be just as legitimate candidates as any for inclusion in causal explanatory models of reality. Even if they were conventional only, these kinds of models would allow us to use the concepts of *Tathāgata*, *nirvāṇa* and *saṃsāra* as reified subjects and predicates in propositional assertions for the benefit of the learning masses. Candrakīrti will have none of it. He is faithful to his master, who had devoted so much time to the "deconstruction" of these categories as referential terms in causal relationship with one another.[20] Candrakīrti devotes himself to the Prāsaṅgika principle that there are no explanatory models, no theoretical formulations that a Buddhist will endure; there are only either empty views or the acknowledgement that all views are empty.[21] In his counterattack, Candrakīrti critically examines sentences such as "*Tathāgata* speaks the *dharma*" and "*Tathāgata* exists" and concludes that these most basic forms attributing agency are tautological, for they only predicate agency to a being who by definition possesses the capacity to act. These sentences reduce, according to Candrakīrti to "the speaking *Tathāgata* speaks the *dharma*" and "The existing *Tathāgata* exists" where all action verbs are only possible if adjectival capacities are assumed of the subject (Yadav 1992: 157–60).[22] Even our simplest sentences can metaphysically reify their grammatical parts. Candrakīrti believes that we must remain vigilant about such claims, for as Yadav says, "the shift from the grammatical to the logical is made in the interests of an ontological stance" (Yadav 1992: 158).

To allow ontology into Buddhism is to corrupt the mission of the *bodhisattva*. Nāgārjuna had enunciated in the *Kārikā* that the Buddha had never preached anything to anyone at any place anytime,[23] and that there were no boundaries between *nirvāṇa* and *saṃsāra*.[24] This does not only mean that there should be no metaphysical dualisms constructed through the use of Buddhist terminology, or any terminology, but also, as Yadav puts it, the Buddha cannot be separated from the very worldly concerns of the Buddhists.

> What then does "*Tathāgata*" signify? If it does not refer to the agent of "speaks," then whose words did the people hear in Shravasti? Who spoke the *dharma*, a ghost or a real person born of Shuddhodana and Māyā? Does not Chandrakīrti steal *Tathāgata* from the Buddhists? The questions have an ontic slant, implying the belief that if *Tathāgata* was not there to speak then the people could not have heard a word (of) the *dharma* at all. Chandrakīrti responds to the questions in light of his stance on ontology…The panic of identity seeks shelter in decisive transcendence…The desire for religious certainty gives itself a spatial anchorage, incarnating itself in the claim that "*Tathāgata* is over there and speaks the *dharma* for us." This assertion implies that *Tathāgata* is over there, the listeners here, and that a distance prevails between the speaker and the listeners. Hence the duality between the Buddha and the Buddhists for egological reasons…It projects *Tathāgata* as an "other" in space, ascribes ontological independence to the other, clings to the words that it itself has ascribed to the other and gives the words the power to define the true and the false…There is no point in stealing the referent of "*Tathāgata*," of Buddha from the Buddhist. There indeed is no such referent, no Buddha apart from the Buddhists…It is not that there are people who are Buddhists by virtue of hearing the words of *Tathāgata*. The opposite is the case. It is because there are people who wish to establish their identity by thinking in categories and speaking the language that they do, that there is an ontic *Tathāgata* who speaks about the things he does, in the language he does and in the place that he does. The underworld is older than the world, the listeners prior to the speaker. (Yadav 1992: 160–1)

It is by tracing the ontological compulsions of human beings to their psychological desire to affirm their own identity, even if as here this is attempted through the difference posited between *Tathāgata* and the world, that the *bodhisattva* justifies his return. "His mission is to "discern the mutual dependence of the *ego* and the *cogito*, of *eros* and *logos*, of 'I' and 'other'" (Yadav 1992: 155) "His aim is to return transcendence to the everyday world, the referents to the self-referential ego, and the ontology of being and non-being to the anxiety of living and dying" (Yadav 1992: 155–6). To use language in Buddhism is not to make *nirvāṇa* into an object of practice, *Tathāgata* into a being who achieved enlightenment and then left the world behind, and Buddhism into a discipline that rejects the affairs of suffering beings. "That would dissolve the worldliness of *Tathāgata* in metaphysical silence, the sociality of truth in institutional secrecy, salvation in elite mysticism. It would be the Vedāntization of Mahāyāna" (Yadav 1992: 162). On the contrary, to use language in Buddhism is to always take one's place within the world, within tradition, history, social relationship, and the radical contingencies of human life. The *bodhisattva*'s task is to "deconstruct ontology" within the world, and this task is the "middle way" (*madhyamā-pratipad*) .

Beyond Identity and Difference: Buddhism and Society

The dilemma of the Prāsaṅga Buddhist as a *vāda-vaitaṇḍika* is for Yadav risky. But in the end it is not really a dilemma at all, but an opportunity to transcend the social implications of ideological essentialism, which has taken so many different forms in Indian ontologies of identity and difference.

> Chandrakīrti...has no language of his own, no methodological independence, no epistemology or syllogistic logic and no center. Nor has he any ontological commitments. He gives no privilege to identity or difference, universal or particular, being or nothingness, self or no-self, eternity or time. He has no alternative set of assumptions, separate criteria of truth and falsity, or standard of criticism alien to the logocentric circle. (Yadav 1992: 147–8)

Hindus and Buddhists united in spurning this approach; Vasubandhu and Diṅnāga and Dharmakīrti joined hands with Vātsyāyana, Kumārila and Udayana in rejecting this method, which is no-method, this stance, which is no-stance. But we must remember, Yadav warns, that they were the champions of ontologies of identity and difference, epistemologies of privilege and elitism, socio-political hierarchy and escapist, irresponsible reclusivism. In this philosophical and social environment, we must appreciate that a rejection of metaphysical alternatives offers new social possibilities.

> Deconstruction is an argument for staying in the middle. It takes a stance against the social implications of either/or

> logic, which is either that one stays in society and accepts its hierarchical structure or finds solace in a metasocial *nirvāṇa*. Consistent with the middle way, the *bodhisattvas* do neither. They do not move into the mountains to save their individual conscience, and in the world they demand social equality on religious grounds. There is no curtain between *nirvana* and *saṃsāra*, between *Tathāgata* and the people... *Tathāgata* keeps on wandering in a multitude of linguistic fields, knowing well that people cannot transcend their language. No meta-language or linguistic hegemony, no silence in a worldless emptiness, only the dispersal of *Tathāgata* in a plurality of texts and tongues. There is a radical sociality between *Tathāgata* and the people. (Yadav 1992: 162–3)

This is Yadav's social vision of Prāsaṅgika Madhyamaka, where criticism goes hand in hand with social belonging, where the Buddha and *nirvāṇa* belong to the people and *saṃsāra*.

> Such is methodic deconstruction. It dissolves questions about beginnings and ends, and lets people face *Tathāgata* in the middle of their world. Being and Nothingness give in to becoming, God to the emancipatory possibility of man. Deconstruction implies courage and hope. People cannot accept death and destruction as their destiny, neither can they harbor illusions about a pure land where the city of *nirvāṇa* is located and where there is a total absence of suffering. There is no such thing as a pure land in the land of human beings... "*Tathāgata*" signifies no more than the inevitability of effort and the risk of faith. The world keeps on dying in spite of *bodhisattvas*, just as *bodhisattvas* keep on returning to the world. (Yadav 1992: 163)

There are many questions that could be asked of Yadav's vision. His Cartesian representation of Nyāya, which has been critiqued in the notes of this chapter, is one point of departure. Another could be his accusation that the Neo-Vedāntins were traditional defenders of caste society, for the early representatives of this tradition in the nineteenth century denied that caste distinctions had any Vedic foundations, and the twentieth century members of the Independence Movement agreed to abolish discrimination on the basis of caste in their first Indian Constitution.[25] In terms of its larger framework, while Ambedkar's idealization of Indian Buddhism as a social justice movement can be seen to override Murti's interpretation of the same as "absolutism" in Yadav's work, there are some obvious European premises there as well. Despite his repeated commitment to "immanent criticism" and "reflection in terms of Sanskrit categories of thought," Yadav's vocabulary abounds with post-modern neologisms. "Logocentric," "deconstruction," "embedded *cogito*" and many other expressions betray the recent trend in Western scholarship, found among other places in David Loy, Harold Coward and Glen Martin, to see strong affinities between classical Indian and contemporary Continental thought. The ever-present suspicion in Yadav's work that the desire for philosophical knowledge is based on a will to political and social power seems to be a deeply Nietzschean and Foucaultian assumption. The notion that a particular ontological doctrine, such as realism or idealism necessarily leads to a philosophy of one type or another of social domination was not merely believed by Yadav to be a fact of Indian philosophical history, but was an inevitable result of doing philosophy as such. To a certain extent then, any overall assessment of Yadav's work depends in part on what sorts of sympathies or disagreements one may have with these more contemporary European traditions of scholarship and thought.

Still, what the essays of Bibhuti Yadav bring to contemporary scholarship is a call to recognize that, within the Sanskrit philosophical heritage, powerful social concerns are inlaid into the intellectual sophistication of ontological and epistemological argument. Furthermore, these concerns are not only paramount in the different schools of Hindu thought, but also within the Buddhist camp, and they are at the forefront of the confrontations between these traditions. Further disclosure and examination of these issues and confrontations in the history of Indian thought will certainly miss Professor Yadav's voice, but they will just as certainly benefit from what his work and life offered.

Notes

1 This essay was first published as: "The Social Meaning of the Middle Way: B.S. Yadav on the Madhyamika Critique of Indian Ontologies of Identity and Difference." in *Journal of Dharma* XXXVI no. 3, July-Sept. 2001, 282–310. It has been reprinted here with the permission of Dharmaram Vidya Kshetram, Bangalore.

2 The major title of this chapter is taken from a quotation of Yadav's most prominent essay, in which he wrote that, according to Buddhism, "existence is relational to the core, and it is in this relationality alone that *Tathāgata* dwells. Such is the social meaning of the middle way" (Yadav 1992: 162).

3 Yadav's vision of the role of Buddhism in Indian intellectual history is very much in the spirit and tradition of Bhim Rao Ambedkar (1891-1956), the former Minister of Law in Nehru's first cabinet and co-drafter of India's Constitution, who resigned his post, and eventually presided over a mass conversion to Buddhism in Nagpur, Maharashtra shortly before his death. Although Yadav never wrote anything extensive on Ambedkar, he did devote some of his lectures on Buddhism to Ambedkar's writings, and quoted him approvingly in places (Yadav 2000: 124).

4 Yadav wrote in many places about the need for "immanent criticism." "I believe in immanent criticism, which means reflection in terms of Sanskrit categories of thought. Nāgārjuna, the founder of Mādhyamika Buddhism, believed that criticism can neither be imported nor performed from outside. Criticism is authentic if it is immanent in its textual field, if it emanates from the problematics it seeks to understand, and if it is done in terms of indigenous categories of thought" (Yadav 2000: 84). India has its own discourse of social justice, in its oldest form from the Buddhist tradition, and therefore does not need to import it from the West. The fact that Buddhism was an indigenous reform movement is also what appealed to Ambedkar (Larson 1995: 26–7). We shall return to this issue of "immanent criticism" later.

5 Yadav's very elegant and supple prose often argues with elliptical metaphors, and the notion of the "circle," or the inventors and defenders of Indian logic, epistemology and ontology, was used liberally. At one point he even calls it the "logocentric" or "syllogistic circle (*hetu cakra*)," punning on the great logical innovation of Diṅnāga (Yadav 1992: 141).

6 See Yadav (1992: 148–52). I have myself defended these objections on technical grounds; see Berger (1998: 7–13).

7 Recall Nāgārjuna's famous 29th verse of the *Vigrahavyāvartanī*, in responding to the accusation that *śunyavāda* must be his logical thesis (*pratijña*): "*nāsti ca mama pratijñā / tasmān naivāsti me doṣaḥ //*" I have gone into these issues in more depth in "Illocution, No-Theory and Practice."

8 In Kumārila's system, it will be remembered, *dravya*-s or substances are only the supports of *guṇa*, *karma* and *samavāya* or *jāti*. One distinguishes among objects as well as among members of different castes, according to Kumārila, based upon the recognition of specific qualities and actions that typify various things or persons. Yadav did not write about these concepts and their implications in Kumārila's system, primarily because the essay he co-authored with William Allen on Kumārila and Vasubandhu was focused on their differing views of consciousness. A thorough explication of the relationship between Kumārila's metaphysics and social philosophy can be found in the last chapter of the late Wilhelm Halbfass' (1993) *Tradition and Reflection: Explorations in Indian Thought*.

9 See Kumārila's *Tantravārtika* I. iii. 2.

10 See Viśvanātha Nyāyapañcānana's *Tarka-saṃgraha*, *Kārikāvalī* 135.

11 J. N. Mohanty has nicely explained the different models of doubt in his "Nyāya Theory of Doubt" (1993: 101–25). These models, *dharmijñāna*, *viśeṣasmṛti* and *prāmāṇya-saṃśayat viṣaya-saṃśayaḥ* are all objective forms of doubt.

12 Yadav's Cartesian representation of doubt in Nyāya has been disputed recently, though in a different context, by Mark Siderits, who has claimed that nothing like a Cartesian formulation of doubt existed in the Indian philosophical tradition (Siderits 1997: 71). As Siderits (1997: 74) says, "to attribute knowledge to a subject is to remark on the causal history of that subject's cognition. It is not to attribute to that subject the ability to grasp whatever evidence would be required to rule out skeptical hypotheses". If Siderits is right, and there are very good grounds for his contention, then Yadav's polemical treatment of Nyāya in this case would have to be questioned.

13 Again, Yadav's continual use of the word "*cogito*" and his representation of how Naiyāyikas eradicate objective doubt does not seem, as Siderits has hinted at, to apply to the actual Nyāya model of selfhood and cognition. True, the logicians thought that the permanent self was the basis for all activity and thought, and the possessor of all the individual's cognitions and feelings. But whether we possess objective knowledge does not depend on anything like a *cogito*, but rather on apprehension (*anuvyavasāya*) of a thing based on sense-object contact, and both of these events were thought by the Naiyāyikas to be contingent and followed strictly on causal factors. Knowledge was not for them affirming the existence of the knowing subject, but rather determining what external causal factors and possibilities for fruitful action existed. The Nyāya school held a theory of truth known in Indian philosophy as *parataḥpramāṇavāda*, which has been long rendered the thesis of "extrinsic validity" and what Siderits (1980: 329) has referred to as an "extensionalist theory of knowledge". Cartesian epistemology is more of an intrinsic model, and Yadav's invocation of it to describe and critique Nyāya epistemology calls to a certain extent into question his commitment to "immanent criticism" of "Sanskrit categories of thought." We will return to this problem again later.

14 "*ātmana upalabdhyābhāsaphalāvasāna*" *Upadeśasāhasrī* 2. 2. 77.

15 Critiques of this kind go all the way back to the famous and powerful one of Rāmānuja of course. Recent treatments dealing with various difficulties of Śaṅkara's *Adhyāsabhāṣyam* can be found in Mohanty (1993: 68–74), notably Krishna (1991: 156–63), and Bilimoria (1997: 252–77).

16 David J. Kalupahana (1992: 161) has long insisted that Nāgarjuna's whole work can be considered to be a commentary on the Buddha's discourse to Kaccāyana, and a systematic logical attempt to eradicate the very kinds of metaphysical questions the Buddha thought hindrances to practice.

17 In this sense, Yadav can certainly be taken as aligned with the notion of "Critical Buddhism," as defined by Hakamaya Noriaki and Matumoto Shiro, which struggles against "substance doctrines" (*dhātuvāda*) within the tradition. This conflict is thoroughly explored from all different perspectives in *Pruning the Bodhi Tree: The Storm over Critical Buddhism* (Hubbalard and Swanson (eds) 1997). But Yadav's alignment with critical Buddhism would have to be qualified by his general rejection of the logical tradition of Diṅnāga and Dharmakīrti based on Candrakīrti. Even some of Yadav's former students had more sympathy with the Yogācāra-Sautrāntika tradition; see Dan Lusthaus (1997: 30–55).

18 It should be noted that Nāgārjuna forgoes the adoption not only of the assumptions of Hindu logic, as Yadav emphasizes, in his *Vigrahavyāvartanī*, but also its method. This is witnessed in this work by his "trilemmic" refutation procedure as well as his insistence that his has no "thesis" (*pratijña*). Once again, this calls into question how seriously we can take the claim Yadav makes that Nāgārjuna deconstructs ontology by using the rules of ontology, for the tetralemmic and trilemmic structures of *prāsaṅga* are clearly his own, and not taken from another system.

19 See his *Prajñāpradīpa* 1:3. Once again, Siderits has recently advocated the case of Bhāvaviveka against the attacks leveled by Candrakīrti, which Yadav goes into in some detail but which are merely rehearsed here. Siderits points out that Candrakīrti merely refutes false theories of causation, but Bhāvaviveka, though he agrees there is no ultimate truth beyond conventional language, defends the conventional truth of some theories (Siderits, 1997: 85).

20 See the *Mūlamadhyamakakārikā*, 25: 1–24.

21 This reaction by Candrakīrti has been seen by some scholars as odd, especially since he seems to endorse the conventional account of the Nyāya *pramāṇa*-s against Diṅnāga's revised version; see *Prasannapadā*, 20: 2–4.

22 Yadav relies here on Candrakīrti's text as well as on Rao's (1969) *The Philosophy of the Sentence and its Parts*. This reduction is obscure and not very compelling, but Yadav finds these objections definitive.

23 *Mūlamadhyamakakārikā*, 25: 25.

24 *Mūlamadhyamakakārikā*, 25: 19–20.

25 Still, even accepting these facts, the nationalism of the Independence leaders, the clashes between Gandhi and Ambedkar over creating separate congressional electorates for untouchables and the acknowledgement of the legal status of Scheduled and Backward Castes through aid programs in the Constitution dull this objection (see Larson 1995: 185–206; 214–26).

6

Deconstruction, *Aporia* and Justice

In Nāgārjuna's Empty Ethics[1]

Nāgārjuna (c. 150-200 CE), the Andhra-born and Nālandā-trained giant of Mahāyāna Buddhist philosophy, is not often consulted for his ideas on ethics or liberating Buddhist practice, despite the fact that three works considered reliably attributable to him, the *Bodhisambāraka*, *Suhṛlekha* and *Ratnāvalī* are entirely concerned with these. Much more common in contemporary scholarship are commentaries that parse his *Mūlamadhyamakakārikā* and *Vigrahavyāvartanī* for their anti-metaphysical and anti-epistemological arguments. Nonetheless, *kārikā*-s eight, seventeen and twenty-four of Nāgārjuna's main work on Buddhist philosophy, the *Mūlamadhyamakakārikā* (MMK) can conceivably be understood as a kind of mini-treatise on the "proper" Buddhist way to think about efficacious virtuous conduct. In these chapters, Nāgārjuna resists various versions of a Buddhist moral dualism between good and bad actions in favor of an admittedly metaphorical explanation of *karma* that draws a powerful parallelism between "common law" (*vyavahāra*) and karmic "debt" (*ṛṇa*).

The claims that are laid out in this mini-treatise are in fact profoundly ethically provocative in the light of contemporary debates in deconstruction on *aporia* or the impossibility of justice as the deconstructability of law (*droit*) as well as the relation between justice and the economy of the "gift" (*cadeau*). Indeed, because he is attempting to valorize the bedrock Buddhist notion of *pratītyasamutpāda*, "causally conditioned co-arising," Nāgārjuna's logic of action is certainly deconstructive in its impetus vis-à-vis other Buddhist views of moral adjudication and achievement, although in a somewhat loose sense. Nonetheless, Nāgārjuna offers a counter-discourse to Derridian deconstruction, as he rejects the oppositional tensions between law and justice or giver and recipient in favor of a visualization of action that places the "paramount aim" (*paramārtha*) of human freedom (*nirvāṇa*) wholly within the transactional chains of the functioning community. In the Derridian model of ethics, justice can only be pursued through an overcoming, through a confrontation with the limits of the present law or with the compulsions of debt created through reciprocity. With Nāgārjuna, one can only realize freedom through the very workings of the social economy itself; there are no limits to transcend in working out one's karmic condition because, as he puts it, "there is no distinction of bondage from freedom; there is no distinction of freedom from bondage. The limit of freedom is but the limit of bondage; between them not even the subtlest thing is recognized" (MMK 25:19-20). For Nāgārjuna, ethics and justice are not "inventional," as Derrida's conception has been labeled, they do not deconstruct social law so that actions more proximal to justice may be carried through, but are rather co-produced as the direct consequences of acts that are inimical to them within the unfolding of life and the transactions of community.[2]

There is, to be sure, a distinctly liberating ring to Derrida's conception of justice, as it continually demands that we acknowledge the other (*taut atre*) and strive after the "impossible" call and unexpected "arrival" of coming justice. This ring is, due to the ever-critical stance of deconstruction, audible only through opposition to present injustice, through battle with the tyranny of the present state of hegemonic capitalist and liberal democratic power, which self-righteously employs in its service the "monster of the law" (Cornell 1992: 167). In *Specters of Marx*, Derrida assails Francis Fukayama's defense of the ideals of liberal democracy, the most fundamental of these ideals being equality before the law, in light of the manifest "empirical" shortcomings of the iniquitous wielding of Western power. Derrida's "ten-point telegram" of indictments against the legacies and consequences of contemporary Western dominance includes the economic burdens the present system of international free-market capitalism foists upon the world's poor, the dissemination of weapons and the wars they enable, drug cartels and the current Western thematization of international law (Derrida 1994: 81–4). Apart from the fact that international law is, despite its claims to equality, monopolized by but a few powerful nation-states, its more immediate flaw is that it is bound up with the modern conception of the state and the "quotidian" enforcement of law that conception insists upon (Derrida 1994: 83). Laws are crafted both on the international stage as well as within nations attempting to control ethnic and political minorities to safeguard the interests of those in power, who often define themselves "homophilically," that is as "genetic brothers" or as a "fraternity of friends" as opposed to the "other" as threat or enemy.[3] "The other," for the dominant discourse of liberal democratic society and the traditional ethical philosophies that buttress it, is not an obligation to be submitted to, but a danger to be resisted. Nonetheless, beyond these overtly political objections to the unjust purview and iniquitous enforcement of law in the post-Cold War world, there are deeper "structural" oppositions between law and justice that go to the very heart of deconstruction, and which involve on the one hand the *aporia* of justice as well as, on the other, its "messianic" promise.[4]

The problems of what we normally conceive to be ethics, responsibility or justice reveal themselves on a number of interrelated levels, those for instance of friendship, of goodness and in the political, but always in the context of whether or not there is really anything ethically intelligible about the assumption of so-called "equality." With regard to friendship, for example, while it is talked of as a loyalty and devotion to the "other" as friend, the quality of friendship is often judged on the basis of the quality of the partner's reciprocity and usefulness to oneself, which establishes "equity" among friends. But Derrida questions what the real ethical value of such an "equity" could possibly be if it demands that the virtue of the other be a pre-condition for my own commitment as a friend (Derrida 1997: 23). The "give and take" of relationships, according to the "logic" or "economy of the gift" (*cadeau*) also demands, according to any existing "conscience" or "science of ethics," whether it be conceived under the name of virtue, deontological or utilitarian ethics, a systematic rule or condition of virtue that we both give with generosity and receive with gratitude, so that our relationships are perpetuated and stabilized through feeding on the cycle of care of others and indebtedness to others. However, Derrida warns, this introduces a crucial problem into the whole phenomenon of gift-giving, beneficience, generosity, because when a gift serves as a mere "bill of exchange," as it were, an investment in the economy of relational reciprocity, it ceases to be a gift as such, a gift in the most genuine sense of something offered purely for the offering, donation (*le don*). Gifts that are only given so that the giver may be recognized and treated reciprocally are not gifs at all (Derrida 1995: 29). These charges of course follow straight to the center of that most cherished assumption of liberal democracy, the assumption of "equality before the law," which conceives justice as the supposedly universalizable and calculable application of law to all citizen/subjects. Derrida reminds us that "Nietzschean geneology" has already uncovered the actual functioning intention behind such a socio-political prioritization of "equality," namely that of the equitability of a transaction which establishes rights of collection and rights of vengeance should collection fail (1997: 64). What is so often self-righteously invoked as a moral principle of protection for "the people" unmasks itself as the power of the state to inflict punishment in exchange for disloyalty.

All of these conceptions of justice as "reciprocity" and "calculable equity" that we have inscribed and encoded within our law harbor within them manifest injustice, for they miss the "singularity" of relationships which is opened by the "other," or which opens one to the other in a manner that confers upon the other not "equality" but priority. As Derrida puts it: authentic friendship involves a recognition of the priority of the other, the greater value of the other compared to oneself, and thus the abandonment of the very assumption of equity (Derrida 1997: 92). In like manner, the "gift," if it is to be a true "gift" (*le don*), must be given as it were "in secret," hidden from the recipient so as not to evoke a sense of indebtedness from the recipient and hidden from the giver too so as not to tempt the expectations of recognition and return in the giver. If the gift can be renounced as soon as it is given, and thus removed from the economy of calculation, then the gift becomes an act of "infinite love" (Derrida 1995: 50–1). Love can achieve infinity, even between finite beings, when goodness, rather than demanding loyalty as the price of beneficence, offers itself to the other through the cancellation of "debt-consciousness," which is to say, "ethics" heretofore conceived. Responsibility as a meaningful act of intention is only exhibited by a giver who not only does not require a response, but who will not respond when asked why he offers his gift, in the manner of Abraham's sacrifice of Isaac in the Biblical narrative.

The demands of "infinite love" and "infinite gift" that the singularities, the unique and concrete events of our lives, enjoin upon us on behalf of the other also inspire that spirit of Marxism that deconstruction continues to embrace. That deconstructive spirit of Marxism Derrida invokes should continue to "haunt" Europe and the "New World Order" with the calls for social and global justice. Were we to treat goodness as a "transcendental objective," a duty that would lend itself to formulaic fulfillment, we would forfeit the actual call of social justice that always tugs at us through the singular other before our eyes, with this forfeit making available to us only a counterfeit "good conscience." The openness to the other and their future, precisely because it resists closure or fulfillment, is "undeconstructable," and is the "messianic" element in Marxism. Messianic expectation is the expectation of the other's arrival, and with that arrival, it is perfect generosity and not reciprocity that establishes a new order of the world, and it is precisely this brand of messianism that Marxism presages (Derrida 1994: 28).

Of course, all this drives a wedge, an ethically necessary and enabling one, between law and justice, ethics and goodness, responsibility and alterity, a wedge that Derrida not only acknowledge as presenting us with several facets of *aporia*, but also as preserving the "messianic" character, a universal, "undeconstructible" of justice. For one thing, while my ethical duty conventionally conceived makes "responsibility" incumbent on me an answerability for my deeds and a conscious knowledge of what I am doing, the goodness of truly giving in a relationship requires that I maintain a "secrecy," a hiding from myself of my giving in order to preserve it as giving, making "irresponsibility" just as necessary for me as responsibility (Derrida 1994: 27).[5] Secondly, and certainly most poignantly, the calls to selfless and pure giving to the other that each singular event, each particular other, make to me render it impossible for me to see to justice for everyone. I must be selective, exclusive, and hence iniquitous, in my duties to others.[6] But these painful and dreadful *aporias* of friendship, generosity, justice and politics are thrown upon so as to be preserved, for what is preserved with them is the hope of the *arrivant*, the unexpected coming of the other, the call of justice itself.

There is, beyond these issues, one of the fundamental *aporias* of justice, namely that while it demands a suspension of closure, an ever vigilant and critical openness to the other and the other's future, the urgency of present circumstances also requires decision, a decision that would enforce a closure on matters at hand. That moment of decision that every event throws upon me preserves this mutually enabling tension between justice and law. Here is where the "other hand," as Critchley puts it, the genuinely deconstructive maneuver of Derridian thought comes in (Critchley 1999: 18). "Determination," "closure," "ethical choices" have been rendered hopelessly problematic through a first-hit deconstructive critique of the role they actually play in traditional moral thought. But on the other hand, once the call to justice as gift, openness to the other, has through criticism rendered calculable decision-making intractably problematic, decisions must still be made in order for any justice to be done. But such decisions interrupt the possibility of justice that made their very consideration possible. In turn, these decisions, determinations to act, and the new calculations and economies of moral exchange they set in motion provoke another iteration of the tension between the indeterminate "perhaps" and the moral exigencies of decision. This is what Derrida refers to as "the *aporia* that all things must face" (1997: 67). There is a mutuality of a sort then in Derrida's representation of the relationship between justice and law, but their mutually enabling interaction is energized, prompted, provoked by their aporetic tension. The demand for justice, the call of responsibility to the other, is fueled by this tension, for the possibility of justice will always be "beyond right, calculation and commerce," as well as beyond law (Derrida 1995: 27). Yet calculations are still to made afresh, and laws are still to be made better. It is because justice and law are irreconcilable, because they cannot penetrate one another, that they provoke one another.

The *Mūlamadhyamakakārikā*'s entire project for its own part seems to be to overturn the very notion that any sense of "opposition" or "tension" is in fact the mechanism for impelling human beings to the cause of justice. Obviously, given its composition in the midst of a rapidly developing Sarvāstivāda and Vaibhāṣika Buddhist scholasticism, the terms of the moral opposition Nāgārjuna is trying to overturn are vastly different, and it is crucial that these varying terms be clarified.[7] This task is not easy, not merely because of the hermeneutic difficulties of contrasting the worldviews of a second century Indian Buddhist and twentieth century French philosopher, but because the term that most securely underpins the moral dualism Nāgārjuna attacks has itself been rather poorly translated and understood. That term is *svabhāva*.

The MMK has in English scholarship been seen so often as an "anti-metaphysical" tract because of its unrelenting denial of *svabhāva*, with *svabhāva* translated most often as "self-nature" and "essence" in some vaguely "Western substantialist" vein.[8] There seem to be no good etymological or philosophical reasons for this however. "Substance," from the Latin *substare* (support or presence) and "essence," from Latin *est*, which is a cognate term of the Greek *estī* and Sanskrit *as* (to be here) do not correspond to the verbal root of *bhāva*, *bhū*, which means primarily to "become" or "to be brought about."[9] The Sarvāstivāda and Vaibhāṣika Buddhist literature that makes *svabhāva* a widespread philosophical term discusses it in the context of how different states of being or entities are brought about, how they are conditioned and can be distinguished in a causal sense. Indeed, the larger context of the philosophical debate about *svabhāva* in early Buddhist scholasticism was intimately tied to questions regarding the general efficacy (*kāritra*) of changing phenomena (*bhāva*) upon one another given varying causal theories and portrayals of time.[10] Though much of the discourse regarding the "efficacy" of *svabhāva* is couched in either psychological, phenomenological or atomistic terms in the Buddhist scholastic literature, its real import is moral, because ultimately early Buddhist philosophers invoked *svabhāva* in order to give viable explications of the mechanics of *karma*, or how our intentions and actions determine our quality of bondage to the world or liberation from attachment.

Buddhism starts with an accounting of how things come to be the way they are (*yathābhūthaṃ*), or, more specifically, a causal-biographical account of how we as particularly unique individuals have come to assume the karmic state in which we presently find ourselves. With regard to ordinary entities, the Vaibhāṣikas argued that each particular thing we cognize must contain its own unique set of "self-replicating" characteristics, for if we are to assume that not all effects of our cognitions upon us, such as their memory or their karmic contribution to our consciousness, are immediate but are rather delayed, then some "solely self-replicating" (*sasvabhāvamātra*) features of entities must persist through all time dimensions, past, present and future.[11] The Sarvāstivādins in their turn posited that certain elementary things in the world, that is to say, certain elements that are not compounded out of other elements (*asaṃskṛta dharma*-s) must have their own "self-sustaining power" (*svabhāva*), since the Sarvāstivādins account for the regularity and predictability of causal production based on the fact that certain capacities (*samārthya*), conditions (*pratyaya*) and powers (*śakti*) regularly bring about effects that correspond in kind to their precedents.[12] The upshot of all this metaphysical theorizing is that, for select events in our psychic encounter with the world, their constitution and causal efficacy, the manner in which they are brought about and continue to be brought about even within the framework of pervasive impermanence, belong uniquely to their own self-production or self-sustenance (*svabhāva*).

This picture of the world has palpable ethical relevance. On the soteriological plane, for both of these schools, *saṃsāra* or the "world of rebirth" and *nirvāṇa* or "freedom" are distinct ethical forms of life and so cannot be brought about by the same causes or behaviors; rather, each respective state of being is brought about by its own constituent behavioral causes or factors. This principle of states of affairs that are brought about or produced only by states of affairs of distinctly like kinds applies then to both the physical and moral spheres in these scholastic treatments, for just as the molecules that constitute fire cannot quench the thirst produced in my body, and water does not have the chemical components that would allow it to burn down a building, so *saṃsāra* is construed as a set of mutually reinforcing and facilitating behaviors that cannot quench desire and *nirvāṇa* consists of another set of mutually reinforcing and facilitating behaviors that cannot arouse attachment. This was, the early scholastic Buddhists believed, the most cogent way to interpret the bedrock Buddhist doctrine of "co-arising" (*pratītyasamutpāda*), which was articulated in the earliest Buddhist *sūtras* as a strictly causally conditional depiction of how attachment overcomes a person, and how that attachment itself can be behaviorally dissolved.[13]

Entities therefore do not "have" or "possess" or "exhibit" *svabhāva* as many English translations of the Buddhist thought of this period so misleadingly present the concept. *Svabhāva*, at least in the Buddhist context, is rather verbal and causal, it means to "self-produce" or "self-create," or to "come about according to (one's) own principle." *Svabhāva* in both its metaphysical and ethical senses is much closer, at least in a conceptual sense, to "autonomy," where the latter means "to have one's own laws, principles or norms," to be a "being from and unto oneself." To translate *svabhāva* as autonomy or self-production would be especially fortunate when it is remembered that these terms can be considered synonymous with "independence," not to be conditioned or influenced by environing factors but to define and determine oneself. Sarvāstivāda philosophers indeed equate the capacity of a person to be autonomous with their ability to bring about virtuous conduct and attain perfect enlightenment.[14] What the notion of *svabhāva* does in the end, its performative function, is to fuel a fundamental moral opposition, to create a tension between forms of life that lead to bondage and forms of life that release one from it, to give us a standard of how to distinguish between acts of *saṃsāra* or *adharma* (attachment or wrong) and acts of *nirvāṇa* or *dharma* (freedom or righteousness). This tension between these two poles is what, according to the scholastic Buddhist movements that were gaining ascendancy in the monastic "universities" of Nāgārjuna time, supposedly impels us to walk the path of virtue.

The daring "deconstructive" drive of Nāgārjuna lies precisely in wanting to resolve this tension, to dissolve this opposition, to overturn this trenchant moral dualism between justice and injustice with the subversive notion of *śūnyatā* or "emptiness."[15] Like Derrida in our own era, Nāgārjuna was viewed by philosophical opponents in India with loyalties to both the Vedic and Buddhist camps as a philosopher of mere and thoroughgoing negativity. *Ŝūnyatā* earned for itself and its major Indian philosophical purveyor a very unsavory reputation. "*Ŝūnya*," given the fact that its primary meaning in Sanskrit is the shape in which the number "zero" is written, was associated with connotations of negation, privation and absence (*abhāva*). Nāgārjuna was constantly branded a "closet nihilist" and was charged with being a "refutation-only" debater, as having "no philosophical thesis" to build a positive program of life upon. Like Derrida, Nāgārjuna, despite these charges, has an affirmative agenda in mind, but that agenda at least overtly allies itself with an already centuries-old program of Buddhist practice. However, because of its association with "co-arising" (*pratītyasamutpāda*), the notion of emptiness is actually solicited to dissolve moralisms of opposition between righteousness and unrighteousness in favor of a morality of the interdependence of the two that makes possible the transition of the latter into the former. If the Vaibhāṣika and Sarvāstivāda schools represent metaphysics of independent existence and autonomous functionings of *saṃsāric* and *nirvāṇic* activities that in the end bring into relief a sharp moral dualism, then the MMK constitutes in its entirety a rigorous deconstruction of autonomy and freedom conceived as detachment from influences in favor of a relational vision of interactional interdependence and mutual freedom. Confronting the Sarvāstivāda and Vaibhāṣika interpretation of Abhidharma metaphysical categories (*padārtha*-s), Nāgārjuna is especially adamant in his advocacy of relationality over autonomy in those chapters of the MMK concerned with the possibility of efficacious Buddhist praxis. And this vision of relational and mutual action, the organic whole that a person's deeds make up, the relatedness of the practitioner to social norms and through that relatedness the enhancement of her ability to transform them is Nāgārjuna's idea of how righteousness is born.

Nāgārjuna attempts to accomplish this task with three maneuvers. First, he exchanges the mechanical depictions of karmic economy that represent action in terms of causal chains governed by morally dualistic productive forces for a metaphorical revisioning of action as debt (*ṛṇa*) and Buddhist practice (*bhāvanā*) as its repayment. Second, Nāgārjuna portrays Buddhist practice, the bringing about and carrying out of virtue, not as the scholastic Buddhists had, as the discipline of a reclusive community at a remove from common social activities (*saṃvṛti*), but rather as a mirror of the "transactional conduct" established by "common law" (*vyavahāra*). Finally, Nāgārjuna refuses to see right or justice (*dharma*) and wrong or injustice (*adharma*) as polar opposites in tension, in battle with one another, each vying as it were for the other's destruction, but rather as a genealogical co-production of right-and-wrong (*dharmādharma-samutpannam*) in which, apart from the performance of wrong, the right cannot come about. These maneuvers, it would seem, enable Nāgārjuna to avoid, to circumvent, an ethical *aporia* such as is encountered in Derrida's thought, since for Nāgārjuna, notions of "transactional law," "debt and repayment through practice" and the "co-production" of injustice and justice, while they do not serve as fixed, transcendental principles of moral judgment, provide nonetheless what he considers good examples, a faithful template, for how ultimate liberation from attachment is made possible.

Nāgārjuna begins the seventeenth *parīkṣā* of the MMK with the forthright announcement that he is actively attempting to articulate the theory that best represents the Buddha's teachings about virtue. But in order to clarify his view of the genuine import of the *karma* theory, Nāgārjuna feels compelled to discard two alternative scholastic treatments.[16] What these alternative theories in their own respective fashions are trying to provide is a transcendentally explanatory baseline, a fixed locus or standard upon which one can sensibly demarcate between meritorious and deleterious acts. Both of these views feed off what can palpably be characterized as a moral dualism, a dualism between meritorious and impure seed-intentions in the first case and good and bad principles of conduct in the second.[17] Nāgārjuna travels down a different road that, in its own remarkably daring fashion, militates against the search for a fixed standard of adjudicating an act, or trades in the hoped-for fixed standard in exchange for a visualization of action that preserves its connection to common-sense notions of causality and the *sensus communis* of appropriate social conduct (*vyavahāra*). If the flaw of the instant theories was to attempt mechanical or transcendental descriptions of action that would allow us to rely on fixed standards for judging its merit or demerit, Nāgārjuna's articulation will employ a combination of a powerful metaphor with a concession to a certain degree of inexplicability.

Planted, perhaps appropriately enough, in the middle of these Vaibhāṣika and Sarvāstivāda architectonics of *karma* is Nāgārjuna's own trope, which he justifies on the authority of the Buddha, awakened teachers and the earliest Buddhist disciples.[18]

> I will now proclaim that idea that is fitting here,
> authorized by the Buddhas, *Pratyeka*-Buddhas and disciples.
> *Karma* (action) is like a document (*pattra*) or a debt (*ṛṇa*)
> that remains unexpired;
> being of the four realms, its nature is inexpressible (*avyākṭa*).
> It is abandoned not through (mere) abandonment,
> but only through constant practice (*bhāvanā heya*).
> Therefore, through the unexpired arises the fruit of action. MMK 17:13-15[19]

Nāgārjuna, having set aside moral conceptions of action that try to capture its features through the language of psychic seeds, continuity or autonomy, chooses an entirely different metaphorical vocabulary to discuss it. Indeed, this Nāgārjunian move of exchanging theory of moral efficacy for moral practice in the MMK is of a piece with the project of the entire work. He writes in the stanzas above that the real material nature of action, how its mechanics actually function in the world, simply cannot be explained (*prakṛtyā 'vyākṛta*). The metaphorical terms he uses to speak of properly Buddhist ethics are that of a debt (*ṛṇa*) or a document witnessing to a debt (*pattra*). When one acts, one inscribes one's name, as it were, on the act in such a way as to acknowledge that the consequences of the act will remain in force, will not be cancelled (*avipraṇāśa*) until one makes good on the debt incurred. To act is to own one's act. But this notion of act, insofar as it is comparable to a document witnessing to a debt, also preserves the interpersonal, social and even environmental relation of action, for debts not only give the borrower an obligation to repay, but the debt is repaid to someone, to the community, to the world, and so Nāgārjuna says that the effects of an action belong to all the four realms (*caturvidho dhātuta*) of existence. Nāgārjuna, unlike Derrida, does not infer the consequence that a sense of reciprocal obligation somehow cheapens or diminishes the "purity" of an act, a perceived cheapening that led Derrida to characterize true beneficence as a true "gift." On the contrary, for Nāgārjuna, it is precisely because action can be thought of as "debt" either incurred or paid to others that the interpersonal bond, the commitment to the other, could be strengthened. This is especially evident in the fact that Nāgārjuna's "documented-debt" conception of *karma* takes into account what he found lacking in the Vaibhāṣika and Sarvāstivāda models, namely an explanation of how action can be abandoned (*prabhāṇa*), or how *karma* is eliminated and one is released from rebirth. A debt cannot be resolved by merely ignoring it or adding nothing more to it, for the document that witnesses to the debt remains in force. In like manner, actions (*karma*) cannot merely be eliminated if one does not repeat them or simply resolves that one has escaped their consequences. The debts that action incurs must be paid somehow. Nāgārjuna insists that, just as a debt has to be "worked off," the borrower has to do the work of acquiring the currency sufficient for another act of "paying off" the debt, so fruits of action are only "worked out" through "constant practice" (*bhāvanā-heya*). Moral cultivation as self-transformation here is inextricably bound to obligation to the other, and so is the very possibility of freedom. To formulate this in all its apparent, but only apparent, paradoxicality, the hope for freedom is bound through a sense of indebtedness to the other, and can be gained only through the work of fulfilling one's obligations to the other.

There is, furthermore, another powerful social resonance in these verses about debt, for the resolution of debts was in traditional India part of "legal trade" or "transaction law" (*vyavahāra*), as we are told in no small number of ancient legal and political texts of the period."[20] This needs looking at, for it unlocks an ever-elusive but indispensable key to Nāgārjuna's thought. *Vyavahāra* is often translated somewhat generically and vaguely as merely social "convention," "practical action" or "custom." This is undoubtedly one of the most prevalent senses of the term, but the "commerce" or "interaction" that *vyavahāra* connotes is more often than not of the "regulated" variety. The most widely disseminated scholarly rendering of *vyavahāra* in Nāgārjuna scholarship in English has much to do with Candrakīrti's commentary *Prasannapadā* where he observes in reference to MMK 24:8 that one of the possible meanings of *saṃvṛti* is ""social convention, that is, the world of ordinary language (*loka-vyavahāra*) and of transactions between individuals which is characterized by the distinction between knowing and the thing known, naming (*abhidāna*) and the thing named (*abhideya*), and so on" (Sprung 1979: 230). Candrakīrti most often boils the notion of *vyavahāra* down to the epistemological and linguistic conditions for the possibility of social interaction. The term however carries a palpable moral and even legal force in Sanskrit literature. The *Arthaśāstra* specifically and repeatedly identifies *vyavahāra* in terms of "legal transaction" and "legal trade."[21] In his version of the *Dharmasūtras*, Gautama lists a series of offenses ranging from abuse and assault to property transfer and economic issues as possible areas requiring "legal action" (*vyavahāra*) (Gautama's *Dharmaśūstras* 11-13; Olivelle 1999: 97–102). This is what informs my translation of *vyavahāra* for the purposes of this essay as "transactional conduct," for it has wrapped up within it moral, social and legal implications. At least in one instance in his commentary on MMK 8:6, Candrakīrti even points out the legal dimensions of *vyavahāra* as it pertains to regulated transactions when he clarifies it with the examples "farming, commerce and governing" (Sprung 1979: 119). This meaning then sheds much needed light on Nāgārjuna's own adamant insistence that the "paramount aim" of freedom could not be attained without reliance on the moral model of mutual obligations enjoined in socially constructed "transactional conduct" (*vyavahāram anāśritya paramārtho na deśyate / paramārtham anāgamya nirvāṇaṃ nādhigamyate //* MMK 24:10; "Without relying on transactional conduct, the paramount aim is not taught; without comprehending the paramount aim, freedom (*nirvāṇa*) is not understood either."). Once again, in contrast to Derrida, Nāgārjuna has no reticence in making worldly law a model for righteousness, for it mandates the recognized obligations of people toward one another.

Nāgārjuna does not bring up in this context any hint that such "common transactional law" may be in its present form in any way unjust, and were a Derridian counter-critique of Nāgārjuna to focus on any particular point, it may be precisely this one.[22] This lack of attention to the possible injustice of present common law does not of course exclude the possibility that certain laws may be unjust and need reform, for while Nāgārjuna does not criticize legal shortcomings, no demand is placed by him on the fixity of present law either. Another feature of *vyavahāra* that provides a contrast to the kind of law that Derrida critiques is that, unlike the latter, *vyavahāra* is not really the law of the state, but it is communal or traditional law, even when it involves testimony in public hearings. It does not have any apparent ideology that undergirds it beyond its support from traditional precedent, and so *vyavahārika* laws are, once again, revisable and not transcendental. Indeed, the categories of *dharma* or "divine law" and *vyavahāra* or "transactional law" are clearly distinct in classical Sanskrit legal texts; the distinction being based on the assumption that the former cannot be changed while the latter can be. Worldly law serves nonetheless, being as it is a model of transactional obligation, as a model of justice, a model that is reflected and not rejected by the practices of Buddhism that strive for freely-engaged righteousness.

The theme of "emptiness" and its relation to the Four Noble Truths of Buddhist praxis is of course the topic of the much-discussed twenty-fourth *parīkṣā* of the MMK, and as such the chapter has been considered in recent scholarship the *locus classicus* of Nāgārjuna's deconstruction of metaphysics. However, in the context of the present topic, it should not be surprising to the reader who considers the *parīkṣā* closely that it is actually predominantly about practice and its intelligibility and possibility. Indeed, the first six verses of the chapter, addressing a *pūrva-pakṣa* or contrary view, represent Nāgārjuna as trading insults with an interlocutor who posits that the principle of emptiness *(śūnyatā)* would lead to the implication that, if all things were empty, so must be the person of the Buddha, the Four Noble Truths, the eightfold path and any conception of particular beings who would attain enlightenment and freedom. Such an assessment of Nāgārjuna's thought seems to have been the default one among Brāhmiṇical and rival Buddhist systems. The most important verses of the chapter are devoted to nothing else but undermining this misconception, and in a way that follows from all Nāgārjuna has said so far in the treatise about action and its moral consequences.

> If you perceive these phenomena as entities
> that are self-produced,
> you will perceive these very phenomena
> as uncaused and unconditioned,
> you will contradict the (notions of) cause, effect,
> the agent itself, instrument, act, arising, ceasing and fruit.
> We proclaim that whatever is causally conditioned co-arising,
> that is emptiness;
> That ("emptiness") is a designation derived from ("co-arising").
> This is precisely the middle path.
> Any particular thing that is not conditionally
> co-arisen is not acknowledged;
> for this reason, any particular thing that is not empty
> is not acknowledged either.
> If all this is not empty, there exists no arising nor extinction,
> (and) this would imply the non-existence of the four noble truths.
> MMK 24:16-20[23]

Attaining the middle path (*madhyamā pratipad*) taught by the Buddha requires one to understand that the real meaning of the designation (*prajñapti*) "emptiness" (*śūnyatā*) is not "absence" or "non-existence" but is instead "causally conditioned co-arising" (*pratītyasamutpāda*). But what exactly does it mean for ethics to be "empty?" What sorts of conceptual implications does equating "co-arising" with "emptiness" have for ethics? In another characteristically radical move, Nāgārjuna ends up, in rejecting the Sarvāstivāda and Vaibhāṣika rhetoric of *svabhāva* that would make good and bad deeds the fruits of disconnected causal chains of action, insisting in a very concrete way that injustice and justice, impurity and purity, unrighteousness and righteousness, exist only in a co-productive relationship. A commitment to *svabhāva* would leave the unenlightened unable to liberate themselves and the enlightened unjustly removed from the suffering of the world that is their moral charge.

> Whosoever is by nature unenlightened, if he pursues enlightenment,
> he will not attain it even through *bodhisattva* practice;
> nor would even a single person do either right or wrong.
> How could the non-empty, much less the self-created, do anything?
> To you, the fruit is acknowledged even without right and wrong,
> though you would not acknowledge a fruit
> produced by right and wrong.
> If you did acknowledge a fruit produced by right and wrong,
> how could that fruit, co-arising from right and wrong, be non-empty?
> You contradict all worldly transactional conduct
> when you contradict the emptiness of causally conditioned co-arising. MMK 24: 32-36

The first several verses above illustrate in a rather poignant and concrete way the consequences to people of propagating a theory of "self-produced" moral outcomes. Nāgārjuna draws the implication that, if actions have in the end their own autonomous characters or self-generated capacities, then a person who finds himself at the moment unawakened can have no hope at all of reaching enlightenment, for *nirvāṇa* and the state in which he lives are such entirely different realms of conduct that effecting the change from one to the other is practically impossible. The same story could be told of a person who was fortunate enough to achieve enlightenment, for they under the *svabhāva* explanation could be tempted to think of themselves as always having carried the virtues of awakening within them, and so the fact that they are now so awakened could lead them to the conceit that enlightenment was no achievement at all, but rather an elite state of potential that they have lived out. Where, we find Nāgārjuna asking in these stanzas, is the morality in such a vision of practice? What kind of moral explanation of the world depicts it as constituted by one set of noble beings destined for awakening and another set of ignoble ones bound to suffering; is this not the very Brāhmiṇical classism that Buddhism as a social phenomenon was trying to reform?[24] A properly moral theory, on the contrary, allows for the possibility of change, change in the person's behaviors, habits and conduct and the change to the world offered by practicing communities; indeed a properly moral theory does more than allow for such change, it enjoins such change.

However, Nāgārjuna's case goes even past these limits. The moral claim being made in these verses is indeed radical from a conventional scholastic Buddhist point of view. If we assume actions are adjudicable by some fixed moral standard, if we can pronounce any given act as moral or immoral only within the framework of a systematic theoretical dualism between good and evil, Nāgārjuna asserts, we actually rob it of its moral worth, a moral worth that is once again "worked out" in the long run of praxis. For acts have extraordinarily complex genealogies that carry with them some incalculable measure of right-and-wrong (*dharmādharma*), a measure which is only created in the circumstance of the act's production or co-arising (*nimitta*, *samutpanna*). This entails of course that right-and-wrong (*dharmādharma*), being ever co-produced through action, are empty (*śūnya*), which means exactly that they do not exist in isolation from one another. But, the MMK warns, empty ethics is the only kind of ethics we can embrace, for ethical absolutism, which in the Buddhist context Nāgārjuna knew entails unmitigated distinctions between wrong and right acts, leads merely to a disassociation of right and wrong that is so great that it effectively leaves us powerless to understand how one may change into the other, and thus powerless to bridge the gap that such a moral absolutism creates between the interdependent world in which one lives and the freedom for which one strives. It is only through the actual performance of acts by agents interacting with the world and with other agents that fruits or moral consequences arise. And it is only through ongoing, unmitigated practice and discipline, practice and discipline which also inevitably involve others and one's environment, that freedom is possible. Freedom can, within the indistinguishably overlapping spheres of worldly transactional conduct (*laukika-vyavahāra*) and the community of practitioners (*saṇgha*), only be attained mutually. After all, to cite this pivotal verse once more, as Nāgārjuna proclaims, "without relying on transactional conduct, the paramount aim is not taught; without comprehending the paramount aim, freedom (*nirvāṇa*) is not understood either" (MMK 24:10)

The point is an extremely significant one to comprehend as Nāgārjuna intimates it. For in saying that ethical absolutism is flawed, he does not mean that calling one action "right" and the other "wrong" has either no meaning or an arbitrary meaning that only serves the ends of power sought after by the social elites. Nāgārjuna has no demonstrable wish, as we saw above, to implicate customary social ethics or laws as they stand. Nor does he mean to reverse the meanings of "right" and "wrong" actions as these are commonly understood in the communally constructed life. The emptiness of ethics is not one that "re-evaluates" or reaches "beyond good and evil" in any way that violates known social practices, but is an ethics only insofar as it is of "good-and-evil." Empty ethics does not denote that ethics is meaningless, but rather that ethics is only meaningful insofar as it allows for the untrammeled interaction of wrong and right, the possibility of the former helping to give rise to, and occasion for, the latter. Does that imply, an incredulous scholastic critic may be tempted to ask, that one somehow attains enlightenment rather than further bondage by performing evil deeds? It means, Nāgārjuna is responding, that without wrong action there will be no pain, with no pain there will be no understanding of pain, with no understanding of pain, there will be no remedy for it nor any facilitator of compassion, and with no remedy of pain or compassion there will be no virtue, and if there is no virtue there will accrue no merit, and were there no merit, we could call nothing good. Morality here is only freed to operate when it is liberated from any construal of dualistic tension.

What Nāgārjuna shares with Derrida then is a vision of justice that deconstructs, overturns, transcendental principles of conduct while retaining a steadfast commitment to the other, the suffering other who demands an affirmative, selfless duty from us. Derrida's indictment of the frequent shortcomings of any given system of civil law as it stands raises a challenge on which Nāgārjuna, it certainly seems, is in this treatise silent. The question that Nāgārjuna's particular handling of ethics however brings before Derrida's thought is whether the latter has, through his insistence on the irreconcilability of the artificially systematized law to the absolute demands of justice, the purity of the offered gift as opposed to the calculative reciprocity of the merely moral, the "universal structure of the messianic" over and above the economy of rights, created an *aporia* that people actually do penetrate in their obligated commitments to one another in everyday life. Does Derrida, in his ethical demands of pure giving and absolute hospitality, expect too much from human beings? Or does Derrida, in his messianism of justice and disjointure of goodness, merely leave human beings with no better option but to expect? While making it incumbent on people to give, Derrida forthrightly admits that such giving is, in his special sense of the term, "impossible;" he asks of them a sacrifice so perfect that they themselves will have no consciousness that they are giving. Nāgārjuna's project seems for its part to point to the deduction that all moral dualisms can only lead to a kind of ethical paralysis that disables one's ability to move from attachment to justice. Nāgārjuna's equation of *saṃsāra* and *nirvāṇa* lays aside any possible distinctions between purely pure and purely impure acts, and along with these any need to posit an aporetic character to human goodness. Nāgārjuna places good giving within relationships, where people have always experienced it, its examples being so abundantly plentiful in human social life that models of it do not have to be looked for in either awaited messiahs or recondite metaphysical formulas, but can be seen everywhere and practiced by everyone. If a "Derridian messianism" leaves us longing for the fulfillment of the prophecy, the promise of justice in our openness to the future, perhaps a "Nāgārjunian Buddhahood" reaches forth a boon-bestowing hand to help a society that prompted, in both unintended and intended ways, the vow that its beneficence makes good on from one eon to the next.

Notes

1 This chapter was first published as "Deconstruction, *Aporia* and Justice in Nāgārjuna's Empty Ethics" in *Deconstruction and the Ethical in Asian Thought*, Youru Wang, ed., London: Routledge, 2007, 35–52. It is reprinted here with the permission of Taylor and Francis, Ltd., U.K.

2 Caputo (1997a: 136–8) enumerates three senses of what is described as Derrida's "inventionalism" in the face of ethical *aporias*, namely how justice must suspend present law in order to improve it, how a just decision must suspend formulaic legal judgment in order to establish the justice of "singular," individually unique cases and the urgency and haste which the need for justice forces on decisions that at the same time require calculative deliberation.

3 Derrida has a fascinating discussion of these dimensions of political organization through an engagement with the texts of the political philosopher Carl Schmidt and the philologist Émile Benveniste in *Politics of Friendship* (1997: 83–104).

4 Simon Critchley (1999: 13–20) has emphasized in his reading of Derrida's critique of Levinas the "two-handed" approach of deconstruction, which both locates "ethics" in the problematic history of Western ontology and yet "displaces" the obligation to the other from that context where it can viably serve as the "condition of the possibility of the ethical."

5 Derrida discusses this problem at length in trying to explicate Abraham's seemingly supremely unethical secrecy to his family and to his own son about God's demand that he sacrifice Isaac (Derrida 1994: 58–69).

6 This is elaborated by Derrida in moving language in both *The Gift of Death* (1994: 68–9) and especially in its relation to "democratic societies" as "rules of the majority" in *Politics of Friendship* (1997: 20–2).

7 Robert Magliola has suggested that Nāgārjuna's notion of *śūnyatā* and Derrida's *différance* could be fruitfully seen as aligned (1984: 89). David Loy pushed this argument a step further, suggesting that Nāgārjuna, because his metaphysical critiques deconstructed both identity and difference, moved beyond Derrida's purely textual approach to criticism (1987: 59–80). Harold Coward, based on later revisionist suggestions from Loy, thought that Nāgārjuna and Derrida could perhaps be reconciled on the basis of the positive functioning of language for spiritual realization in the space of Zen dialogues (1990: 145–6). The late B.S. Yadav, though in the process of writing about Nāgārjuna never mentioned Derrida explicitly, had no apparent hesitation about seeing Nāgārjuna as engaged in a "methodic deconstruction" of various strands of Hindu and Buddhist "logocentrism" (1992: 132–3). The earlier comparisons struck me as in need of far more philosophical contextualization of both philosophers. Yadav's appropriation of deconstructive language in order to represent Nāgārjuna's thought, as I have written elsewhere, eloquent and evocative as it certainly was and even with all its obvious promise to enhance and deepen future scholarship in this area, seemed to beg the comparative question rather than resolve it.

8 The three major translations of the text into English concur on this rendering. Inada has it as alternatively "self-nature, self-existence, self-essence, own-being" (1970: 184). Kalupahana translates *svabhāva* as "self-nature" and its adjectival form *svabāhavato* as "substantially" (1986: 32–4; 36). Jay Garfeild, who depends on the Tibetan, *rang bzhin*, gives *svabhāva* with some qualification as "essence" (1995: 89). The peculiarly Western metaphysical biases of the translations themselves, as Andrew Tuck (1990) has so effectively demonstrated, have tended to reflect the assumptions of transcendentalism, analytic philosophy or deconstruction, depending on whatever philosophical movement happened to be in vogue in the West. The most important departure from this in recent writings has been the work of John Schroeder, who effectively points out that the real targets of the MMK are the various hermeneutics of Abhidharma (2000: 559–72). In Schroeder's depiction, Nāgārjuna's aim is to thematize a more faithfully Buddhist view of specifically meditative practice. While I wholeheartedly concur with Schroeder's corrected emphasis, it seems to me that Nāgārjuna's frequent invocation of the Four Noble Truths as a whole, which encompass not only meditation but conduct as well, implies that his conception of practice is much more broadly ethical in its interests

9 Halbfass notes this difference between these two verbal forms in Sanskrit, but does not think it of too much import with regard to their common general sense of "being" (1992: 22). In certain philosophical contexts such as the Buddhist, however, I think the difference is significant.

10 See Frauwallner (1995: 185–208).

11 A detailed exposition as well as Sautrāntika critique of these views is found in Vasubandhu's *Abhidharmakośabhāṣya* (see V. 25c-27), as is referenced in Burton (1999: 113) and in Williams (1981: 227–57).

12 Saṅghabhadra, a younger contemporary and opponent of Vasubandhu, has the definitive philosophical treatment of the Sarvāstivāda explanation of these processes in his *Nyāyānusāra* (see the reconstruction of verses 46:a-b in Cox 1999: 695–701).

13 "*imasmiṃ sati idaṃ hoti imassa uppādā idaṃ uppajjati / imasmiṃ asati idaṃ na hoti imassa nirodhā idaṃ nirujjhatti //*" ("That existing, this comes to be; that arising, this is born; that not existing, this does not come to be, that ceasing, this perishes." (from the *Majjhima-nikāya* I:262ff, qtd. in Kalupahana 1992: 56 but my English translation).

14 In his monumental *Nyāyānusāra*, Saṅghabhadra introduces the treatise by reminding his readers that the whole point of Abhidharma analysis is to explicate the difference between "contaminated" and "uncontaminated" *dharma*-s in order to attain enlightenment (verses 2-6) and after a brief introductory overview of the aggregates of personality and consciousness, proclaims that only those beings that have the capacity to self-produce (*svabhāva*) are ultimately real (*paramārthasatya*), while those that do not exhibit *svabhāva* are only nominally real (*prajñāptisatya*) (verse 15); see the reconstruction in Cox (1999: 651; 655). It is of course one of the main aims of Nāgārjuna to turn this assessment on its head,

15 Despite the widespread classical Indian view of Nāgārjuna as a "refutation-only" (*vāda-vaitaṇḍika*) debater (see Matilal 1998: 51–6) and the current Western penchant to see him as a thoroughgoing "deconstructionist of ontology" (see Martin 1995: 98–109), Nāgārjuna often forthrightly states his intention to proclaim "right views" in the MMK, which is not, as is the *Vigrahavyāvartanī*, written in the *genre* of *vāda-vitāṇda* (refutation-only debate).

16 The present *parīkṣā* has been the subject of considerable interpretive debate among the MMK's English translators. Inada speculates that Nāgārjuna is out to refute two rival theories of *karma*, one which sees the transition from act to moral fruit as one of continuity (*śāśvata*) and the other which sees it terms of interruption (*ucceda*), making verse 20 the announcement of the *prāsaṅga* method of refuting these rival explanations (1970: 104–5). Garfield, who concurs with Inada that verse 20 and not verse 13 is the pivot verse of the chapter, outlines four different Buddhist theories of *karma* that Nāgārjuna is after, though he does not detail who the representatives of these views are supposed to be (1995: 231–44). For reasons I will explain further shortly, it seems to me that the *parikṣā* can be divided up into roughly four sections; verses 1-5 clarifying the terms and moral goals of the basic Buddhist view of *karma-phala*, verses 6-12 rejecting a decidedly early Vaibhāṣika view, verses 21-33 refuting two possible Sarvāstivāda interpretations, and sandwiched in the middle of

the chapter in verses 13-20 is Nāgārjuna's own highly metaphorical view of *karma* interspersed with a few remaining rejoinders of the just-dispensed-with initial Vaibhāṣika position.

17 Nāgārjuna characterizes and refutes these views in MMK 17:6-12 and 17:21-24, and space limitations prevent me from entering into details about these arguments. Significantly however, the polemic of Nāgārjuna against the latter view in verses 28-33, which famously ends by comparing all agents and acts and fruits to "the cities of the *gandharva*-s, the illusions of sleep," is solely directed at the *pratyaya-samutanna karma* depiction and is not, as Inada (1970: 105) takes it, a general denial of any conception of moral agency.

18 Kalupahana is basically right, contra Inada and Garfield, in seeing these stanzas as representing Nāgārjuna's genuine view (1986: 249–54). Nowhere else in the MMK can what Nāgārjuna defends be found to depart from views of the "Buddhas" and *Pratyeka*-Buddhas he relies on, and his citation of enlightened beings in both verses 13 and 20 provide the proper frame for his own position, not to mention the fact that verse 13 declares the idea he sets forth there to be "fitting" (*yojyate*), an appellation his does not grant to any of the other purported notions in the *parīkṣā*.

19 All translated passages from the MMK in this essay are my own.

20 See for instance the third century BCE *Arthaśāstra*, 3:1:39-40, where *vyavahāra* is deemed to be witness given in a court proceeding (Rangarajan 1992: 380), the first century CE's *Manusmṛti*, 8 where the term clearly is meant in the sense of a court proceeding and the "eighteen titles of law" are called *vyavahāra-pada* (Sharma 2003: 314–90) and the third century *Dharmasūtras* of Gautama, 11-13 where the term refers to a number of areas of regulated trade (see Olivelle 1999: 97–102).

21 The entire first three books of the *Arthaśāstra* define *vyavahāra* alternatively as a legal transaction, a contract stipulating the terms of a transaction and as either live or documented testimony given in a court proceeding. The fact that the term was in such widespread usage some four centuries before Nāgārjuna should leave us little doubt that, in employing the term, he had at minimum moral and legal senses of it in mind.

22 Caputo hints at this critique when he points out that Derrida's vision of the gift, messianic in spirit, "is concerned with the possibilities that open up for the outsiders, the political, social, national, sexual outsiders" in a way that Nāgārjuna's "gentle play of harmony and benignity" could never be (1997b: 186–8). Caputo's understanding of Nāgārjuna appears rather uninformed and his impression even somewhat Orientalist, but against the backdrop of this difference between the thinkers, the critique of Nāgārjuna may be available.

23 I translate the second line of MMK 24:18; *sā prajñaptir upādāya pratipat saiva madhyamā* in an importantly different way from most other modern renditions. In my view, the line only contributes to the general point the entire chapter is trying to

make, emphasizing the synonymy of "conditioned co-arising" and "emptiness rather than claiming that "emptiness" is also some species of mere "designation." I justify this translation in a previous chapter of this volume, "What Kind of Designation is 'Emptiness?: Reconsidering Nāgārjuna's MMK 24:18.'"

24 In the works of the late B.S. Yadav, Buddhism in general, and its Madhyamaka strand in particular, are primarily a protest against the pervasive castism of Brāhmiṇical systems, a hermeneutic self-consciously redolent of that of B.R. Ambedkar (See Yadav 1992).

Part III

Indian and Intercultural Philosophy

7

Early Brāhmiṇical and Confucian Ideas of Duty

Continuing an Intercultural Debate

This chapter undertakes an attempt to make intercultural philosophy truly intercultural, which entails enabling many different philosophical traditions to enter into dialogue and debate with one another without Western thought providing the standards which evaluate them. Here, the widely hailed second-century CE Brāhmiṇical and devotional text, the Bhagavad Gītā, will be put into conversation with the third-century BCE Confucian classic, the *Mengzi* (*Mencius*). I will examine how the two works morally evaluate liminal circumstances in which family duty appears to come into direct conflict with the larger social good. In both cases, the grounds for determining one's ethical obligations are sought in the makeup of one's personhood. The ways in which the Gītā's and *Mengzi*'s depictions of the constitution of personhood diverge lead, in quite direct ways, to how they respectively assess which obligations, to one's intimates or to society as a whole, are paramount. But this chapter will go beyond the merely exegetical conclusions that this comparison will uncover. It will argue that the amelioration of conflicting duties, which is advocated for by both the Confucian *Mengzi* and the far-too-often maligned Arjuna in the Gītā, is morally preferable to abrogation of one duty for another, which is insisted on by the Gītā's Kṛṣṇa.

The argument of this chapter has a history. In a special issue of *Dao: A Journal of Comparative Philosophy* in 2007, Liu Qingping 劉清平 and Guo Qiyong 郭齊勇 recapitulated an ongoing conflict which had appeared in exclusively Chinese venues earlier. Liu maintained that primary Confucian texts like *Lun Yu* (*Analects*) 13:18, *Mengzi* 5A3 and 7A35, insofar as they dogmatically assert that all other duties even the most widely construed duties of 仁 *ren* or "care" for the general public, must be set aside if that is necessary in order to preserve the requirements of 孝 *xiao* or "dependability" to one's family members

(2007: 5–7). For Liu, this unbreakable principle of Confucianism explained much of the political and social corruption, underwriting loyalty to kin and intimates, that can be found in Chinese history and contemporary life (2007: 2–3). Guo countered this set of charges with the standard Confucian argument that, far from recommending unqualified family loyalty, the *Mengzi* itself and Confucian thought in general council that a conflict of family and social duties should be met by all attempts to satisfy the demands of both (2007: 32–3). My initial publication on this topic, appearing in a later installment of the *Journal of Dao*, attempted to illuminate this debate by setting the *Mengzi* into confrontation with the Gītā. It came to the conclusion that both Guo's reading of the *Mengzi* and the Confucian aspiration to reconcile conflicting moral duties, even when personally costly, are more easily vindicated than either Liu's polemics against Confucianism or the "intrinsically" founded conception of duty in the Gītā (Berger 2008: 157–63). Since then, however, a brilliant analysis dramatizing this very debate between the Gītā and *Mengzi* was written by Geoffrey Ashton (2014: 1–21). In Ashton's straightforward reading of the Gītā, Arjuna is struggling with the discord between affection for his family and the broader social duty which the war between cousins has prompted. In the midst of this discord, Kṛṣṇa's teaching of *niṣkāma karma* or "desireless action" enables Arjuna to reconcile this conflict by empowering him to carry out his larger social duty without attachment to his cousins (2014: 7–9). But even more important for Arjuna's transformation, according to Ashton, is Kṛṣṇa's revelation of his divine body, enveloping all outcomes and all worlds, in the eleventh chapter of the work. For Ashton, the Gītā, by revealing to Arjuna what the gruesome outcome of the war will be in all its honest horror, opens a space where social roles may be "played" but not "lived." And this in turn enables Arjuna to meet the demands of moral duty in times when family and social affections have been overcome by family and social strife (Ashton 2017: 17–20). Ashton's contribution adds, in my view, some weighty insights into any comparative evaluation of the Gītā and the *Mencius* on the basis and aims of moral duty.

In what follows, I will examine the most important relevant arguments of the Gītā and *Mengzi* in detail and take Ashton's points and other important aspects of the issue into serious consideration. In one respect, Ashton's arguments have compelled me to reevaluate my position and subject it to some important qualification. Though each text portrays extreme circumstances which seemingly demand we choose between our obligations to our most cherished ones and society as a whole, neither, I now think, successfully establishes how even the most cultivated human feelings can help us resolve our dilemmas. The Gītā's advice that we surrender all attachments to our own individually pre-made duties is no more a realistic depiction of how we conduct ourselves or evaluate moral problems than is the implausible narrative of the *Mengzi*, which enjoins an untarnished love for murderous family members as indispensable to social solidarity. Ultimately, neither of these works offers us a way to retrain our feelings or perspectives in ways that will enable us to attain their respective ultimate moral ideals. Instead, each text grounds its final moral goals in arguments about what persons most fundamentally are. Once this basis for their respective moral visions has been established, I will, once again, argue that the *Mencius* has a stronger case to make with respect both to the constitution of human existence and to envisioning morally redeemable aspirations than does the Gītā.

The Gītā: Gauging Results or Playing at Roles?

The Gītā is of course the sixth chapter of the magnificent and sprawling epic of the Mahābhārata, which narrates the great war between the protagonist Pāndava family and their cousins, the Kauravas, who have usurped the rightful succession of the Pāndavas to rulership by deceit and trickery. Consigned to thirteen years of exile, the Pāndavas follow the council of the clan general Kṛṣṇa, still unbeknownst as God in human form, to resolve the ongoing conflict with the Kauravas through diplomacy and concession, so that the realm does not suffer the cataclysm of an all-out war. Each of these successive attempts ultimately fails, until finally the dreaded conflagration can no longer be avoided. The reader is convinced, by the time the Gītā commences, that every self-sacrificial effort has been made to preserve the family harmony and secure the peace, reaffirming the genuine value of family duty (*kuladharma*) in classical Brāhmiṇical society. We find ourselves faced then, as the Gītā opens, with entirely extreme circumstances, when family duty must ultimately be set aside so that the just order of the world can be maintained (*lokasaṃgraha*). It is now Kṛṣṇa's task, instead of advising for peace, to give Arjuna, the Pāndava's leading general, the fortitude to lead the battle.

However, just before the first confrontation on the field of Kuru starts, Arjuna falters when he looks upon his arrayed cousins and remembers how noble and dear to him so many of them are. He despairingly slumps into his chariot. Though he is distraught, he lays out several arguments to his charioteer Kṛṣṇa which are meant to demonstrate that going forward with the battle will be gravely wrong. The Gītā itself gives these arguments quite short shrift, and the text's classical and modern commentators almost uniformly dismiss them as excuses for Arjuna's uncharacteristic faint-heartedness. In all the secondary literature devoted to this topic in English, as well as in most classical Indian commentary, Arjuna's arguments receive almost no regard, except for one essay by M. M. Agrawal (1992). I will, however, give these arguments more attention here, as I think their moral weight is worthy of serious consideration and because they have some surprising resonances with what we will see is the position articulated in the *Mengzi*.

What Arjuna first recognizes when he looks across the battlefield at the arrayed Kauravas is no longer a horde of enemies, but relatives he has known all his life, with intimate relations to him and intimate relations to one another.

ācāryāḥ pitaraḥ putrās tathaiva ca pitāmahāḥ /
mātulāḥ śvaśurāḥ pautrāḥ śyālāḥ sambandhinas tathā //
etān na hantum icchhāmi ghnato 'pi madhusūdana /
api trailokya-rājyasya hetoḥ kiṃ nu mahī kṛte //

Here are teachers, fathers, sons, and even grandfathers,
maternal uncles, grandsons, fathers-in-law, grand uncles, kin;
I do not wish to kill them, Madhusūdana, even if they slay me;
If rulership of all the three worlds comes from killing
what can be gotten from it at all? (Bhagavad Gītā 1:34–5)

The thickness of intimacy with his cousins grips Arjuna strongly at the moment when the prospect of cutting them down hand-to-hand, rather than the abstract demands of rightful succession to the throne, overtakes him. On the field, Arjuna sees masters who have taught him, and family members with love and loyalty for one another, as well as family members for whom Arjuna himself feels much affection. Arjuna feels revulsion at all of this, but such revulsion is not just pusillanimous, sentimental gushing. Instead, the life of feeling is acknowledged here to be morally informative. For Arjuna will soon point out that caring for and protecting one's family members is a linchpin of the obligations of *dharma* itself. Arjuna, it should be noticed, adds rhetorical potency to each of his pleas by addressing Kṛṣṇa through one of his many divine names. In this instance, he calls Kṛṣṇa "Madhusūdana," a form of Viṣnu who brought down a demon in order to protect *Brahma*, the creator of the world. The true spiritual warrior does not bring about the demise of being, but protects it.

Arjuna moves on to point out that, while the Kauravas are clearly in the wrong for obtaining their sovereignty by deception and, if it is permitted, slaughter, should the Pāndavas enter into battle and win the throne through war, it will be the Pāndavas on whom defilement will fall.

yady apy ete na paśyanti lobhopahata cetasaḥ /
kula-kṣaya-kṛtaṃ doṣhaṃ mitra-drohe ca pātakam //
kathaṃ na jñeyam asmābhiḥ pāpād asmān nivartitum /
kula-kṣaya-kṛtaṃ doṣhaṃ prapaśyadbhir janārdana //

Even if their thoughts, overtaken by greed, do not see
the error in killing their family or in cheating their friends,
how can we, Janārdana, not know that impurity will undo us,
since we understand the error of killing our family? (Bhagavad Gītā 1:38–9)

Kṛṣṇa is now addressed as Janārdana, the one who punishes wrongdoing. If wrongdoing leads to demise, then, Arjuna points out, we must ever take care that even the most adverse circumstances do not prompt us into misconduct. There is no denying that the Kauravas are guilty of great sin. However, Arjuna points out, their responsibility for their conduct might be somewhat mitigated by the fact that their minds are so overwhelmed by avarice that they cannot comprehend what they are doing. The Pāndavas, however, are not confused; they know fully well that slaying their cousins, in every other conceivable context, could be nothing less than a horrid violation of *kuladharma* or family duty. A knowing violation of the obligations to family must surely be a far worse taint (*pāpa*) than an unknowing one. So, what can possibly become of the goal of restoring the rightful succession of the Pāndavas to the throne when this can only be achieved through a worse offense than the theft of the Kauravas? Even if the Pāndavas win through these means, it will amount to no more, Arjuna suddenly realizes, than the replacement of one injustice by an even graver injustice. We have now gone beyond the significant but purely emotional dread of killing to fully formed moral deliberation.

The third argument Arjuna proffers is, however, the most significant one. Up to now, we have found ourselves on the horns of an apparent dilemma, where a fateful choice between family and society at large must be made. Arjuna suddenly points out that these two sets of duties are not in conflict in the first place. They are mutually supporting such that, to undermine the family is to undermine society.

kula-kṣaye praṇaśyanti kula-dharmāḥ sanātanāḥ /
dharme naṣṭe kulaṃ kṛtsnam adharmo 'bhibhavaty uta //
adharmābhibhavāt kṛṣna praduṣyanti kula-striyaḥ /

strīṣu dushṭāsu vārṣṇeya jāyate varṇa-saṃkaraḥ //
saṃkaro narakāyaiva kula-ghnānāṃ kulasya ca /
patanti pitaro hy eṣāṃ lupta-piṇḍodaka-kriyāḥ //
doṣhair etaiḥ kula-ghnānāṃ varṇa-saṃkara-kārakaiḥ /
utsādyante jāti-dharmāḥ kula-dharmāśca śāśvatāḥ //
utsanna-kula-dharmāṇāṃ manuṣyāṇāṃ janārdana /
narake niyataṃ vāso bhavatītyanuśuśruma //

When families demise and continuous family *dharma* is vanquished,
in that annihilation of *dharma*, *adharma* prevails
with the remainder of the family.
Kṛṣṇa, the prevalence of *adharma* brings impurity
to the women of the family.
Those that are born of impure women, descendent of Vṛṣṇi,
are of mixed caste,
and this mixture leads both the family and its destroyers to hell.
Without the *piṇda* offerings, the family ancestors surely vanish.
Those who destroy the family and bring about the mixing of castes
ruin the continuity of lineage and family duties.
Janārdana, the successors have said that
they who ruin family and human *dharma*
dwell in hell forever. (Bhagavad Gītā 1:40–4)

Arjuna now addresses Kṛṣṇa as a descendent of Vṛṣṇi, and so also the progeny of a virtuous family. Were Kṛṣṇa's family at some earlier point to have fallen into grave sin (they eventually will), the lineage would not have continued and the world would lack a powerful and needed protector. These dual roles of Kṛṣṇa as both the inheritor of a family legacy and the responsibility for guarding the world at large are invoked to persuade him that war will be disastrous for both family and society. For one thing, since it is normally the duty of the eldest son of a family to offer *piṇda* or riceball sacrifices to their ancestors in order to maintain the latter's existence in the ancestor-realm, the deaths of large numbers of eldest sons in the ensuing battle will lead to the dissolution of the family's lineage. A war between relatives will destroy the family's past, present, and future. Beyond this, while the modern reader may surely reject the notions of caste and the defilement imputed to women in this passage, its overriding purpose is to draw attention to how a war between relatives will, in the long run, destroy both family and society. One result of the pending and cataclysmic battle will be that many wives of the *kṣatriya varṇa* or warrior caste will be widowed and left without any other male relatives who could serve as caretakers. In order to secure their own lives, the new widows will be left with no choice but to enter into *pratiloma* or "against the grain" caste marriages. Such marriages will both ruin the social status of the women and cause any children born of their new marriages to be treated as outcastes for an unknown number of generations. These are almost unimaginably, yet entirely predictable, grievous consequences of a war between the Pāndavas and Kauravas, and these consequences themselves should be avoided. But, Arjuna goes on, those who destroy family lineages and bring on the conditions of inter-generational social suffering are themselves consigned to hell, and rightly so. Again, what becomes of the whole aim of restoring justice to rulership with a Pāndava victory when the means of that victory result only in the collapse of *dharma*, first for the family and by direct implication, for the human world as a whole? This last argument also deserves special attention because it resolves the apparent conflict between family duty and larger social duty. It does so by arguing forthrightly that the undermining of family duty will lead to the collapse of social stability at large. The two duties, in Arjuna's estimation, do not conflict with one another, but are continuous with and interdependent upon one another. This also means that, for Arjuna, not fighting the battle represents an ameliorative solution; it fulfills the interdependent duties to family and society, as refusing to destroy the former will also preserve the latter. The refusal to fight will involve the concession of accepting some injustice, surely. The righteous side of the family will be denied their rightful place as rulers, while the deceitful Kauravas will continue to occupy the throne. But this will, Arjuna surmises, involve much less destruction than the immanent war will.

Kṛṣṇa's initial response to these briefly stated yet detailed and serious moral concerns is to belittle Arjuna. Arjuna is not only, according to Kṛṣṇa, expressing the kind of hesitancy and cowardliness that is unbecoming of a warrior, but he is also displaying *klaibyaṃ*, "impotence" (Bhagavad Gītā 2:3). Classical and even modern Indian commentators have seized quite enthusiastically at this belittlement. Rāmānuja takes no notice of Arjuna's arguments at all and merely comments on his weakness, fear, and complete incomprehension of the difference between *dharma* and *adharma* (1992: 54–61). Even Gandhi, who read the Gītā as a symbolic text about the inner conflict between fear and courage, chastises Arjuna for duplicity, since Arjuna only hesitates to fight his cousins and never those who are unrelated to him (2009: 32–7). Of course, Kṛṣṇa moves on, in the manner of an *Upaniṣad* sage, to progressively challenging provocations designed to give Arjuna more worldly and spiritual motivation to the lead the charge. He appeals to Arjuna's sense of reputation, points to the metaphysical difference between the eternal self and temporary bodies of all beings in order to dull Arjuna's despair at killing, implores Arjuna that desireless *karma* fulfillment of duty, while renouncing the *phala* or results of action is the kernel of holy sacrifice (Bhagavad Gītā 2:19, 22, 33–7, 47; 3:17–18, 36–41).

None of Kṛṣṇa's arguments are persuasive in any moral sense. Some are mutually contradictory; Arjuna is expected both to consider how his reputation as a mighty and heroic *kṣatriya* will suffer if he does not fight and to disregard the fruits of his deeds. Some of what are supposedly the central arguments Kṛṣṇa proffers are morally irrelevant. Even if we accept the Gītā's metaphysics of selfhood, for which the *ātman* is eternal and only the body and its passing ego-identity perish, this tells us absolutely nothing about the circumstances in which it is permissible to kill and in which it is not, and serves as little more than psychological reinforcement. Arjuna's possible refusal to fight, provided it rightly recognizes the difference between *ātman* and body, should be just as meritorious as this realization in battle. The cumulative force of these arguments cannot amount to much for anyone who takes the moral dangers of the great battle seriously, for a battery of poor arguments is not strengthened by collecting them all into one unit, it is instead only a poor battery. Chapter after chapter of the Gītā's litany of inducements for Arjuna to rise in his chariot, take up his *gāndīva*, and assail his cousins, follow, but none of them does the trick.

And let us make some important observations regarding the Gītā's idealization of *niṣkāma karma* or desireless action. A state of mind which allows one to carry out one's moral duties without regard to the results has two primary functions. The first of these, as just noted, is psychological. In this case, Arjuna suddenly finds himself paralyzed on the battlefield because his supposed enemies are people he actually loves, and the prospect of killing them in hand-to-hand combat is horrific. Arjuna's reluctance is completely understandable, and his consideration of intimacy is something we can intuitively deem as morally appropriate—we would have a hard time thinking Arjuna is in any respect a good person were he not to emotionally dread slaying his relatives. So, if it is Arjuna's moral duty to carry on with the battle, then Kṛṣṇa must teach him how to disregard these emotional bonds and fight anyway. But the other function that *niṣkāma karma* is supposed to have is a moral one, since as the theory goes, *karma* which leads to rebirth is determined primarily by intention, whether that intention be to harm or to benefit. So, if Arjuna is to be truly virtuous in fulfilling his soldierly obligations, there must be a way for him to perform them without accumulating karmic residue (*karmaphalahetur*) that can only be dissolved in a later life. And so, desireless action must perforce be a fundamental element in Kṛṣṇa's moral council. But is it? Tara Chatterjea has argued that the kinds of fruits or consequences (*phala*) of action that the *niṣkāma karma* theory involves should be narrowly conceived, since both Gītā commentators and general scholastic explanations have focused on the fruits of pleasure or the absence of pain (2002: 126–30). That is to say, in this case, Arjuna should not be focused on the pain that killing his relatives will cause him alone, or whether the act will land him in heaven or hell alone. Arjuna can be found to worry about these things above. But even if we accept these narrow parameters, Chatterjea argues, while the Gītā otherwise insists that no being in the natural realm, including gods, can escape action, it requires the engaged person in the world trying to solve a moral problem to divest themselves of every component of agency, the ego, motive, expected benefits, and any sense of responsibility (2002: 140–1). But is such a complete negation of agency even feasible for people who are constantly acting and interacting in the world? And even if it is possible, how desirable is it? Chatterjea notes accurately enough, though she does not find much fault in it, that *niṣkāma karma* or "desireless action" is a directive about the state of mind required to perform actions that do not bind one to selfhood, while all the moral dimensions of actions are accounted for by the Gītā through its associations between psychophysical energies and specific forms of duty (2002: 142). We will examine the latter association later. But, as Chatterjea puts it, while this representation of things allows every person in every occupation to perform their duties selflessly, it apparently does not call for any moral deliberation. *Niṣkāma karma* empowers one to do whatever they do free of ego, but if we are looking for an answer to the question "what is the moral thing to do in this situation?" the possibility of egolessness does not confer any moral sanction on or prohibition of what is finally done. In other words, all the Gītā's talk about desireless action is, like Kṛṣṇa's other arguments so far, morally irrelevant. It is merely a felicitous technique for acting when one's moral duty has already been decided, and fulfilling that moral duty will involve otherwise painful consequences.

In alignment with many classical and modern commentators, but adding his own insights, Ashton claims that the Gītā's eleventh chapter, where Kṛṣṇa reveals himself in his complete divine embodiment, changes everything. The culmination of this astounding revelation occurs when the outcome of the war is manifested for Arjuna in all the frankness of its horror. But faced with the undiluted reality of the massacre as it is enveloped within the already-decided unfolding of all things, Arjuna can now agree to be the tool of God's intentions, and not his own.

śrī-bhagavān uvāca
kālo 'smi loka-kṣaya-kṛt pravṛiddho /
lokān samāhartum iha pravṛttaḥ //
ṛte 'pi tvā na bhaviṣyanti sarve /
ye 'vasthitāḥ pratyanīkeṣu yodhāḥ //

tasmāt tvam uttiṣṭha yaśo labhasva /
jitvā śatrūn bhuṅkṣva rājyaṃ samṛddham //
mayaivaite nihatāḥ pūrvam eva /
nimitta-mātraṃ bhava savya-sācin //

The blessed one said:
"I am time, the mighty cause of the world's dissolution,
the activity that completely annihilates this world and all the worlds.
Even without you, all these foes gathered here
to do battle against you will cease to exist.
Thus, you are to arise and attain your honor,
conquering your enemies, relishing kingship.
It is indeed by me that these (warriors) have already been struck down.
Ambidextrous archer, be only an instrument!" (Bhagavad Gītā 11:32–3)

Often this revelation has been thought to awaken Arjuna to the fact that he is not in control of the outcome of the war, no matter what he does. The end has been pre-ordained by God, and so he should relieve himself of any responsibility he might feel for striking down his cousins. If this were the moral content of the argument, it would, like the rest of Kṛṣṇa's rhetorical serves, not be persuasive in the least. Active participation in the realization of an outcome is an assumption of a share of responsibility for that outcome. If the outcome is ruinous, and one refused to participate in bringing it about, or better, if one tried to prevent the ruin, only then could one credibly be pardoned of accountability. But this is not what Ashton sees happening in this passage. It is here, Ashton contends, that, despite the rhetorical flights of abstraction into *ātman* and the eradication of desire, Kṛṣṇa has elected to hide nothing from Arjuna, but instead immerses him into the gore and morbidity of his cousins' fate. It is only in the space opened out to Arjuna by this theophany that he can attain to an indispensable kind of "moral freedom" (Ashton 2014: 19). For Arjuna and the Pāndavas as a whole, observing the obligations of family duty and attempting for more than a decade to resolve the ongoing conflict with the Kauravas through deference and concession have only prolonged the injustice and not resolved it. The only just resolution can be achieved if, in these truly liminal conditions, Arjuna can be liberated from fully inhabiting his roles as both a family member and a warrior, and instead can be an instrument (*nimitta*) of a tragic but necessary outcome. Arjuna need not be subjected to merely "live his role," but can acquire the "power over his roles" needed for "identity-play" and genuine moral choice (Ashton 2014: 19).

There is no doubt that Ashton has put his finger on a crucially important moral consideration with his analysis. We must acknowledge the reality and gravity of genuine moral dilemmas. After all, irreparable breeches of family affection do happen in life, far more frequently than anyone would like. Moral obligations of the most demanding sort, sometimes requiring the sacrifice of one's very life, may be duly owed to people beyond the family. And there are times when various duties to different people conflict so completely and starkly with duties to intimates that one needs to be chosen over the other. And since we must acknowledge these possibilities, which are frequently more than just possibilities but present, daunting challenges, human beings must cultivate the abilities that will allow them to overcome the proximities of intimacy that have been fed by the soil of feeling and courageously fulfill greater goods. To the extent that Ashton is right, to the extent to which Kṛṣṇa's awe-inspiring manifestation has given Arjuna moral fortitude, it has empowered Arjuna to face down the most extreme, and yet most real, of life's ordeals.

Be all this as it is, we still have not addressed the specific moral questions that Arjuna has posed to us. Since bringing harm to our own family members does seem to tear at the very roots of human intimacy itself, should we not exercise the greatest care, and most precise judgment, to distinguish which circumstances require such an uprooting and which may not? Are we not obliged to first determine whether violating the most-deeply felt of social bonds is required immediately or whether it will create more injustice than may already be afoot? The most trying of times may demand the most effort on our part to identify an ameliorative solution, rather than impel us to just give up and reach for mortal means. These concrete and specific questions are simply left unanswered, whether by the formulaic contrast between soul and body, the principled weighing of intention against consequences on the scale of ideas, or the possible fortitude we will need in case our bonds of affection fail to mobilize our better angels, but only forestall what we must do.

We would do well to remember at this juncture that Arjuna's forebodings about the fruits of war with his cousins were more than justified. Before the Gītā closes, as we have seen, Kṛṣṇa acknowledges through forthright revelation that the most lamentable and horrific deaths await those very beloved relatives that Arjuna now looks upon with such love. By the end of the Mahābhārata epic, mass slaughter has wiped out the Kauravas and decimated the Pāndavas, whose leaders soon renounce their thrones and go off to a mountain retreat where they are to die. The entire drama inaugurates the *kāliyuga*, our present age in history, when even the best deeds human beings can muster unravel to tragic ends. Most poignantly, in the *Mausala Parva* of the Mahābhārata, shortly after the end of the eighteen days of battle, Gāndhāri, who has lost every one of her hundred Kaurava sons and in compassion consoled the Pāndavas for their own losses, movingly curses Kṛṣṇa for allowing the Armageddon to take place, and condemns him and his entire clan to a demise that Kṛṣṇa must accept. Arjuna's deep consideration for the thick bonds of intimate human association and his insistence that broader social solidarity must be tied to them have been shunted aside. But neither Kṛṣṇa's too-lofty arguments nor even his divine body have been able to prevent total collapse.

The *Mengzi*: Intimacy and Amelioration

Now, in comparison, on what ground does the Confucian *Mengzi* set us? There are two episodes in particular that highlight situations in which duties to intimates and society as a whole seem to conflict. These have drawn significant classical attention and were highlighted in the Liu-Guo debate with which this chapter opened. In the first, Mengzi's students question him about a seeming failure of the legendary emperor Shun in impartial rulership. Despite the fact that Shun's half-brother, Xiang, was murderous and participated in an attempt to take Shun's own life, the emperor enfeoffed him in the neighboring state of Youbi, while other men unrelated to Shun, and guilty of far milder offenses, met with execution. Shun seems to have sacrificed the public good, for which he is primarily responsible as ruler, for a private good in unjustly favoring his brother. Mengzi offers a moral explanation for a purportedly historical event.

> 仁人之於弟也，不藏怒焉，不宿怨焉，親愛之而已矣。
> 親之欲其貴也，愛之欲其富也。封之有庳，富貴之也。
> 身為天子，弟為匹夫，可謂親愛之乎？ ...
> 象不得有為於其國，天子使吏治其國，而納其貢稅焉，
> 故謂之放，豈得暴彼民哉？ 雖然，欲常常而見之，
> 故源源而來。『不及貢，以政接于有庳,』此之謂也。

> A caring person does not harbor indignation or nurse accusations
> toward his younger brother, but only treats him with affectionate care.
> Affectionate, he desires nobility for him. Caring, he desires wealth
> for him. His constant wish is to care for him. The conferral of
> Youbi secured his honor and wealth. While Shun was the son of
> heaven, if his younger brother was a commoner, could this be
> deemed affectionate care for him? . . .
> Xiang was not allowed to own or manage the country.

> The son of heaven commissioned minor officials to govern the country and transfer its revenues to him. It is therefore said (of Xiang) that he was banished, for how could he be permitted to oppress the people? Anyway, Shun wanted always to keep him under scrutiny, and thus came incessantly (to his court). As it was said: "he obtained tribute and applied policies in Youbi." (*Mengzi* 5A3)

In a situation that would seemingly force emperor Shun to choose between loyalty to his brother and evenhanded justice in his kingdom, he instead finds a way to fulfill the demands of both duties. He does not permit his sibling Xiang to be prosecuted, and honors his inherited station of "prince" by placing him in a palace in a controlled adjoining state. This is not merely done out of genuine care and affection, but because the ruler of a morally just polity cannot model the abandonment of family obligations to his citizens, for this would be deemed (謂 *wei*) unjust by the masses. For Shun to model the abandonment of family care to the empire at large would be tantamount, in the estimation of the Confucian Mengzi, to undermining the very root of social bonds, namely family dependability (孝 *xiao*) But the enfeoffment of his younger brother at Youbi also constitutes a punishment, for Xiang is not allowed to keep any of the state's revenues or actively govern the state, for if he were permitted these things, his rulership would surely be a disaster for the innocent populace. Xiang maintains his nominal princely status under this arrangement, and has all his personal needs provided for by his brother, and these conditions fulfill the requirements of 孝 *xiao*. But his enfeoffment is at the same time effectively a form of house-arrest, as the regent appointed by Shun and Shun himself keep unrelenting tabs on him and leave him no opportunity for mischief. This, presumably, fulfills the ruler's requirements of protecting the public from a dangerous criminal.

The emperor Shun portrayed in the *Mengzi* opts for an amelioration even in far more extreme circumstances. The discussion surrounding *Mengzi* 7A35 is controversial and difficult to assess, but on close examination and in consultation with Confucian commentary, its import is consistent with the preceding case. In the present passage, however, Mengzi acknowledges the supposed historicity of the actual outcome of a case and compares that outcome to what a sage would have done in the circumstances. Here, the conversation concerns Shun's father Gu Sou, a man so "blinded" by evil that he would have his own son killed if he could.

> 桃應問曰：「舜為天子，皋陶為士，瞽瞍殺人，則如之何？」
> 孟子曰：「執之而已矣。」

> 「然則舜不禁與？」
> 曰：「夫舜惡得而禁之？夫有所受之也。」
> 「然則舜如之何？」
> 曰：「舜視棄天下，猶棄敝蹝也。竊負而逃，遵海濱而處，
> 終身訢然，樂而忘天下。」

> Tao Ying asked: "(When) Shun was the son of heaven, and Gao Yao was his minister (of crime), if Gu Suo had murdered someone, what would have been done in this case?"
> Mengzi said: "(Gao Yao) would have merely apprehended him.
> "Would Shun not have forbade this?"
> (The master) said: "How could Shun possibly have forbade it? He had what he had received."
> "What would Shun have done in this case?"
> (The master) said: "Shun would regard relinquishing the empire like throwing away worn-out sandals. He would steal his father away on his back, travel to the coast and dwell there. He would stay there till the end of his life, joyful, even forgetting the empire." (*Mengzi* 7A35)

At first glance, this reply by Mencius would seem to indicate that, when the chips are really down and an either-or decision is unavoidable, the Confucian sage would never betray a parent to the state, no matter how malevolent the parent was and no matter how justified the state may be in seeking to punish the parent's wrongdoing. This judgment appears consistent with other famous, or infamous, passages in the Confucian classical corpus such as *Analects* 13:18, where Kongzi avers that a filial son would never betray the thefts of his father to the authorities. But the obviousness of this preference, in the broad discussions of Confucian literature, is deceptive. Regarding the *Analects* 13:18 passage, other passages in the text such as 4:18 seem to depart from this. Furthermore, a wide variety of selections in the *Xunzi*, *Li Ji*, *Kongzi Jingyu*, Song Dynasty commentators like Xing Bing and Zhu Xi and Qing Dynasty exegetes like Cai Yuanpei council remonstration with the parents and other means of family restitution for a crime be undertaken in place of public punishment (Huang 2017: 15–41). There are other instances in Confucian commentary, for instance in the *Zuozhuan*, when various authors assert that, when more weighty crimes than the stealing of a sheep in *Analects* 13:18 are committed, children are permitted to make such infractions known (Ni 2017: 311). The Confucian commentarial tradition therefore acknowledges what Ashton has argued about the Bhagavad Gītā, namely that there are cases in which the social good must be preferred to family ties. But even in the case of the instant passage of the *Mengzi*, commentators have disclosed the respects in which Shun's solution to the dilemma presented in 7A35 is a case of the amelioration of conflicting duties.

There are at least two details of this passage which show how, in this hypothetical situation, Shun does not merely prefer protecting his father over the public requirements of his rulership, but that his choice protects the public order. Firstly, as ruler, as the discussant Tao Ying points out, Shun had the power to simply dissuade the righteous law minister Gao Yao from pursuing his father and keeping the whole affair under wraps. But a ruler who would do this could only be corrupt and contemptuous of the proper administration of justice in the realm, as Mengzi sees it. If Gao Yao did apprehend Shun's father, Shun could not in any way morally intervene. There is an interesting disagreement in the commentarial literature over the grammar of the sentence 夫有所受之也 (*fu you suo shou zhi ye*) in the text. Jiao Shun argues that it acknowledges Gao Yao's appropriate legal authority over crimes committed even by the emperor's family, and Zhao Qi insists that the sentence is about Shun's strict responsibility as ruler to see that misdeeds are properly punished (van Norden 2009: 128–9). In either case, part of Mengzi's answer to the question at hand is that, were Gao Yao to apprehend and execute Shun's father for a murder, Shun would have no moral choice but to acquiesce to this outcome. Instead of deterring Gao Yao from his rightful mission, however, Shun would gladly prefer to give up his rule and dwell with his father in exile.

But is this itself not a contravention of the public good in deference to family loyalty? After all, while Shun may not have compromised his law minister's rightful authority of office, he still prevented his father from being arrested and punished, and saved his life. Are then Shun's actions still not tantamount to preserving his intimate loyalties and turning his back on the public good? The Confucian commentarial tradition does not generally concede this, even during the Song Dynasty, when Confucian equations between the larger public good and the most expansive principles of ethics led to either great criticisms of or refined apologetics for *Mengzi* 7A35 (Huang 2010: 83–7. In the Song literature, the most remarkable argument is given by the eleventh-century scholar Yang Shi. He maintains that the father–son relationship is concerned with the personal kindnesses between specific human beings (一人之私恩 *yi ren si en*) while the standards and laws (法 *fa*) of society have to do with the public at large (天下之公 *tianxia zhi gong*). These two spheres of relationships are both moral in nature and thus of utmost importance (義 *yi*), and both must be upheld without any diminishment to either (相為輕重不可偏舉 *xiang wei qing chong bu ke pian ju*). In the case of Shun and Gu Suo, the entire context of events is required in order to fulfill the needs of both private and public good. Yang Shi therefore observes that "the world cannot be without law even for a day, nor can a son be without his father even for a day" (天下不可一日而無法人子亦不可一日) (Huang 2010: 86). Therefore, Gao Yao must be permitted to play his role as minister of crime, unimpeded from pursuing the punishment of Gu Suo, while Shun must be permitted to protect his father. However, because Shun occupies the dual roles of father and ruler, his response to the circumstances must address the exigencies of both the private and public realms. Yang Shi indeed understands Shun's relinquishing of the throne as fulfilling both the duties of intimacy and public justice. The intimacy requirement is obviously met by Shun saving his father's life. The public justice requirement is fulfilled in two ways. Shun, in this hypothetical scenario, hands over power to a righteous successor so that the maintenance of law in the kingdom might continue unabated. Furthermore, he goes into exile and takes his father into exile with him. This is a considerable penalty, as Shun pays for his father's infraction with his abdication. In addition, as in the case of *Mengzi* 5A3 given earlier, Shun removes his father from the empire and thus removes the threat his father represents to the rest of the populace. Because Shun's imperial abdication serves the public good in these ways, Shun's actions are best seen as upholding both the private and public requirements of rightness (Huang 2010: 86). This kind of analysis is quite typical of classical Chinese moral thinking in general, for which the correct assessment of a problem lies not in determining the agency and responsibility of only one actor in a scenario, but in comprehending the respective needs of and most satisfactory solution for all involved in a situation.

Now certainly one may still question whether this was the maximally just solution. Can Yang Shi really be correct when he insists that Shun's abdication of the throne in order to save his father would actually enhance the cause of justice in the empire? Would not the populace be more likely to see Shun's abandonment as an outright betrayal of public trust when he was in a tough spot, an admission that he does not really deserve to be ruler after all because he is unable to put the public's needs above those of his avaricious family? The Song Dynasty reformists Wang Anshi and Sima Guang certainly thought so. And one may wonder whether Yang Shi or other like-minded commentators have fully considered what Mengzi means at the very end of his reply to Tao Ying, intimating that Shun would be happy to forget about the kingdom entirely after leaving it. Some argue that this happiness reflects the fact that Shun was a reluctant ruler in the first place and had no political ambitions, and others may chalk it up to the unreserved faithfulness Shun has to his father despite his father's wretched hatred for him. All these questions are perfectly justified, and one may persist in asking whether the cases we find in *Mengzi* 5A3 and 7A35 are morally justifiable. In any case, the extended Confucian exegesis of *Mengzi* 7A35 demonstrates that, even here, what is being praised is Shun's attempt to meet the demands off all his duties to his family and the public, and does not represent an abandonment of one duty for another.

As in the case of the Gītā discussed earlier, we have every reason to wonder about how realistic either of these famed narratives of the *Mengzi* are, and with that, how sound the attendant moral judgments are. If the narratives about Shun and his family in the *Mengzi* are to be believed, both Shun's half-brother and father wanted to murder him when he was young. They have no loyalty or family feeling toward him. They simply want to see Shun dead so they can confiscate the wealth that he has accumulated as a successful farmer, and they make several attempts to accomplish this. In response, we are told, Shun merely pines for his parents' approval, and offers equal terms of rulership to his half-brother Xiang immediately after Xiang tried to bury him alive, only because Xiang greeted him with obviously feigned deference (*Mengzi* 5A1). There was eventually a reward for all this humility, we are told, for not only was Yao so impressed with Shun's filial devotion that he arranged to have Shun installed as emperor, but once installed, Shun's father was reconciled to him, and the entire kingdom became filial (*Mengzi* 4A28). Even so, are we, as the audience to these stories, actually supposed to believe that either Shun or any human being could return unrelenting mortal hatred with selfless and doting love? It is obvious from other chronicles that the *Mengzi* is both rewriting the details of other accounts of Shun and engaging in hypotheticals which were not part of the foregoing Shun mythology. And the particular ways in which the *Mengzi* dresses up the stories of Shun and his parents, which seem outlandish on their face, have led to many hypotheses about why the text goes to the trouble of defending these contortions. The scholarly theories run the gamut of possible assessments of the historical figure of Mengzi and the Confucian lineages that follow him. Some guess that the stories Mengzi tells about Shun are attempts at dynastic apologetics, others believe the tales of Shun reflect the extremely cultivated virtue of Mengzi rather than Shun, and still others have supposed that they are defensive reactions to perceptions of Mengzi's folly, trying laughably to make errant beliefs and actions by Mengzi seem at bottom virtuous. The sheer volume of interpretive efforts devoted to explicating the *Mengzi*'s construal of emperor Shun's loyalty to his family can only confirm our impression that the text's emotional explanations for Shun's behavior are just not convincing.

The Natural Roots of Duty: Intrinsic or Relational?

So, if neither the Gītā nor the *Mengzi* provide us with credible explanations of the emotional states out of which virtuous actions arise, and if neither text paints a compelling picture of the consequential justifications of certain courses of conduct, then where are we to go? How are we to decide, in the absence of these, whether we should prefer a moral framework which forces us to choose only one obligation in liminal cases of conflicting duties or whether we should find some means to fulfill as much of all of our duties as we can, even in the most extreme cases? As it turns out, the Gītā and *Mengzi* ultimately ground their respective moral standards in varying conceptions of personhood, in the makeup of human character. It is only by seeing the continuity between these conspicuously differing portraits of human nature and the moral directives each text gives us that we can have some basis on which to evaluate their relative merits.

It should be remembered that the consummating argument Kṛṣṇa makes to Arjuna in the Gītā is found in its eighteenth and final chapter. It serves as the last flourish, the clincher, in all that Kṛṣṇa has said and revealed. In that crucial argument, Kṛṣṇa makes a case for the ultimate metaphysical coherence of a person's nature, their basic inclinations and their most fundamental moral commitments in the world. After reminding Arjuna of the alignment between virtuous action and desirelessness *karma*, Kṛṣṇa returns to the *triguṇa* theory.

na tad asti pṛthivyāṁ vā divi deveṣu vā punaḥ /
sattvaṃ prakṛti-jair muktaṃ yad ebhiḥ syāt tribhir guṇaiḥ //
brāhmaṇa-kṣatriya-viśāṃ śūdrāṇāṃ ca paraṃtapa /
karmāṇi pravibhaktāni svabhāva-prabhavair guṇaiḥ //
śamo damas tapaḥ śaucaṃ kṣāntir ārjavam eva ca /
jñānaṃ vijñānam āstikyaṃ brahma-karma svabhāva-jam //
śauryaṃ tejo dhṛtir dākṣyaṃ-yuddhe cāpy apalāyanam /
dānam īśvara-bhāvaśca kṣatra karma svabhāva-jam //
kṛṣi gau-rakṣya vāṇijyaṃ vaiśya-karma svabhāva-jam /
paricaryātmakaṃ karma śūdrasyāpi svabhāva-jam //
sve sve karmaṇy abhirataḥ saṃsiddhiṃ labhate naraḥ /

sva-karma-nirataḥ siddhiṃ yathā vindati tacchṛṇu //
yataḥ pravṛttir bhūtānāṃ yena sarvam idaṃ tatam /
sva-karmaṇā tam abhyarcya siddhiṃ vindati mānavaḥ //
śreyān sva-dharmo viguṇaḥ para-dharmāt svanuṣṭhitāt /
svabhāva-niyataṃ karma kurvan nāpnoti kilbiṣam //
saha-jaṃ karma kaunteya sa-doṣam api na tyajet /
sarvārambhā hi doṣeṇa dhūmenāgnir ivāvṛtāḥ //

Nothing that is on the earth or in the divine heavens
of material existence can be free from the three energies.
Subduer, the actions of priests, warriors, merchants and labourers
differentially ensue from the basis of their own-nature,
from the three energies.
Tranquility, restraint, asceticism, purity, patience, and indeed
knowledge, discernment, and orthodoxy are the doings of priests
originating in (their) self-nature.
Might, vigor, courage, and skill with arms along with implacability,
service and qualities of lordship are the doings of warriors,
originating in (their) self-nature.
Cultivation, cow-keeping, and commerce, these are the doings of
merchants, originating in (their) self-nature.
All that constitutes the servile practices, these are the doings of
labourers, originating in (their) self-nature.
A human being delights in the success of his specific doings;
so hear how dedication to one's own-action leads to success.
A human being who attains success through his own-action
is worshipping him who generated all worldly beings
Failure of own-duty is better than perfection of another's duty.
From the performance of action in accord with own-nature,
no taint is incurred.
Son of Kunti, acts that are born from what one is,
even when errant, are not to be abandoned;
indeed, as fire is concealed by smoke,
all new undertakings are concealed by error. (Bhagavad Gītā 18:40–8)

The assertion that one's own duty done without merit is morally superior to doing another's duty to perfection is repeated several times in the Gītā, but here that assertion is given a full metaphysical explanation. The explanation draws its warrant from the Sāṃkhya framework of the "three energies" (*triguṇa*). The word "*guṇa*" in Sanskrit denotes a "string," such as the strings of a musical or mathematical instrument. Primordial matter (*prakṛti*) is accounted for by three distinct energetic resonances: *sattva*, which is luminescence or brilliance; *rajas*, which is activity and movement; and *tamas*, which is stolidity and "dark" inertia. All material beings are made up of dynamic but predominant accumulations of these three bands of activity. A warrior like Arjuna takes on the birth and form of a warrior because he is predominantly driven by the "fiery" (*teja*) *guṇa*, which gives him courage, determination, aggression, and an unwillingness to retreat from challenge (*apalyāna*). These traits are what the warrior is born with, they are his unique nature, his *svabhāva*. That *svabhāva* impels one to a uniquely prompted set of actions (*svakarmanā*), which flow from the qualities that are their basis, and so equip a warrior to all the valor and skill that are needed on a battlefield. The actions of which one is most readily capable, which flow from their inborn nature, properly determine one's unique moral duties to society at large. In the Gītā, these prescribed duties specific to one's nature are said to be one's *svadharma*, a synonym for caste duty (*varṇadharma*). Under the overarching theoretical framework of *karma*, even one's birth is a moral event, a moral outcome of intentions and deeds of previous lives. That moral outcome that eventuates in what one is, in the present natural constitution of one's specific and concrete personhood, also maps out one's overriding obligations to society at large. There is then a seamless continuity between one's *svabhāva* (own-nature), *svakarmanā* (own-action), and *svadharma* (own-duty). But what is announced at the close of this explanation is perhaps the most striking statement of all. Recall that, in his initial objections to going to war, Arjuna was most troubled about the wide-ranging and grievous kinds of moral error (*doṣa*) that would attend killing his relatives, undermining the family and bringing about generations of social suffering. Kṛṣṇa now tells him that practically all actions that are undertaken by human beings, regardless of their intentions and outcomes, produce some moral error. That brute fact does not dilute the moral obligations that are appropriate to one's social station, however. Kṛṣṇa insists that, even if Arjuna did refuse to fight and wandered off to the forest to carry Brāhmiṇic duties to perfection, this would acquire more taint than his own warrior obligations even if the latter were entirely without virtuosity (*viguṇa*). In the final analysis, Arjuna's only morally justified course of conduct in this lamentable circumstance is to act in accord with the makeup of his personhood.

We can make the same case with the *Mengzi*. Of course, Mengzi is renowned in Warring States Chinese thought for being the only thinker who believed that, in addition to its capacity to approve and disapprove of environing circumstances, the human heart has of its own natural accord the capacity to feel certain basically moral emotions, namely compassion, shame, and respect (*Mengzi*

2A6). However, this is not precisely what underwrites the deeds of emperor Shun in the stories examined earlier. Shun's two inescapable duties, we recall, are care for his family and rightness in rulership. Like any good Confucian, Mengzi holds that what makes these two duties both possible and consistent with one another is that the latter organically grows from the former. In his recrimination of Mohist thought, Mengzi gives us an origin story for funerary rights, which were originally introduced by human beings in extended care-taking for their deceased parents, but which now are the conduit of the enduring connection between a society and its ancestral past.

> 天之生物也，使之一本，而夷子二本故也。蓋上世嘗有
> 不葬其親者。其親死，則舉而委之於壑。他日過之，狐狸食之，
> 蠅蚋姑嘬之。其顙有泚，睨而不視。夫泚也，非為人泚，
> 中心達於面目。蓋歸反虆梩而掩之。掩之誠是也，則孝子
> 仁人之掩其親，亦必有道矣。

> Things produced by heaven are given one root, but Yizi concludes they have two roots. In primeval times, (people) did not bury their dear parents. When their parents died, they just left them in gullies. After some days, they passed by and foxes and cats were eating them, and flies and gnats were gnawing at them. Sweat dripped from their foreheads and they looked away, utterly unable to bear it. Their sweat did not fall due to other people; their faces and eyes were effected by the hearts within them. They went home, and returned with spades to cover the bodies. In the sincerity of this burial, see that the dependable son's and caring person's internment of their dear relatives must be *dao*. (*Mengzi* 3A5)

The Yizi referred to by the passage was supposedly a Mohist practitioner. As such, Yizi was committed to the foremost Mohist doctrine of inclusive care (兼愛 *jian ai*), which requires everyone to be treated equitably. One implication of the standard of inclusive care is that burials for all, whether they be rulers or peasants, relatives or strangers, should be equally modest, and that mourning periods for them should not be so prolonged as to deter the surviving family members from getting on with their lives and keeping their livelihoods. The principle of inclusive care and the ways in which it should be practiced do not necessarily come naturally and immediately to us; they must be discovered through prolonged deliberation and judgment. However, in the verses leading up to the passage just quoted, it is noticed that the Mohist Yizi, despite his rational commitment to impartial care, gave his own parents a lavish funeral when they died. Mengzi therefore comments that Yizi must believe that the human heart has two roots (二本 *er ben*), one being the judgment that people should treat one another impartially and the other the special affection one has for one's parents and kin. But such a belief in two roots may cause them to come into conflict and impel the person to hypocritical behavior, just as Yizi himself engages in with a preferential funeral for his parents. Mengzi is probably either uncomprehending of or quite uncharitable to the Mohists' position on these matters. For the Mohists only argued that even distant acquaintances entrusted to one's care should be treated with the same regard as one's own kin, and if everyone in society did this, justice would prevail in the world (Fraser 2016: 143–9; 169–73; 179–82). Regardless, Mengzi's own argument is clear. The human heart does not grow from two roots, but one, and the incubator of all moral inclinations is the kind of spontaneous feeling of compassion that the primeval people in 3A5 suddenly feel for their dead relatives. The basis of these moral norms is not explained by social pressure, nor the expectations of others, but rather by the need to care for loved ones even beyond their deaths. The entire edifice of the moral and social 道 *dao* emerges from this single root of feeling for one's intimates, and wider social justice is only attained by extending these feelings to others. The dispositions of the human heart are where we find the basis for the continuity between family loyalty and social rightness. And that is why ameliorations between family and social duties are sought by the Confucians, for family and society are the root and branch of one organically whole existence.

A Case for Outcomes

And so, for both the Gītā and the *Mengzi*, the ultimate justification for moral directives lies in their divergent but fundamental depictions of what constitutes the human character. But the variance of these portrayals is precisely what accounts for their differing moral assessments about what we should do in extreme cases where loyalty to intimates and responsibility to the greater good appear to be mutually exclusive. The consistency between one's unique nature (*svabhāva*) and one's caste duties (*svadharma*) in the Gītā is one I will continue to characterize as intrinsic. The *guṇa*-s or "strands of energy" that constitute all material things take up a specific configuration in a particular person's psychophysical embodiment, and that unique configuration, inherited not from one's parents or culture but from intentions and deeds of past lives, form one's personality and inclinations and equip one for an ideal occupation.

An occupation here is not merely a way to make a living, but is a form of moral service to society at large. The obvious discomfort that modern Indian reformers felt for this long-beloved and philosophically prized work elevating the obligations of caste prompted them to reformulate the Gītā's relevance to their and our times. According to their reframings, we should think of the *guṇa*-s as empowering us with unique "talents," and those talents will inspire us to make "commitments" to an occupation in which those talents are best suited to benefit society (Chatterjea 2002: 111–23). Even allowing for this liberal formulation, the motivations to duty that this reinterpreted Gītā describes are intrinsic. And this intrinsic makeup of persons cannot be abandoned in one's adult moral commitments, since our interactions with others and our duties to them track with what we most basically are. This by no means, as we have acknowledged, amounts to a disregard of family intimacy, thick social relations, and a denial of the emotional and community ties that bind us. But, as Kṛṣṇa took great and lengthy pains to argue, the externals may all unravel and spiral out of one's control; the family may rupture, friendships can be betrayed, community loyalties may be rent, all attempts at peace-making might explode into wanton carnage, outcomes may escape all our efforts to control them and guide them toward happier conditions. The moral advantage of the Gītā's revelatory stanzas, as Ashton has compellingly argued, is that it gives us the "hermeneutic" agency and "moral freedom" we will need to creatively respond to the breakdown of one of our assumed "roles" and search more deliberately for what the situation demands of us.

However, to the degree that this advantage does not speak to the specifics of a moral dilemma, the Gītā's position as it is stated is vulnerable to at least two paralyzing objections. For one, its intrinsic metaphysics demands that we believe that there is some fixed proportion of personality traits within us that, once we are aware of them, provides us a template for those obligations which we cannot under the most trying of circumstances abandon or change. Even if Ashton is right, and I believe he is, that the theophany of Kṛṣṇa extended the hand of moral deliberation to Arjuna, the other hand that ties together one's nature and one's duty in one continuous string places an incorrigible limit on that very deliberation. Of what value is the choice Kṛṣṇa offers Arjuna at the very end of the text when everything has not only been predetermined by Kṛṣṇa's divine will, but has also been predetermined by a logically cultivated discernment of what makes Arjuna a steadfast, manly warrior and not an "impotent" would-be ascetic? The second major problem with the Gītā's resolution of Arjuna's moral quandary is that it enshrines fidelity to intrinsically determined duty even if that duty is errant, even if it causes the very dystopia that Arjuna had the keen foresight to dread. Arjuna knows what wretched and enduring suffering the war with the Kauravas will cause, not just to his "enemies" but to the even-more-numerous innocent victims, Kṛṣṇa admits that the war will bring about precisely these results, and the Mahābhārata tells us the heart-wrenching details of the sadly predictable outcome. But, it seems, none of that matters for Kṛṣṇa's intrinsic ethics. Such a total disregard for the consequences of actions cannot be a hallmark of a worthy moral theory. Kṛṣṇa, it seems to me, has only captured one feature of egolessness, namely the lack of possessiveness or pride we should have in our dealings with others. But he has missed the more important dimension of egolessness, the morally and not just psychologically crucial one, which requires us to search for resolutions to problems that do the least necessary harm and the most necessary good to others.

The *Mengzi*'s approach to moral rightness is also made by connecting the natural configuration of our personhood to the duties we owe to others. We might at first glance be quite tempted to label the *Mengzi*'s model as a variant of intrinsic metaphysical ethics, due to the work's distinctive view that all social virtues have their roots in the innermost heart. But I will persist in calling it a relational model, for several important reasons. For one thing, though in the text Mengzi argues that certain moral feelings are inborn in the human heart, he also consistently maintains that, in order for these feelings to be transformed into virtuous behaviors, they must be educated, cultivated, ritualized, be nurtured by intimacy, and expanded to ever-broadening circles of association. If these feelings are damaged or obfuscated by deleterious environments or improper training, they can become completely ineffectual and dominated by baser desires and captivations. Second, the *Mengzi*'s obsession with cases of family dependability (孝 *xiao*), an obsession that even at important junctures in the text can stagger into comedic incredulity, at least shows that moral feelings only count for something when they have acquired enough power to transform perilous dangers into fortunate outcomes. Duties in the Confucian perspective are not ends-in-themselves, they are not to be clung to until the bitter end, but are instead features of personal character that are built to produce better ends. This intense focus of the *Mengzi* on relational goods, therefore, cannot envision abstracting the application of moral feelings, even if they are presumed to be inborn, from the situations to which they are to be applied. And so, in contrast to the Gītā, where one's deeds are to flow from one's nature regardless of consequences, the *Mengzi* sees virtuous feelings as always aimed at optimizing consequences. Here, the fruits of action matter. And because those consequences involve not just the isolated agency and responsibility of one person but envelop the needs of all concerned, solutions that ameliorate between the demands of different responsibilities are what are sought, in small things and in large ones. Such an amelioration was what Arjuna, though he himself does not appear to realize it, seems to at least lay the groundwork for. Had he been allowed, to imagine an ameliorative solution, and had this become known to the crafters and exegetes of Confucian lore, it would have been Arjuna, and not Kṛṣṇa, who would have been the Gītā's moral hero.

8

Indian and Chinese Notions of Luminous Awareness

Five years ago, my second major independent monograph appeared on the "luminosity of consciousness" (*prabhāsvaram cittaṃ*, 明心) that arose in the Indian Vijñānavāda tradition and greatly influenced Chinese thought. This idea emerged out of the general context of early Brāhmiṇical and Buddhist thought, and was appropriated by various Chinese Buddhist schools and eventually transformed Song and Ming Dynasty Confucian reflection (Berger 2015). At the outset of that volume, I declared it necessary to bracket my own present philosophical perspectives in order to reveal the most important South and East Asian shifting conceptual frameworks of "luminosity" and its significance for thinking about personhood and the potentials of human conduct. Though, toward the opening and closing of that work, and in a few papers since then, I have briefly commented on what I believe are the merits and shortcomings of this notion of luminous awareness, I have preferred to maintain a largely exegetical stance with regard to it. I did so because I was convinced by the eight years of study and teaching leading up to that book that the idea was the most significant philosophical bridge from classical Indian to Chinese thought, and I still hold this to be the case. I therefore did not want to interfere with the idea as much as I wanted to adequately comprehend it, and in order to do that, I had to remain focused on what the ancient texts were telling me.

This chapter, by contrast, will articulate my own estimation of the classical Indian and Chinese recensions of luminosity, and what value I think that idea might have for renewed dialogue between scholarly representatives of South and East Asian thought. In order to do this, I will address four distinct, but historically related, conceptions of the luminosity of awareness, namely the general Brāhmiṇical idea of *prakāśatva*, the Buddhist variant of *prabhāsvaram cittaṃ*, the early Chinese Buddhist formulations of 清净心 *qing jing xin* and the more mature Chinese Buddhist notion of 明心*ming xin*. In some, though not all, respects, these four concepts develop through confrontation and interaction with one another. But they each require their own particular kind of ontological commitments, fundamental depictions of what personhood consists in and ideals of human potentiality. All of them, in my view, have their own philosophical problems. But they also all have powerful and provocative relevance to contemporary philosophical discussions.

Before proceeding to the analytical tasks I give myself in this chapter, I think it is necessary to address one important exegetical matter. Space permits me to deal with this interpretive issue only briefly here, but what the treatment lacks in detail I hope to make up for in concision. In my work on this issue in recent years and here, I argue that the luminosity of awareness was the most philosophically crucial concept that effected the transition of Buddhism from South Asia to East Asia. A number of people have criticized this approach, arguing that it was the idea of Buddha Nature, first formulated in Indian Gupta Period *tathāgatagarbha* texts and developed in the 佛性 *fo xing* literature in China, that is the right place to locate the connecting link between South and East Asian Buddhisms (Jorgensen 2018: 48). After all, Buddha Nature texts in both India and China predated the translations and commentaries of the sixth-century Paramārtha / Zhen Di on whose works I place so much emphasis in my narrative about how Buddhist notions of consciousness are transformed in the Chinese context. Indeed, presumably earlier texts that are of Buddha Nature provenance, like the *Sāriputrābhidharma* and *Ratnagotravibhāga* make mention of "luminous mind" which is by its nature undefiled (Anālayo 2017: 35–8). In addition, much of the language surrounding "original awakening" and the "brightness of mind" that is embraced by Hua Yen and Chan authors in Tang and Song Dynasty China is adopted much more consistently from the vocabulary surrounding Buddha Nature than from anything in Paramārtha's treatises. Since this is the case, the fundamental arguments between classical Indian and Chinese forms of Buddhism, which can be traced to traditional discussions and have been revived in the "Critical Buddhism" debate of recent decades, are the following. Is Buddha Nature a legitimately Buddhist concept, or does it reintroduce a kind of essentialism into reflections on human awareness that the earliest Buddhist philosophers in India had forthrightly rejected (Hubbard and Swanson 1997)?

To rectify this issue, I will make only the most pertinent points. Neither in my original study nor now do I deny that Buddha Nature texts were produced in India and China prior to Paramārtha's work, nor that they were a major generator of Buddhist thought and reflection regarding awakening in both of these cultural spheres, even though the notion predominates in East Asia far more palpably. And it is certainly the case, in the significant early Chan texts of the Tang period, notably in Guifeng Zongmi's works and the *Platform Sūtra*, that the vocabulary of Buddha Nature is freely used when discussing original awakening. All these points are well-taken indeed. However, I maintain that the notion of "luminous awareness" is where the real philosophical goods of Buddha Nature theory itself lie. Early textual thematizations of Buddha Nature tended to be elusive, rarified, and often inconsistent with one another. The third- and fourth-century *Ratnagotravibhāga Sūtra* refers to an originally pure nature and even a few times to a mind that is "luminous" by nature, but also insists that the mind must be purified before that nature can manifest (Johnston 1950: 36–7). The *Śrīmālādevīsiṃhanāda Sūtra*, from roughly the same period, while witnessing to the "embryo of thusness," claims that it is not the purview of deluded or attached beings and that it is difficult to comprehend (Reid 2014: 98–9). In the highly controversial *Mahāparinirvāṇa* Sūtra, we find that the Buddha Nature is identified with the true self of all beings, in what, on the face of it, seems to be a patently un-Buddhist doctrine (Habata 2007: 87). The *Tathāgatagarbha Sūtra*, its earliest extant translation being from the ninth century, asserts at once that all beings have a pure Buddha Nature free of defilements but that the Buddha preached the *dharma* in order to remove defilements (Takasaki 1966: 51). In the all-important *Fo Xing Lun*, though it is unequivocally argued that all beings at their root possess (本有) the Buddha Nature, also called the 道理 *dao li*, it is explained that the fundamental cause of this possession is the emptiness of things and persons, and this emptiness makes the mind amenable to cultivation (King 1991: 32, 40–1). Finally, in the *Da Sheng Qi Xin Lun*, though there is a pure mind lying at the fundament of all things, it is merely asserted, and not shown how, it is both empty and non-empty, and that it is never defiled but acquires defilements (Hakeda 1967: 35, 50). The earliest Sanskrit texts dealing with Buddha Nature seem to have been largely composed in the Gupta Period, during which there may have been some incentive to compete with Brāhmiṇical doctrines positing an essence of consciousness or being, and at any rate, the ideas of those texts had little to no purchase among scholastic Buddhists (Westerhoff 2018: 186–93). In the case of early Chinese *Fo Xing* translations and literature, there is discernable admixture of Daoist and Buddhist vocabulary and ideas, and while there prevails with time a consistency of diction with regard to how to refer to Buddha Nature, there is no clear consistency of views about what it is and how it functions. My focus on Paramārtha's works, and in particular his commentaries on Vijñānavāda, is based on the clarity of rationale for the readings he gives of Vasubandhu's texts as well as the robust character of the justifications he offers for arriving as his notion of an "untainted" basis of all awareness. It is this latter idea, in my view, that becomes the substantive core of later Buddha Nature and original awakening discourse. Now that this attempt to clarify my position on the Buddha Nature literature has been articulated, I move on to the notions of luminosity I will evaluate.

The Brāhmiṇical conception of awareness as *prakāśatva* is clearly the most essentialist of the four varieties of luminosity examined here. This idea of consciousness predominates in the schools of Sāṃkhya, Yoga, and Vedānta. Insofar as awareness or consciousness can be experienced or understood at all, its very nature must be the capacity to manifest to us both outer states of affairs and internal sensations and reflections. Classical Brāmiṇical systems across the board hold that the physical body, its matter, its vital fluids and organs, and its sensory and feeling apparatus, though they casually interact with the environment and with one another internally, are of their own accord unconscious. A dead body, after all, has these vital fluids and sensory organs just as living bodies do, but they do not confer awareness in that case. Consciousness is therefore its own ontological type of spiritual substance. The Sāṃkhya, Yoga, and Vedānta traditions refer to this core of all awareness and describe it alternatively as *puruṣa* (the "man" or "person") and the *ātman* (self) of any sentient creature. But these associations should not tempt us into thinking that the *prakāśatva* of awareness is a specific sort of "knowledge" or "subjectivity." The idea of *cit* or consciousness in general, of which *prakāśatva* is the essence, supervenes on knowing cognitions. Knowing cognitions are only one variety of conscious experience, the myriad other examples of which are pleasures, pains, desires, eversions, meditative states, dreams, and, for some, even dreamless sleep. There was of course an ongoing separate debate about whether knowing cognitions themselves were justified by "external" correlates (*parataḥ prakāśa*), a position held by Naiyāyikas, or "internal" criteria (*svataḥ prakāśa*), a view advocated by Mīṃāmsākas, Vedāntins, and Buddhists. But the light (*prakāśa*) of consciousness in general manifests all of our experiences, not merely epistemically grounded ones. Further, the "personhood" or "selfhood" of consciousness is not an individual subject or embodied ego, as it was for Nyāya and Vaiśeṣika thinkers, but instead is the pervasive wellspring of awareness within which both epistemic and individual subjectivities themselves appear. Thus, for Sāṃkhya, Yoga, and Vedānta, *prakāśatva* is the very nature, the very fact and feat of consciousness simpliciter. And because consciousness as such is not material, it is partless and incapable of destruction, it is eternal in the sense of being both beginningless and endless. The Advaita Vedāntins were unique in believing that consciousness is utterly ontologically unitary, and therefore is the consciousness of all beings at once and for all time, while all other schools of Brāhmiṇical thought held that even consciousness was individuated—that there are countless discrete foci of consciousness. These foci undergo countless generational histories of rebirths, redeaths, and releases from embodiment. But, for all the Brāhmins, wherever one finds life, sentience, and self-initiated action, one sees the luminescence of consciousness.

In large part, Indian Buddhists rejected this depiction of consciousness. Their primary objection was to the continuity or permanence (*nitya*) of consciousness that is attributed to it by the Brāhmiṇical schools. The Buddhist theories of causality definitionally linked the existence of something to its production, and since all conscious states are produced by the interaction of an external or internal sensory organ with some stimulating circumstance, we must understand awareness in terms of specific and impermanent cognitions (*vijñāna*) rather than as some unchanging and abiding spiritual substance. Cognitions do not endure forever; the objects of cognitions change, our senses of ourselves and the modalities of our subjectivity change, and even memories are often distorted and transformed when recalled, rather than present static kernels of previous experiences. However, the most idealized instance of cognition, which, when accompanied by cultivated practical and reflective virtues, becomes a lasting disposition, is awakening (*bodhi*). The awakened person acquires a comprehensive understanding of the perils and limitations of desire-driven action, how to liberate people from the bonds of desire and the invulnerable contentment that results from such freedom. Descriptions of this awakened state are legion, but one of them, invoked only a few times in the Buddha's own discourses, is *prabhāsvaram cittaṃ*. In the early discourses, *prabhāsvaram cittaṃ* is an achieved, not substantial, state of awareness that is "light-possessing," or "luminous" (*prabhāsvaram*). It is a form of insight that results from meditative cultivation (*bhavaṅga*) (Harvey 1995: 170–3; Anālayo 2017). And this is, in more elaborate but still rather elusive form, the sense of *prabhāsvaram cittaṃ* that Vasubandhu invokes in his *Madhyānta Vibhāga*. He claims there that cognitions are neither of their own accord pure or impure, but like all things, gain their specific character from the circumstances of their causal production. Things that are causally produced are empty or void (*śūnya*) of any ever-present and static feature. And so, it is only through cultivation that a cognitive state can become *prabhāsvaram* (Kochumuttom 1982: 84–9). For the Indian Buddhist scholastics, then, awareness as such is not its own abiding substance whose very nature is to manifest its world that otherwise would exist in cognitive darkness, as the Brāhmins would have it. Instead, a specific cognition that thoroughly comprehends the relation between the world and human activity can only arise from a certain program of moral and meditative praxis, and it is that cognition that deserves the name of "luminous."

The first major Chinese recension of Vijñānavāda is offered by the sixth-century translator and commentator Paramārtha / Zhen Di. Paramārtha was, to note a crucial fact, fully informed about both of the foregoing Indian conceptions of the luminosity of awareness, as he translated and commented on not only the major Vijñānavāda works but also the *Sāṃkhyakārikā*. His interpretation of Vasubandhu had the latter claiming that the mere dynamic interplay of pure and impure tendencies in unfolding human experience was not sufficient to explain how primordially ancient forms of desire and attachment could be undone merely by aspirations for and halting attempts to attain purity. For Paramārtha, the "causal root" (根本 *gen ben*) of purified consciousness had to be an ever-untainted basis of pure awareness (Radich 2008: 54). This "pure and luminous awareness" (清净心 *qing jing xin*), Paramārtha's translation of the expression *prabhāsvaram cittaṃ*, not only provided the ground of causal potentiality for perfected awareness to be attained in practice, but took over the body's sensing and acting functions once the attainment of awakening effectively shut down the previously operative ego-identity and the "storehouse" of previously accreted habits and motivations (*ālayavijñāna*) (Radich 2008: 52–3). Now, the notion of a 清净心 *qing jing xin* had both dictional and conceptual precedent in Chinese thought with a partial or fully aligned Daoist pedigree. The expression *qing jing* itself is found in a few passages of the *Huainanzi* where it describes 道 *dao* in the chapter *Tan Ming Jun* and qualifies 愉愉 *tianyu*, or the peaceful contentedness of sages in the *Ren Xian Xun* chapter. In the second- to fourth-century Wei-Jin Period, discussions of whether spiritual luminosity (神明 *shen ming*) was inborn only for certain people, a position held by Liu Shao, or whether it could be attained by anyone through practice, a view Wang Bi defended, were prominent. Paramārtha appropriates this vocabulary for the purposes of transforming it into a full-blown Buddhist doctrine of a fundamental level of awareness that is ever-revealing, undistorting, and the very possibility for perfection in practice. In succeeding centuries of Buddhist literature, this formulation of the luminous mind would become inflated to cosmic proportions. The ninth-century Huayen and Chan master Guifeng Zongmi portrayed the entire natural order as emerging from two fundamental types of existent, the primordial *qi* (元氣 *yuan qi*) from which matter is derived and primordial consciousness (識 *shi*), the intrinsically awakened genuine mind, from which all sentience comes (Gregory 1995: 205–6).

It is debatable whether there was ever a sharp distinction between body and consciousness in early Chinese thought. While early Confucian and Mohist philosophers seemed to believe that the bodily sense organs, including the heart, were conscious of their own accord, there does appear in the *Zhuangzi* the notion that spirit (神 *shen*) is at once the body's most basic kind of vitality and actional capacity, but that it is also separated from the body at death. This was a detail noticed even by Ming Dynasty Buddhist commentators like Hanshan Deqing. But the proclivity to give the luminous mind control over the body, and to see it even as ontologically distinct from material substance which we see developed from Paramārtha to Zongmi finds its way even into seminal Song Dynasty Chan works which otherwise reject doctrine and emphasize practice. In the received compilation of the *Linji Yulu*, the bodily sense organs can only become aware of things if the "singular, pure luminosity" (一精明 *yi jing ming*) of the mind is focused at (在 *zai*) or through them (Sasaki and Kirchner 2009: 165). Indeed in a number of the text's passages, the mind is said to be distinct from the physical elements of the body, representing the authentic "you" of every person, and is therefore in a position to use the body for its own purposes rather than being dominated by psychophysical impulses (Sasaki and Kirchner 2009: 162). These descriptive passages are, to be fair, overshadowed by the much larger number of instructions in the work imploring the Buddhist practitioner to shine that light of the mind on its immediate circumstances and illuminate them. This emphasis retains the overarching Chan insistence that it is activity and not abstract distinction-drawing that is the real occurrence of awakening in life. That being understood, even in Chan classics, the degree to which the Buddhist conception of the "luminous mind" has been made over the centuries into its own autonomous capacity is evident, even when it is said to be "without form" (無形 *wu xing*).

Having summarized these four distinct but historically and conceptually related varieties of luminosity in *prakāśatva*, *prabhāsvaram cittaṃ*, *qing jing xin*, and *ming xin*, it is time to make some comparative observations and suggest some frameworks for understanding their general features. We will then move into an analysis of their relative philosophical merits. I will begin by associating two pairs of these ideas of luminosity, arguing that, while they are by no means identical formulations within the pairs, they are close enough to one another to constitute some paradigmatic contrast with the other pair.

The first and third of these variations, the Brāhmiṇical *prakāśatva* and the reformulated idea of *qing jing xin*, appear to be the most metaphysically loaded of the group. They postulate a unique ground in nature for the most fundamental capacity of awareness to manifest reality to sentient beings. For both, consciousness in its most basic form is its own ontological type, irreducible to matter and rendering all embodied, living beings the powers to perceive their external and internal circumstances. Indeed, it is tempting to speculate, precisely because Paramārtha translated the *Sāṃkhyakārikā* into Chinese, that at least in his case, the notion of *prakāśatva* partly influenced the way he thought about the Buddhist variant *qing jing xin*, though the latter idea certainly did have some native Chinese precedents. Perhaps there is a more general similarity between these conceptions, since even in Indian Vijñānavāda, a more serious and detailed attempt was made than by any other Indian Buddhist school to account for how we ended up with our ultimately false ideation of a continuous subjective and personal identity, a false sense of self (*ātman*). The basis for ego-identity was explained by positing that the seventh mode of cognition, the "deliberatively naming cognition" (*manonāmavijñāna*) reifies a certain preferred set of attachments and habits residing in the "storehouse cognition" (*ālayavijñāna*) and calls them "I" and "mine." In the case of subjectivity, our accreted attachments and habits are stored in the form of "seeds" (*bijā*) in the storehouse cognition, and there they can be preserved and either triggered by present experiences or actively objectified or recalled. Though, Vasubandhu insists, there is no real continuity to the *ālayavijñāna* since even its own activity is as persistent as onrushing water, its preservation of seeds of experience gives it both the appearance and function of continuity. All Paramārtha really does in his reception of Vijñānavāda is to postulate an even more basic, and genuinely continuous, level of subjectivity beneath the storehouse cognition, the awareness of which is never distorted and so provides the foundation for fully awakened realization. But in a strongly resonant, though not identical way, this latter role is precisely what is performed by the *prakāśatva* of consciousness in Sāṃkhya, Yoga, and Vedānta. After all, the continuity of *prakāśatva* is not a continuity of ego-identity, as that is supplied for each embodied being by other processes and mechanisms. Instead, the continuity of *prakāśatva* lies in its unique ontological character as the source of cognitive revealing, the manifestation of things via the light of awareness itself. The very distinctness of *prakāśatva* and *qing jing xin* from physical matter, though this distinction is more radical in the former than in the latter, assures luminous awareness in both of these cases its abiding character and its unadulterated purity as awareness. And this is also why both of these notions of luminous mind make of supreme knowledge or awakening a kind of recovery, for in attaining these we are merely going back to the root of what we are as conscious beings, a root which has always existed within us, to be tapped, and in no need of production.

By contrast, the ideas of *prabhāsvaram cittaṃ* in its earliest Indian Buddhist forms and the *yi ming xin* or "singular, pure mind" of Chan texts are far more closely associated with production and activation through praxis. Before emphasizing this commonality, it is important to note the differences between these ideas; they are more distinct from one another than the *prakāśatva-qing jing xin* pair. For one thing, there is really nothing in either the early Buddhist or Vijñānavāda treatments of *prabhāsvaram cittaṃ* to suggest that it is anything other than the achieved state of comprehensive understanding that is the culmination of moral and meditative cultivation. There may be some exceptions to this rule in the early *Tathāgataghārba* literature, but they are, as noted earlier, vague and not well-developed. The few available references to *prabhāsvaram cittaṃ* in the Theravāda *Nikāya*-s simply tell us that the luminous or "splendorous" realization of awakening results from ongoing *bhavaṅga* or deep states of meditation. Vasubandhu in his turn tells us that the *prabhāsvaram cittaṃ* is possible because the mind is empty of its own nature, and as such, when nurtured and disciplined in the right fashion, can shuffle off all of its contingent impurities and become untrammeled. The Indian variety of *prabhāsvaram cittaṃ* therefore represents a discovery model of awakening, in the sense that awakening accomplishes something new, confers upon us a state of awareness we did not possess before in any respect. The Chan *ming xin*, by comparison, shares some characteristics with the *prakāśatva / qing jing xin* conceptual pair. It appears, at least in some important places, to be irreducible to mere bodily or psychophysically sensory functions, and in fact the body can only be conscious when the *xin* is located at specific sensory organs. And since, as the *Linji Yulu* constantly insists, the *ming xin* is what we most basically are, and thus serves as the reason we can have trust in ourselves and our own capacities for awakening, it fits within the recovery category of how enlightenment is envisioned. If one prefers, and as I have done in earlier work, one could associate *prakāśatva*, *qing jing xin*, and *ming xin* with one another, insofar as they are all depictions of awakening as recovery, leaving the Indian Buddhist idea of *prabhāsvaram cittaṃ* as a discovery approach. But here, I have specific philosophical reasons for arranging *ming xin* with *prabhāsvaram cittaṃ*, since both the second entirely and the first predominantly are associated with bodily practice. Though we are overtly told little about the generation of *prabhāsvaram cittaṃ* from embodied cultivation in Indian texts, its coupling with *bhavaṅga* in Theravāda and with the intentionally transforming effects that purification works on consciousness in Indian Vijñānavāda leave little doubt of this. Deep meditative states are accomplished in Theravāda through certain bodily postures, breathing patterns, concrete exercises of concentration, and disciplines leading to equanimity. *Prabhāsvaram cittaṃ*, though certainly subtle and not necessarily visible to others under this formulation, is effected by a specific set of behaviors. In like manner, in the *Linji Yulu*, what is most vital about our *yi ming xin* are the ways in which we use it, the practiced fashions in which we call upon it, or shine it, on our ever-changing "environments" (境 *jing*). There are in Chan methods for helping us to do these things. Among these methods are the *gong an* and "*dharma* war" (*fa zhan*) verbal encounters with fellow monastics, the strategies used for mastering our emotional states, the concentration we devote to performing one task or one narrowing of attention at a time, even the tedium of ritual of temple life, which strip away habit, distraction, and attachment and return us to our most unconstructed yet responsive selves. Chan thinkers may believe we stand in possession of this *yi ming xin* all along, but it takes both being in the right environments and training to use (用 *yong*) it. And it is what happens to us and those around us when we use that portion of our awareness unshaped by preconceived social priorities that matters the most. Of the varieties of luminous awareness under consideration here, *prabhāsvaram cittaṃ* and *ming xin* are, though they fit into the causal chain of events, less metaphysically loaded and, in that way, closer to our other experiences of attaining new abilities through practice.

Let us refer for the sake of ease to these two groupings of the idea of the luminous mind from classical Indian and Chinese traditions as the metaphysical and practical models, with the metaphysical referring to the *prakāśatva* and *qing jing xin* descriptions and the practical to the *prabhāsvaram cittaṃ* and *ming xin* portrayals. To address the practical model first, it has an appeal that is multi-faceted and fairly obvious. For one thing, the relative proximity of early Indian Buddhist thought and Chan in placing the emphasis with regard to the possibility of awakening on praxis to some degree deflates the charge of Critical Buddhists that East Asian forms of Buddhism are too essentialist or substantialist to be true to the historical Buddha's own teachings. This is perhaps the case with East Asian versions of the metaphysical model to which we will shortly return. But, even though Chan Buddhists occasionally maintain some metaphysical commitments regarding the luminous mind, they are surrounded on every side, as it were, by a resistance to doctrinaire distinctions. And so, their concern with cultivation and interaction makes it often seem that the remaining metaphysical language is far more motivational than descriptive. What we mostly get from both Theravāda and Chan depictions of the luminous mind is that incorrigible brand of Buddhist optimism about human potential. It proclaims that, even though we are profoundly limited, damaged, deluded, and sinful creatures, we can, assuming we have gathered enough from our pain, marshal our virtues, which have also been sedimented from past experiences, to the end of perfecting ourselves through a certain program of conduct. The path to such a dramatic transformation of our habits is hardly easy, since it demands that we purge away our naturally and socially acquired thirst for possession, recognition, and invulnerability to demise. Still, the possibility of achieving luminous awareness does not itself overtax our intuitions about human improvement. Just as we master other things through acquaintance, skill-acquisition, and reinforcement, so we could, with the right means, remold our orientations in the world from ones of passion to compassion, from ones of taking to giving, from ones of seeing only what we believe to seeing. The practical model of the luminous mind is in this respect merely an extension of the general confidence we have in our ability to learn. It does not necessarily broach any mind–body issues and it does not necessarily require that we carve out a special and distinct metaphysical category of consciousness. On the whole, the practical model, which claims merely that a program of praxis can produce a luminous mind, is philosophically well-behaved. That is its major appeal, and the appeal is considerable. The practical model offers us a plausible scenario of human moral and axiological improvement, and even perfection, and that allows for an optimistic view of human capacities. That optimistic view is indeed perhaps something the world as a whole greatly needs at this moment, after about a century and a half of dark philosophical and psychological views about the hindering forces and destructive recesses of consciousness. In the midst of conditions that progressively threaten human existence, which include global climate change, global pandemics, and the progressive hardening of social identities and political allegiances, credible grounds for belief in our capacities for bettering our individual and collective lives are urgently on call.

There is a hard nub to the practical model, however, and that is precisely in the postulation that we can achieve such a thing as a luminous mind. Buddhist and Brāhmiṇical philosophers were not by any stretch of the imagination naïve. They acknowledged that human beings were capable of incredible self-delusion, unmitigated selfishness and cruelty to others, and willful evil. Indeed, under "normal" circumstances, most of the thinkers representing these traditions would concede that human beings in their daily activities fall somewhere within a spectrum of uncomprehending and exclusively desire-driven conduct. If we are indeed starting from these basic circumstances, and even allowing for the occurrence of many rebirths and a wealth of learning from experience and eons of civilizational history, are they really warranted in expecting that we could, in both moral and sapiential ways, make ourselves as perfect as human beings can be?

It was precisely the problematic prospects of this belief that inspired the crafters of the metaphysical model of the luminous mind to be so bold. If we are capable of consummate awakening and thoroughgoing transformation of our characters, there must be something more than just an admixture of pure and impure tendencies accreted from the past to serve as the soil from which unsullied and invulnerable virtue could spring. Our potential for the behavioral perfection of consciousness, according to the purveyors of the metaphysical model, must lie in the fact that, at some core level, the nature, the natural function, of consciousness is to reveal the world to us as it is. Now, to be sure, that daring proclamation entails a host of metaphysical problems which may not, to say the least, be amenable to satisfactory resolution. For instance, the degree to which we have proven over the last century and a half that human consciousness can be eliminated, damaged, attenuated, altered, enhanced, and expanded through corresponding neurological and physiological changes leaves little reasonable doubt that some variety of physicalism, more likely of the emergentist type, is the correct framework for comprehending consciousness. The ancients were, at least in some quarters, aware of this, which explains why thinkers such as the Cārvākas and, I would argue, many early Chinese philosophers, put no distance between physiology and awareness. Moreover, explanations that were suggested in the ancient Brāmiṇical and Buddhist literature of how consciousness, supposedly its own independent ontological substance, first became enmeshed with physical material and activity were never convincing. The "how" or even "why" of that process received no compelling systematic account. Solving the potentiality problem that the practical model of the luminous mind saddles us with seems to entail too many philosophical costs that cannot be adequately paid by the metaphysical model. Perhaps we can only solve them by either pointing to certain exemplars of sagehood whom we believe have mastered themselves and attained surpassing sagacity or, should we be personally inclined, we may turn to practice ourselves, to give ourselves that most worthy of endeavors.

Still, a too-hasty abandonment of the metaphysical model may in its own right let us off the hook of a philosophical challenge that we really ought to face. That challenge, in its most straightforward terms, demands that we think more deeply than we yet have about the relationship between consciousness and the natural phenomenon of life. I do not wish to defend some kind of panpsychism here, since panpsychism draws in effect no distinctions between mechanical or chemical reactions and awareness. However, there may be something fundamentally conscious about natural life as we presently understand it. Nucleic acids, after all, are assemblages of constitutive information, and it is that information which enables organisms to initiate various kinds of activity in the environment, such as seeking nutrition and procuring opportunities to reproduce. It may not be entirely unreasonable to characterize a situation in which chemicals and the structures they maintain are information-driven and oriented toward their environments as conscious processes rather than merely mechanical or "instinctual" reactions. If that is allowed, then consciousness, as a unique natural phenomenon, is fundamentally the capacity to sense in some fashion and actively engage with the environment in some fashion. And that capacity is one we could metaphorically label "luminosity," insofar as consciousness on this account manifests, sheds light on, the environing external and internal world for beings which, in varying ways, experience those manifestations and intentionally navigate within them. Here, consciousness would not be, as it was for many of the ancients, an ontological type that was categorically distinct from physical processes. Its appearance would depend on the configuration of physical activities. But it would, nonetheless, be a metaphysically distinct and unique phenomenon, and would exist in varying degrees and with varying potentialities in creatures of different structures and in a variety of states. Classical notions such as *prakāśatva* and *qing jing xin* could have therefore been, so to speak, robust intuitions that life and sentience are inextricably intertwined. And that entanglement could in its turn confer on living beings not just the possibility of survival, but special abilities to learn, purposefully rather than passively adapt, and, effectively, become new sorts of beings. And so, it is in the fundamental capacities of consciousness, to sense rightly and successfully navigate in the environment, that rests our continued prerogatives to learn and grow, and, should we be sufficiently devoted, to become wise and good.

I am not willing at this point to declare that either the classical metaphysical model of the luminosity of consciousness, or the updated variant I have just described, are true. I am not sure enough evidence is available at this moment to underwrite the contemporary version, and I continue to think the classical depictions of *prakāśatva* and *qing jing xin* leave an unbridgeable chasm between physicality and consciousness. But the philosophical debate on whether or not our awareness is at its roots or can become luminous was one not only worth having from the early centuries of the Common Era until late medieval times. It is one entirely worth rekindling now. And the resources that the classical Indian and Chinese traditions provide for us in rekindling that discussion are precious, and have not lost one bit of their value. Indeed, the enormity of challenges that human beings have set themselves in the contemporary world makes the value of the luminous mind as real and possibility perhaps more precious than it has ever been.

9

The Unlikely Commentator

The Hermeneutic Reception of Śaṅkara's Thought in the Interpretation of Dārā Shukøh[1]

The legend, established for centuries now, has it that the justification for the humiliating execution of Prince Dārā Shukøh by his brother Aurungzeb in 1659 was Dārā's heresy. Of all his works dealing with the relation between Brāhmiṇical and Islamic thought, we are told by contemporary sources that his original work *Majma'-ul Bahrain* and his translation of the *Sirr-i Akbar* were what provoked the charge (Kazim 1865–73: 179). Indeed, after the public punishment was carried out in the streets of Delhi, when the decapitated head of Dārā was brought to his younger brother inside of a box, the new Shah is reported to have uttered the eulogy: "as I did not look at this infidel's face during his lifetime, I have no wish to do so now." (Sarkar 1912–24: 219). Of course, the fate of Dārā Shukøh as a historical matter is much more attributable to his political and military misjudgment, having spent seven years thwarting the expansion campaigns of Aurungzeb and ineptly contesting his forces in the final battle for dynastic succession (Gascoigne 1971: 193–215). But the return of orthodox Islam to the Mughal court was to be the major legitimization for Aurungzeb's rule. And so the perpetuation of the legend has made Dārā appear to his centuries of detractors as a decadent apostate in his great-grandfather Akbar's tradition, and to his supporters as a tragic martyr for Hindu-Muslim concord in Indian civilization. It is quite ironic then that, as far as we know, Dārā had a much more hermeneutically self-conscious appraisal of his own scholarship. He combined his personal spiritual interests with a desire to vindicate the universality of the Qur'ānic worldview through a demonstration of how its monotheism was echoed in classical Brāhmiṇical religious and philosophical texts. Though this agenda inspired him to see to the translations of sacred Vedic scriptures and practices into the then open intellectual world of the empire, it also made him their unlikely commentator.

This can be gleaned most clearly from Dārā Shukøh's supervision of the translation of some fifty *Upaniṣads* during a six-month period in 1657, the *Sirr-i Akbar*.[2] Dārā was a Qādiri Sufi, admittedly one whose associations with ascetics of other traditions steadily increased during the intellectual ferment which followed Akbar's reign. Still, his primary audience for these historic translations were members of the *Ulema* of the imperial court. As such, Dārā becomes a commentator on ancient Sanskrit philosophy, but he is a Muslim commentator who selects and presents texts and concepts for fellow Muslims. This seemingly elementary but very powerful fact is borne out in two pivotal ways. The first lies in the brutally frank reasons he states in the work's preface, which is argued in the manner of an *apologia*. Dārā does not merely claim that he is offering up a noble example of religious syncretism so that the Muslim and Hindu communities of the empire can aspire to mutual understanding and toleration. In addition, he sets out to defend the *Islamic orthodoxy* of the *Upaniṣads*, claims even that they are themselves Islamic texts, witnessed by the Qur'ān and bearing witness to true and untarnished monotheism. This argument leads to the second hallmark of Dārā's commentarial stance, namely the interpretive contortions that are expended in casting the *Upaniṣads* as the "works of God" in a monotheistic light through reliance on the commentaries of the Advaita Vedāntin Śaṅkarācārya. Advaita was certainly not the most doctrinally congenial *darśana* to declare equivalent to monotheism. This was a fact of which the prince ought to have been conscious given his previous, extensive studies of the traditions of Yoga, Viśiṣṭādvaita and popular *bhakti* movements such as that of Bābā Lāl's Kabiri Vaiṣnavas.[3] As it turns out however, the choice of Śaṅkara may have been conveniently deliberate, as the interpretive lens through which he sees Brāhmiṇical philosophy provides a rationale for both Dārā's esoteric reading and his wish for some doctrinal cover. It is after all on Śaṅkarācarya's authority that the *Upaniṣads* are understood as "secret teachings," hidden from both the views of most practicing Hindus and Muslims alike. This detail provided the heir-apparent the space to pursue his translation projects and religious interests in safety, without the court needing to worry overmuch about possible popular consequences.

These quite overtly political dimensions of Dārā Shukøh's readings and explications of classical Indian thought are not highlighted here for the purpose of impuning his genuine spiritual interests and apparently sincere religious eclecticism.[4] Indeed, close scrutiny will reveal that, in taking up these commentarial positions with all their political implications, though he denies political motives, Dārā validates not merely the orthodoxy of the *Sirr-i Akbar*, but his very own doctrinal compliance. He sets before his readers in the Mughal court the argument that, since religion is a gift of God, religious inclusivism is God's expectation of Islamic rulership. The tragic irony of the mission of this unlikely commentator is that the strategy played, like so many of his other designs, right into the hands of his rival younger brother.

In his striking and revealing preface to the *Sirr-i Akbar*, Dārā begins by celebrating God and the revelations of the *Qur'ān*, as well as paying respects to his Qādiri preceptors. He describes his studies as the single-minded and pure-hearted pursuit of the "oceans" of truth emanating forth from the *Tawhid*, or the doctrine of God's unity (Hasrat 1982: 284–5). It is under these banners, devotion to the *Qur'ān* and a desire to more perfectly comprehend *Tawhid*, that Dārā is first drawn to the investigation of non-Islamic religious traditions.[5] He acknowledges that these academic efforts on his part have met resistance among certain *Ulema* scholars and theologians. But Dārā dismisses such opposition as being directed against, not him, but "all the words of Unitarianism, which are most evident from the glorious Qur'ān and the authentic traditions of indubitable prophecy" (Hasrat 1982: 285). He finds in the course of his studies however that the *Veda*s and *Upaniṣads*, the classical religious texts of "this most ancient people" of India, also testify to monotheism and God's uncompromised unity (Hasrat 1982: 285). Lest anyone should object that immersion into texts which stand outside the orthodox schema of Revelation itself signals heresy, Dārā Shukøh preempts with quotations from the Qur'ān testifying to a wider dissemination of spiritual wisdom. He cites passages that demonstrate, to the satisfaction of his own hermeneutic, that God is sure to send prophets to every nation and people, for only when the message has been communicated can any fair judgment be rendered.[6] He closes the preface by recounting how, when he and his team had finished the translations, he turned once again to the *Qur'ān* for an omen of God's blessing on his project, and his eyes fell on the opening verses of *al-A'rāf*, "This Book has been revealed to you—let not your heart be troubled about it—so that you may thereby give warning and admonish the faithful" (Hasrat 1982: 287). It turns out that more than half of the text of Dārā's preface to his translation of the *Upaniṣad*s is devoted to dawning what he hopes will be perceived as an orthodox mantle of commentator. This mantle can be worn because the *Upaniṣad*s themselves have presumably been sent by God, as the prince believes the Qur'ān shows; they are in his estimation *bona fide* Islamic texts.

Part of understanding the significance of this ardent wish on his part to be seen as conforming to manifest orthodoxy depends on recalling Dārā Shukøh's political situation and reputation among the *Ulema* at the time of the translations. He had already caused stirs in the Mughal court for his existing works on Brāhmiṇcal thought, and this is well documented. But the appearance of the *Sirr-i Akbar* also coincides with Dārā's *de facto* ascension to the Mughal throne. In September of 1657, Shah Jahan fell ill with an incapacitating urine retention, and his eldest son, the only one of the Shah's sons present at Delhi, restricted access to his father, provoking some suspicion.[7] In fact, Shah Jahan at this point retired to Agra and conferred authority on Dārā, just as his brothers Shuja and Aurungzeb began to mobilize their forces (Gascoigne 1971: 200–1). It was Aurungzeb in particular who had a vendetta against Dārā, for his elder brother had in the previous year accepted bribes from local administrators to prevent Aurungzeb from completely overrunning the wealthy outpost kingdoms of Golconda and Bijapur (Gascoigne 1971: 200–1). Aware that the outwardly more pious Aurungzeb might be favored by the *Ulema*, Dārā Shukøh would only be acting wisely to have his bases covered, as it were, with them. These facts do not in any way dilute the heir-apparent's sincere spiritual interests, nor his hope that the translations would enlighten himself, his children and "all seekers of Truth." But they do point to the fact that his repeated claims that his translations "had no worldly motive" do require some historical qualification (Hasrat 1982: 266–7). Most significantly for our purposes, these circumstances further reveal Dārā's clear self-consciousness as a Muslim addressing himself and his inter-religious openness to Muslims.

In an attempt to balance the defense of the *Sirr-i Akbar* as in seamless accordance with orthodox Islam, Dārā tries to quell possible fears he senses will arise in the court about the texts gaining popular acclaim and leading Muslims away from the fold. He does this through the very name he translates into Persian for the term *Upaniṣad*, "The Great Secret," and through the way he explicates the nature of the Vedic scriptures' secrecy. The *Upaniṣads*, he notes, are texts of extreme obscurity and profundity, so difficult indeed to grasp the import of that "there are few conversant with it even among the Indians" (Hasrat 1982: 266). These sacred texts, the earliest and most recondite expression of monotheism in the history of religious literature, are according to Dārā so protected among the holy Brāhmaṇas that one of his motivations for delving into their difficulties became a desire "to solve the mystery which underlies their effort to conceal it from the Muslims," though he does not explain or support this oblique accusation (Hasrat 1982: 266). Cementing this line of argument about the *Upaniṣads'* "secrecy," and in methodological consonance with his soliciting of textual evidence from the Qur'ān about the nature of these classical philosophical treatises, Dārā alludes to a passage from *al-Waqi'an*. The verses run: "I swear by the shelter of the stars (a mighty oath if you but knew it) that this is a glorious Koran, safeguarded in a book which none may touch except the purified, a revelation from the Lord of the Universe." (Hasrat 1982: 267). Dārā Shukøh deduces, based on his above-mentioned studies of other scriptures, that this passage cannot be referring to the Psalms, the Book of Moses, the Gospels or even the *Lawh-i-Mafuz*, for while he does not state it explicitly, the former were laid open before the masses and the latter has not yet been revealed (Hasrat 1982: 267) And it is at this most crucial point where the indigenous commentaries on the earliest *Upaniṣads* are summoned from the Advaita Vedāntin Śaṅkarācarya.

Dārā Shukøh and his team of Varanasi paṇḍits offer some fifty *Upaniṣads* up for translation, though the numbers slightly differ in different versions of the manuscript. Some of the *Upaniṣads* are among the oldest, while large numbers come from "middle" and "late" periods.[8] Conspicuously, all translations, whether they are from prose or poetic *Upaniṣads*, lack the internal organizational delimiters, *adhyāya*-s and *khaṇḍa*-s, which all of the original texts contain. This decision seems not to have been haphazard, such that the translators made the editorial decision that this ancient organizational schema was simply not necessary for the Persian recapitulation. On the contrary, this omission allowed the translators to freely insert commentarial texts (*Upaniṣadbhāṣya*-s) into the original narratives. While it is evident that not all of this commentarial material is drawn from the seminal seventh century Advaitin Śaṅkara (Halbfass 1988: 33), significant portions of the Persian texts of the *Aitareya, Bṛhadāraṇyaka, Chāndogya, Īśā, Muṇḍaka, Māṇḍūkya, Kena* and *Kaṭha* are interspersed with the interpretations of the illustrious southern master.[9] The commentarial material selected from Śaṅkarācarya, however, comports very oddly with the predominant number of medieval, "theistic" *Upaniṣads* which comprise the *Sirr-i Akbar*, for the doctrines of Advaita, it is well known, unlike the Viśiṣṭādvaita and Dvaita schools of Vedānta, were hardly monotheistic in any accurate sense. While much is certainly made in Śaṅkara's commentaries of *brahman*, this being the central subject of *Upaniṣadic* literature, "Non-Dualism's" most famous exegete makes distinctions without number in his works between *nirguṇa-brahman* and *saguṇa-brahman*, the latter being only a constructed, dualistic mental projection of divine existence and the former a direct, non-dualistic experience of the unity of *brahman* and the self (*ātman*) or self-luminous awareness.[10] The implication for Advaita philosophy is clear; any conventional or even systematically theological conception of God as is found in other schools of Indian religious thought become relegated to the level of mere mental projection and self-deception. One only gains access to the truth when all projections of God as "other" than one's own innermost consciousness are completely abandoned. In other words, for Advaita, "God" is a practical fantasy for the masses, not the stuff of true philosophical and meditational insight. While many comparisons with Sufi doctrines and formulations of *Tawhid* may freely suggest themselves here, as they certainly did to Dārā Shukøh, Śaṅkara's non-theistic polemic is too constant and clear to be mistaken for theism. And this fact is precisely what provoked the ire of the other theistic schools of Vedānta.[11] The differences between the doctrines were so noticeable in fact that even the audience Dārā was trying to win over, the Mughal *Ulema*, was deeply suspicious that the prince was embracing "pantheism" in his espousal of these texts for spiritual cultivation. And it was not as if Dārā had no choice in the matter of theistic doctrine between the contesting schools of Vedānta, for it is quite well established that there were societies of Viśiṣṭādvaita and Dvaita in Varanasi at the time he set about his translation project in the 1650's (Bernier 1914: 334),[12] traditions of commentary which would have been much theologically safer than his soliciting of Advaita tenets to support monotheism. This begs the question then of why Dārā would choose Śaṅkara's interwoven commentaries on the *Upaniṣads* to validate his conceptualization of *Tawhid*.

The answer may well lie in the use Dārā Shukøh attempted to make of his Qādiri esoteric proclivities, and the correspondence these found in Śaṅkara. It was after all Śaṅkara who first dubbed *Upaniṣadic* teachings as hermetic secrets. Indeed, Śaṅkara in his commentarial literature makes the case that the word *Upaniṣad* is etymologically derived from the same root as *rahasyam*, "secret."[13] The Persian title of Dārā's translation *Sirr-i Akbar* may well then come from Śaṅkara's glosses on quotations from various *Upaniṣads* such as *Kaṭha* I: iii, 17, which characterizes certain spiritually edifying narratives as "*paramaṃ guhyaṃ*" (the greatest secret), where Śaṅkara rephrases *guhyaṃ* as *rahasyam* and then equates the later with the word *upaniṣad*. No other explicitly theistic sects of Vedānta interpret the term in this way. In the sense in which *Upaniṣads* were taught by these other schools, they were not "secret" teachings, but more properly "advanced" teachings for mendicant renunciates or scholarly students of a monastic order. However, despite the relative doctrinal dissimilarity between basic Advaita and Islamic teachings, Śaṅkara's take on *what Upaniṣads are* is more important to Dārā than a precise interpretation of their content. For, as we have just seen, the hermeneutic Dārā employs to claim that the *Sirr-i Akbar* are indeed *bona fide* Islamic texts hinges on his ability to establish that they were first "secretly" revealed to and since entrusted to purified renunciates, as he believes the *Qur'ān*'s *al-Waqi'an* verse reveals. The sacred secrets of the texts he now presents before the Mughal *Ulema* should not, therefore, he deduces, inflict them with worry once they are made part of the library, since the "common folk" will not understand them anyway, and only the most spiritually discerning Muslim will comprehend their depths. Dārā Shukøh's methodology of interpretation here becomes subjected to his project of legitimation. The prince is not merely making with these translations a gift to the empire's body of knowledge out of an antiquarian spirit of preservation or humanitarian impulse of toleration. He has become the unlikely spiritual commentator, advocate and exegete, of the already fourteen-hundred year-old *Upaniṣads* for the Islamic community, calling on his brothers to claim their proud, rightful ownership of civilization's first historical witness to *Tawhid.*

Tragically, the sale did not pass and the wager found the tables turned against him. Aurungzeb had already been convinced for some time that his older brother was an "atheist," and when his forces overran Dārā's army, many of whom were *rajput*-s, the court conducted the "compulsory" *divani-i-khas* debate and rendered their condemnation with its mandated punishment (Gascoinge 1971: 215). And while following centuries would cast his image either as heretical apostate or religious syncretist, the sad irony is that Dārā Shukøh may have understood his own cause more as one about the nature of Islam's spiritual and political heritage. For Dārā, the monotheistic message which God had first sent into the human world with the *Upaniṣads* had, through his scholarly restoration, been made universal and could now be reclaimed through his line of "universal rulers."

Notes

1 This essay was first published as "The Unlikely Commentator: The Hermeneutic Reception of Śaṅkara's Thought in the Interpretive Scholarship of Dārā Shukøh," *Journal of Ecumenical Studies: A Festschrift in Honor of Leonard Swidler* vol. 50, no. 1 (2015), 85–92. It is reprinted here with the permission of University of Pennsylvania Press.

2 That the *Sirr-i Akbar* was a collaborative effort, and not the lone work of Dārā's admittedly unique genius has long been beyond doubt. A.H. Anquetil Duperron, whose translation of the *Sirr-i Akbar* into Latin appeared at the beginning of the 19th century, acknowledged that Dārā Shukøh had in his efforts consulted with the ablest Sanskritists of his day. Despite this, the German philosopher Schopenhauer, who adored Duperron's renderings, credited the Mughal prince with most of the work, provoking his punishment (Schopenhauer [1851] 1988: 347). Only with E. Goebel-Gross' Marburg dissertation of 1962, entitled *Sirr-i Akbar*, did

the composition of the work come under critical scrutiny in the West. The facts that the translations of the some four and a half dozen texts were completed in just a half-year as well as that the heir-apparent, while he does take credit for the translations, admits he employed the help of learned paṇḍits (cited in Hasrat 1982: 267), solidify the inference that the project was a considerable collaboration. But this only brings into sharper relief the hermeneutic questions we will address.

3 Of course, most of Dārā's original works on and translations of Brāhmiṇical texts had been finished by now, the *Seven Discourses with Bābā Lāl* having appeared no later than 1653, the *Majma'-ul Bahrain* in 1656 and the translations of the *Gitā* and the *Yoga-Vāsiṣṭha* in 1656-57 (Hasrat 1982: xxvi–xxv).

4 These virtues are in any event sufficiently extolled in the existing secondary literature so as not to require additional support. Indeed, the tradition has been to link the "mysticism" and "courageous humanism" of Dārā tightly with the spiritual well-being of India as a religiously pluralistic civilization (Massignon [1926] 2003: 94–105).

5 Hasrat 1982: 285 mentions in this regard reading "the Book of Moses, the Gospels, the Psalms and other scriptures". This is significant in the sense that, for deeper comprehension of God's unity, the prince consults first the sacred lore produced by the other recognized and acknowledged "People of the Book" before turning to "other scriptures."

6 Dārā uses the following as prooftexts from the *Qur'ān*: "No soul shall bear another's burden. Nor do we punish until we send forth a messenger" (*al-Isra*, 14–15); "We have sent you with the Truth to give good news and to proclaim a warning, for there is no community that has not had a warner" (*al-Faṭir*, 24); "We have sent forth Our apostles with veritable signs, and through them have brought down scriptures and the scales of justice" (*al-Ḣadīd*, 25) (All translations from *The Koran* 1999). Exegetical issue could obviously be taken with Dārā's interpretations of each of these verses, but as he takes the allegorical approach in his reading, he attempts to bypass such issues.

7 The chronology of events in 1657 alone casts serious doubts on Dārā Shukøoh's claim to have been the major translator of the *Sirr-i Akbar*, for we know that he was in Delhi from July of that year to the end of 1657, tending to the various weighty political matters presently under discussion (Gascoigne 1971: 200–1). This means that the "six months" he is supposed to have spent continuously in Varanasi on the translations must have come in the first half of that year. The number of texts which had to be selected, the amount of commentarial literature which was included in the translations, which we will discuss below, combined with the complexity of scholarly consultations with paṇḍits he freely admits was required for the project make his assertions of primacy in the authorship of the translations strain credulity.

8 About twelve of the fifty-two *Upaniṣads* in the most authoritative MS are genuinely Vedic, coming from the so-called "early" and "middle" periods of composition, while the remaining forty, though they are classified under Vedic categories, are very late medieval compositions and are primarily devotional in character (Hasrat 1982: 270–3).

9 There has been an interminable argument in the scholarship about which *bhāṣya*-s can credibly be attributed to Śaṅkara, and this paper is the wrong venue to enter into such a discussion. Karl H. Potter's estimates can be found in the third volume of *The Encyclopedia of Indian Philosophy* (Potter 1981: 115–16). On Potter's account, only about half of the texts listed above can reliably be said to be Śaṅkara's.

10 See for instance *Brahmasūtrabhāṣya*, i:1,11; i:1, 20. Eliot Deutsch (1973: 13) comments: "This divine status of Brahman is not to be construed, however, in this context, as a personal deity who responds to prayer, bestows grace, or enters into history; rather, in *nirguṇa* Brahman, all distinctions are eliminated…in *saguṇa* Brahman, a duality in unity is present…and, consequently, the power of love… (*bhakti*)".

11 To be fair, these philosophical differences would have been hard to detect were one to merely rely on the Sanskrit of the *Upaniṣads*, whose constant references to *deva* and *Īśvara* are plainly theistic in tone. The anthropomorphic and even gendered depiction of God is still embedded in Śaṅkara's own Sanskrit, for he equates the expressions *paraṃ brahman* and *paramātman* with *Īśvara* (Mayeda 1992: 19).

12 The city of Varanasi, which had been restored under Akbar, was supposedly targeted by Aurungzeb precisely for its wealth of Hindu learning after his capture of the throne.

13 See his *Kenopaniṣadbhāṣya*, iv: 7 and *Upadeśasāhasrī*, xiii. While there is some sense in which the transmission of early *Upaniṣads* was in the context of ritual Vedic practices privy only to the Brāhmaṇa class, this etymology is in itself indefensible. The most likely derivation was in modern commentary first suggested by Louis Renou, who extrapolates it as a synonym for the ancient word *bandhu* or "tie," implying that *upaniṣad* denotes the "connection" or "equivalence" between the constituents of the human self and the substances of cosmic reality (Olivelle (trans.) 1996: xxxii, lli).

10

The Pivot of Nihilism

Buddha Through Nietzsche's Eyes[1]

Nietzsche's occasionally articulated admiration of Buddhism, along with his anticipation that Buddhist thought would soon draw European people to it, has elicited a considerable amount of attention from comparative philosophers in recent decades. A good deal of this attention has come from East Asian and particularly Japanese scholars, such as Kenji Nishitani and Abe Masao, who variously contended that, despite what the late 19th century visionary believed, Zen offers a more compelling solution to nihilism than Nietzsche does. Even more recently, André van der Braak (2011) has attempted to bolster this position by recruiting ancient and medieval Indian and Chinese Buddhist thinkers like Nāgārjuna and Linji Yixuan into the Zen efforts to overcome nihilism. Historically, however, Nietzsche's acquaintance with Buddhism, quite limited in scope even for its time, was restricted to mostly early South Asian Theravāda. But even here, scholars such as Robert G. Morrison (1997) have attempted to argue that Nietzsche's estimation of Buddhism as a laudable but ultimately life-denying kind of nihilism was wrong, and that more affinities existed between the figures of the enlightened sage and the *Übermensch* than Nietzsche estimated. When one looks over some of Nietzsche's observations about Buddhist thought and particularly about the figure of the Buddha himself, one can at times understand why those who represent different schools of the tradition become so intrigued. "I could," Nietzsche (1990: 42) once wrote in a fragment from the early 1880's, "become the Buddha of Europe, but admittedly an antipode for the Indian one."[2] Even more, he speculated that a "European Buddhism might perhaps be indispensable" (Nietzsche 1967c: 80). And yet, at the same time in his published works, as is well-known to all the above-mentioned authors, he openly worries that "a new Buddhism, a European Buddhism" will bring upon the cultural complexes of the continent a weakening of the mind and a debilitating form of nihilism (Nietzsche 1964a: 82). The seemingly irresolvable ambivalence the

Nietzsche articulates about the Buddha and the religious movement he founded spans practically all of his writings. While Nietzsche's references to Buddhism are sparse, they betray profound curiosity with and concern about the values the tradition represents to him.

It should not be thought, of course, that Nietzsche ever studied Buddhist or any other Asian philosophical heritage extensively. As is everywhere acknowledged by now, the single title Nietzsche owned on Buddhist thought by Hermann Oldenberg seems to have been utterly unmarked; Nietzsche never consulted with his lifelong acquaintance and former Schulpforta classmate Paul Deussen about Indian philosophical thinkers in their correspondence. He very rarely cites anything from translations of Buddhist texts. He took Schopenhauer to be more or less a reliable authority on Brāhmiṇical ("Hindu") and Buddhist philosophies despite an ever-growing body of 19th century professional Orientalist literature on them (Sprung 1993: 51–63). And still, Nietzsche's fascination with Buddhism, when he gives expression to it, appears to be persistently poignant and of widely cultural significance. He tends to view Buddhism as a unique "type" of nihilism, one admirable for both its rejection of world-transcending religious ideas such as God, souls and immortality and for its refusal to resort to moralistic dogmatism as a safeguard against the loss of meaning in life. In Nietzsche's view, Buddhism had to occupy a unique position at the culmination of an already long philosophical and ascetic heritage in India in order to embrace these commitments as courageously and "honestly" as it did. In this regard, Nietzsche finds in the figure of Buddha a kind of kindred historical spirit. On the other hand, Buddhism's ultimate idealization of *nirvāṇa*, the "extinguishing" of all desirous attachment to life, was the fateful step to decadence that Nietzsche wished to warn Europe against in its own historical encounter with nihilism. One could, then, walk with the Buddha down the road of nihilism up to a point, but at a crucial moment most pivot away in order to re-enter and reaffirm life in the world. The Buddha, as Nietzsche would have it, shows us both how nihilism can triumph and how it can lead to disaster, and this makes him in the final analysis an indelibly important figure in Nietzsche's thinking and works.

Obviously, Nietzsche's appropriation of Buddhism into a narrative of European thought that makes nihilism its present transformational stage, apart from totalizing the tradition according to a basically Schopenhauerian trope, reveals the degree of self-preoccupation involved in his estimation. It reflects, as Wilhelm Halbfass (1988: 125) pointed out long ago, not so much Nietzsche's interest in Buddhism as a unique and diverse heritage, but more his "deep and passionate concern about modern man and the destiny of Europe." Nietzsche overtly expressed, however, a general disdain for professionalized European Indological scholarship in the 19th century.[3] He did not regard Buddhism as a merely ossified body of texts only to be considered through philological analysis, but rather as a living tradition that challenged foregoing European values. Nietzsche's stance toward Buddhism, then, should be considered a hermeneutically open, and not a closed-minded, one. Perhaps then we can, instead of becoming too preoccupied with Nietzsche's relative unfamiliarity with Buddhist thought in South and East Asia in general or with the degree of "European" interests that prompted his assessments of it, ask the more interesting question of whether his depictions of Buddhism are reasonable ones. Did early Buddhists really reject ideas of transcendence and shed what Nietzsche would consider the stigmas of absolutistic standards of good and evil? Did they see themselves as adjudicating already ancient philosophical and religious views and thus as shaping a new destiny for their own civilization? And, above all, what should we make of Nietzsche's portrayal of the Buddhist conception of *nirvāṇa* as the culmination of "nihilistic" tendencies?

In what follows, we shall see that Nietzsche's perspectives on early Buddhist values are at times vaguely insightful and suggestive, especially with respect to the ways in which Buddhist texts envision how its principles mediate between contesting philosophical and axiological views then at odds in South Asia. Still, in weighing the merits of their own principles and even the ideal of *nirvāṇa*, the early Buddhists vehemently reject the characterization of their tradition, even among ancient contemporaries, as "nihilism." They instead famously see their prescriptions for life as forging a "middle path" (*majjhimā praṭiipadā*) between extreme forms of self-indulgence and self-denial. For its early advocates and practitioners, then, Buddhism was itself already precisely a pivot away from nihilism, not a triumphant emergence from nihilism, or worse, as Nietzsche imagined it, a fateful embrace of it. For the aforementioned commentators on Zen, and particularly as Zen is mediated through twentieth century Kyōto school frameworks, there is more justification for comparative approaches that highlight Buddhism as a conquest over an axiologically nihilistic orientation. But when South Asian Buddhist thought is placed in the spotlight instead of East Asian Zen, what is often too curtly overlooked by comparativists is exactly that both the historical Buddha himself and his early advocates vehemently deny that Buddhism is a nihilism of any sort to begin with. But most telling, as we shall see, is how Buddhists conceive of what they call "nihilism." Indeed, what Nietzsche calls nihilism, the Buddhists label as the error of "eternalism," but what early Buddhists called "nihilism" was precisely the kind of life, and philosophical commitments, that Nietzsche largely valorized. A clear explication of this latter contrast should be sufficient to demonstrate that early South Asian Buddhist and Nietzschean thought cannot viably be seen as philosophical allies.

Nietzsche's Buddha: The Admirable but Weak-Willed Nihilist

Nietzsche adopts wholesale the Schopenhauerian conception of Buddhist *nirvāṇa* as "nothingness" and a "denial of the will to live" already in *The Birth of Tragedy*. In the first culminating section describing the salvifically life-affirming power of Dionysian art, he asserts that it steers the spectator of tragedy clear from the "danger of a Buddhistic longing for a negation of the will" (Nietzsche 1967a: 59). This association of *nirvāṇa* with "nothing" is a constant theme, surviving into his mentions of it fifteen years later in *On the Genealogy of Morals*. It should be noted that the Buddhist version of the "ascetic ideal," the turning away from worldly attachments that the historical Buddha embraced, Nietzsche posited, did not merely infect his greatest ideas, but even his everyday attitudes. This is evidenced, Nietzsche (1967b: 107) surmises, by the Buddha's calling the birth of his son Rahula "a fetter." Buddhism, that is, should be considered a decadent form of human thought because its ultimate rejection of sensuous desire, worldly attachment and creative activity, even, as it were, in its most basic and elemental manifestations, make of *nirvāṇa* or final release form worldly life a logical outcome of its values. In this respect, Buddhism, as a life-denying tradition, is very close to Christianity, for, as Nietzsche says in *The Joyful Science* (Nietzsche 1964b: 286), they both suffer from "an extraordinary malady of the will" (*einer ungeheuren Erkrankung des Willens*). He speculates in *The Antichrist* (Nietzsche 1974: 150) that early Buddhists took this turn toward decadent life-denial because they were "races that" had become "kind, gentle and over-spiritual, and which feel pain too easily."

And yet, as Michael Hulin (1993: 71–2) has astutely pointed out, Nietzsche does not simply maintain a reductionist approach to Buddhism, and one can observe as Nietzsche's writings mature a certain "softening" of attitudes toward even those notions on Buddhism that initially repelled him the most. This observation does appear to obtain with respect to Nietzsche's appreciation of the different resonances of the idea of "nothingness" in Buddhist thought and its larger ramifications for its axiology. At moments, in his late notes pondering the "most scientific hypothesis" of the "eternal recurrence," for example, Nietzsche (1967c: 35–6) plays with the degree to which seeing nature as without beginning or end reveals its "aim- and meaninglessness," and this could be the very "extreme form of nihilism" that a "European Buddhism" could "compel." That is to say that, as he puts it, the Buddhist concept of causality, which Nietzsche does not elaborate on, implies in any case that the universe exists eternally, and so depicts the natural order as ultimately purposeless and should therefore be seen as a philosophically advanced form of nihilism (1967c: 38). So, there does seem to be a subtle shift in Nietzsche's assessment of precisely what kind of "nihilism" Buddhist thought represents.

The picture becomes still more complex when we turn to how Nietzsche measures the more broad-ranging cultural significance of Buddhist philosophy as he understands it. Even in his inaugural work, Nietzsche (1967a: 110–13) associates "Buddhistic" and "Brahminic" religions with a culture of tragedy, which has overcome its optimistic faith in reason and eternal values, with such overcoming accompanied by a determination "to live resolutely." The early Buddhist thinkers (through, he presumes, their adoption of Sāṃkhya) attained to an "honest" atheism that transcends Christian conviction and yet is utterly consistent with the "ascetic ideal" five centuries before the emergence of Christianity (Nietzsche 1967b: 161). This line of thought that depicts Buddhism as an historical precursor and yet superior in spirit to Christianity is continued in a most telling, if brief, way in *Ecce Homo*. Here, Nietzsche declares that the laying aside of moralistic *ressentiment* by the Buddha makes his prescription for life more of a "hygiene" and "physiology" than a religion, and thus clearly distinguishable from what he would classify as more vengeful kinds of "priestly" movements (Nietzsche 1967b: 230). In notes of early 1888, Nietzsche further diagnoses the reasons that Buddhism can demur from the moralism that Christianity maintains on behalf of the "underprivileged." Buddhism, he argues, strides past good and evil by asserting that every act alike, rather than being "good" or "evil" in any absolute sense, is the pursuit of a desire and a means to continue to cling to existence. So, since the overarching point of praxis in Buddhism is to be released from desires no matter what their content, the tradition demands no "revenge" against the society's aristocratic rulers and so requires no "enemy" (Nietzsche 1967c: 96). Nietzsche dramatizes these points powerfully in *The Antichrist*, where he concludes that, despite the fact that both Christianity and Buddhism are religions of decadence, Buddhism offers at least a superior way of being in the world for those still-living, for it makes real happiness possible by promising nothing, while Christianity promises a thousand things, including "justice," and keeps none of its promises (Nietzsche 1974: 184). Hulin (1993: 72–3) is certainly correct then when he claims that

Nietzsche's "domestication" of Buddhism is undertaken because "he needs it as a foil in his interminable polemic against Christianity." But this is not the whole story either, of course, because Nietzsche's peculiar representations of Buddhism also aid him in constructing a certain "type" of nihilism that is far more estimable in his view to foregoing "types" of priestly nihilism (Judaism and Christianity), but one that is still markedly, and even perilously, inferior to his own. What in Buddhism, apart from its already-reviewed formulation of final *nirvāṇa* as an ideal to be striven for, is so dangerous?

Simply put, Nietzsche sees Buddhism as dangerous because when, at the crucial moment that it has the inestimably rare opportunity to re-enter the dynamism and legislative power of life, it turns away from it. It is not enough, after all, to realize that, in constructing our frameworks of knowledge and values, these ordered and pseudo-enduring constructions are merely "fabrications" and "lies." According to Nietzsche's narrative of Vedāntic thought, for which he credits the works of his former classmate Deussen, this rejection of convenient philosophical fabrications led ancient Indian thinkers to even deny the reality of the ego, a denial that students of Buddhism will recognize as well, a "triumph," he says that is perfectly fastidious in its "mockery" of "reason" (Nietzsche 1967b: 118). But this very purity of spirit falls into the fateful philosophers' trap of pretending that there is such a thing as a "pure, will-less, painless, timeless knowing subject" that does not actively interpret and will in the very act of seeing (Nietzsche 1967b: 119). We must also realize that these fabricated frameworks that we construct are "lies that make life possible," since it is precisely such "error" that is a "condition" of life (Nietzsche 1964b: 164). Now, like other priests, in their own particular way of embodying the ascetic ideal, Buddhists only apparently turn away from worldly entanglements, but in actuality gain something. By focusing on the eradication of pain and not the moral legislation of others, Buddhism "prescribes life in the open, a life of travel, moderation" and understands goodness as "health," and thus, despite what they may say, actually makes service to the ego a "duty" (Nietzsche 1974: 148–9). So far, so good; all of this, combined with a long history of cultivating philosophical skepticism toward the ideas of God and "sin" make Buddhism, for Nietzsche, "the only really positive religion to be found in history" (Nietzsche 1974: 147). Setting all this into motion makes the Buddha, furthermore, a genuine "physician of souls." But still, for one thing, as the portrayal comes to a head in *The Antichrist*, the oversensitivity to pain that grounds the motives of Buddhism must be fundamentally a "hatred of reality," an "anguish" and a tendency to become "deprecated by the self-preservative instinct" (Nietzsche 1974: 165–6). This anguish makes Buddhism in the long run a "tired" and "passive" form of nihilism that cannot muster the "enhanced power of spirit" necessary for the revaluation of values that Europe must face.[4] Buddhism refuses, that is, to return to the world of will, perspective, judgment, legislation and creativity with the strength of spirit that would enable it to suffer its losses and ennoble human beings in the effort. This sentiment is fully given expression in *Beyond Good and Evil*, where Nietzsche says that, "no longer like Buddha and Schopenhauer, under the dominion and delusion of morality," he represents "the most world-approving, exuberant and vivacious man" who not only tolerates the world but wills it again and again throughout eternity, for others certainly, but also for himself, because he "always requires himself anew—and makes himself necessary" (Nietzsche 1964a: 74).

And it is at this pivotal juncture that the distinction between "weak" and "strong" forms of pessimism is so meaningful. Nietzsche first makes this distinction in the preface to the second edition of *The Birth of Tragedy*. There, he characterizes a pessimism of weakness as "a sign of decline, decay, degeneration, weary and weak instincts—as it once was in India and now is, to all appearances, among us, 'modern' men and Europeans" (Nietzsche 1967a: 17) By contrast, a pessimism of strength is "an intellectual predilection for the hard, gruesome, evil, problematic nature of existence, prompted by well-being, by overflowing health, by the fullness of existence" (Nietzsche 1967a: 17) Now, is Ivan Soll (1990: 115) pointed out, this distinction does not actually have so much to do with a variance of "descriptive" or "evaluative content" in the two pessimisms, for they both find the world predominantly and inevitably painful and life as lacking in any overarching, objective meaning. Even in *The Birth of Tragedy*, the difference between these kinds of pessimism really comes down to how Schopenhauer thought tragedy was intended to inspire a "denial of the will to live," while Nietzsche found in it a special artistic form, combining the Dionysian and Apollinian aesthetic sensibilities in a triumphant justification of life, even with all its pain. But here, in the mid 1880's, Nietzsche is overtly locating the "pessimism of weakness" in ancient India. In the case of Buddhism, its causes are frequently identified in the philosopher's *corpus* with, as we have already seen, the "over-spiritualized" and "too sensitive" attitude towards pain that focuses all the practitioner's efforts around avoiding it, preventing it, eliminating its root cause in "desire," and turning away from it in a lifestyle of "moderation." Nietzsche just as consistently claims in his late writings that, in Buddhism's case, this hypersensitivity and aversion to pain are rooted in diet; the prolific consumption of rice and strict vegetarianism mandated by Buddhist practice lead to "narcotic modes of thought and feeling," indolence and faint-heartedness in the face of suffering (Nietzsche 1964b: 180).[5] In any event, these central tenets of Buddhism that make of suffering not something to be joyfully embraced, affirmed and triumphed over but the fundamental problem of life that is to be solved, or better dissolved with the eradication of desire, make the teaching, for all its merits, one that Europe must in its coming battle with nihilism forge past, and not accede to.

As mentioned in the opening of this essay, contemporary scholars who have inquired into both Nietzsche's reception of South Asian Buddhism and those who wish to create some comparative bridges between Nietzschean and early Buddhist thought have tended towards a reconciliation of their views. For all his exceptional interpretive critiques of Nietzsche's hermeneutic treatment of Buddhism, Hulin (1993: 72) at some points suggests that Nietzsche's attitude about Buddhist nihilism would have been different had he distinguished between strict monastic Buddhism and lay practice, for which dietary and moral restrictions are far more lenient. Morrison's sometimes strained reading goes so far as to suggest that the elimination of desire was not really the aim of Buddhist practice, but instead they strove for a transformation of desire that would enable individuals to "overcome themselves," that is, to overcome their enslavement to appetite, something that Nietzsche could endorse. These various attempts at rapprochement may not, it seems to me, be able in the end to eradicate the differences between Nietzschean and early Buddhist ideals. It is impossible, given all that Nietzsche writes, to imagine that the *Übermensch* could remain a mendicant who cultivates infinite compassion for all beings. And it is just as impossible to cast the Buddhist *arhant* or *bodhisattva* as a creative artist who takes it upon herself to autonomously legislate and enunciate values for the future of civilization, at least as Nietzsche envisions this. But rather than delve into this contrast directly, it will be more informative and interesting to concentrate on Nietzsche's basic characterization of Buddhism as a "type" of nihilism that commendably shuns ideas of transcendence and morality given the scholastic wisdom it has cultivated, but in the end regrettably fully embraces life-denial in its worldless *nirvāṇa*. As we focus on this issue, comprehending what early Buddhists themselves said about nihilism, or their formulation of what nihilism is, will shed the most light on the intellectual relationship between "the awakened one" and the "philosopher with a hammer." What we will find is that what early Buddhists took to be nihilism was in fact the very kind of life the Nietzsche, with important qualifications to be sure, idealized, namely the world-inhabiting life of constant flux and the affirmation of powers of vitality. In denying that they were "nihilists," it was this world-enmeshed affirmation of impermanent physical life that the Buddhists took to be nihilism. Now, the Buddhists also rejected, and here is what Nietzsche complimented them for, the notion of an enduring soul that had to be liberated from bodily existence. But the Buddhists did not call this latter kind of spiritualism nihilism, but rather described it as the error of "eternalism." This fundamental irreconcilability of Buddha's and Nietzsche's conceptions of nihilism and the stark contrast that this irreconcilability entails for what kind of human life they respectively valued seem to drive a wedge between their thought that no subtleties of comparative prodding can smooth over in any credible way.

The Buddha's Middle Path and the Life of Will as Nihilism

Given the Buddha's own life-story, whether partly mediated through the early *Discourses* of the Pāli scriptures or in the legendary second-century biography *Buddhacārita*, it is surely tempting to represent the founder of the tradition as someone who "overcame" nihilism after a prolonged period of extreme and fruitless asceticism. Giving in to this temptation has been, in part, what has prompted modern scholars to argue that there is more affinity between Buddhist and Nietzschean thought than at first meets the eye. But taking this tack runs up against a stubborn motif of early Buddhist texts and philosophical reflection, namely that the advocates of the tradition in this period rejected the idea that Buddhism was a nihilism of any sort, and insisted that nihilism, as they understood it, was not to be "overcome" but avoided. Though nihilism may have been a stage that Siddārtha Gautama passed through in his own journey toward enlightenment, early Buddhists do not believe it to be a necessary feature or stage of either a person's or a civilization's life, but instead an intellectual and spiritual error that, far from being inevitable, is best ruled out from the beginning.

The very first discourse of the Pāli scriptures, the *Dhammacakkapavattana* (*Turning the Wheel of Dharma*) *Sutta* identifies two "extremes" (*antā*) that represent alternative ways to view and live in the world. The first is "pursuit of sensual enjoyment" (*kāmasukhallikānuyoga*), and, while practiced by "common people," it is ultimately grounded in the philosophical conviction that no permanent soul exists (*natthitā*) that will survive bodily death, and so one should enjoy oneself while one can (Bodhi (trans.) 2005: 75). The other extreme is called "pursuit of ascetic self-mortification" (*atthakillamathānuyoga*), which affirms the existence of an eternal soul (*atthitā*) and so dedicates those who renounce the life of the home to practices that supposedly liberate this soul from impermanent physical existence (Bodhi (trans.) 2005: 75). It is especially important to note, as mentioned above, that both of these supposedly "extremist" ways to live are, the Buddha pleads, "not to be followed" (*na sevitabbā*). We shall return to why these errant ways of living, particularly the "nihilist" way, should not be followed shortly. But it is important, with regard to early Buddhist thinking, to take stock of which of these "extremes" is dubbed "nihilist" and why. Because the hedonic materialist specifically denies the existence of a putative entity, that being an "eternal soul," his conviction is called by the Buddha the view of "non-existence" (*natthitā*).[6] This should not confuse us into thinking that one who holds that an eternal soul does exist (*atthitā*) is correct because of the mere positivity of the thesis, for such a view is considered by Buddhists to be demonstrably and even obviously false, particularly, the Buddhist philosophical commentaries assert, because no one ever experiences such an eternal self. But why, in that case, does the Buddha call someone who believes that only the physical body constitutes a person a "nihilist?"

According to the early Buddhist framework, "nihilism" (*natthitāvāda*) is also often labeled "the doctrine of annihilationism" (*ucchedavāda*). In the simplest sense, *ucchedavāda* represents, as noted, the belief that any given individual's existence and consciousness is terminated upon their bodily death. But much more than this is involved. The *Acela Sutta* clarifies that the annihilationist holds that, because physical matter, including the physical matter the makes up the body, undergoes constant change, and so what we consider a "person" is always in flux, the effects of an individual's deeds do not in any literal way fall on the same individual who initiated the actions leading to them.[7] There is at once a basic philosophical mistake in such a perspective on personhood as well as a practical attitude that undermines the very possibility of moral life. The philosophical problem is that the denial that the effects of an agent's acts fall on the agent is tantamount to a more general a-causlism, as it implies that causal processes cannot be intelligibly discerned or tracked in nature or conduct. More importantly, believing in *ucchedavāda* would uproot any motive for a person to observe moral norms. As the well-known first century Abhidharma interpretation of the Buddhist "no-self" theory, the *Milindapannha*, elaborates, an adherent of "annihilationism" would defend his theft of a neighbor's mangos in a courtroom by saying that the "person" who stole the fruit is not the same "person" who was accused of the crime, and so the defendant should not be convicted (Rhys Davids (trans.) 1890: 112). "Annihilationists" are, owing to their wayward conception of causality, thus given to simply enjoying the hedonic pleasures of life without worrying about their consequences, about moral duties, or about what kinds of conduct do or don't lead to peace of mind.

Now, the corrective to the annihilationist position, for early Buddhists, was not to affirm the substantial and enduring existence of the person or agent, for this would be a concession to the "eternalists" and their conception of the enduring soul. Instead, annihiliationism is exposed as an errant set of beliefs and practices by rightly comprehending the nature of causality. This "right view" of causality was called by the Buddha "causally conditioned co-arising" (*paticcasamuppada*).[8] The most general idea of this formula in early Theravāda literature had to do with causal regularity, the linkage of certain causes with certain effects and the absence of those very effects in the absence of their causes.[9] It is indeed this very kind of causal regularity that underwrites the Buddha's "Four Noble Truths," which claim that pain is always caused by desire, and so if one eliminates desire, one will eliminate the most difficult kind of suffering of life, the suffering we feel about our own impermanence and the impermanence of all we hold dear. More specifically, "causally conditioned co-arising" is for the Buddha the "twelve-limbed" (*dvādasāṅga*) chain of rebirth, beginning with persistent ignorance of the nature of things, proceeding to a persistent clinging to sensation, desire and action and resulting in the persistent iteration of rebirth and redeath in the world (Bodhi (trans.) 2005: 75). It is because psychophysical life can be understood as a consistent connection of causes and effects that one individual's deeds can be distinguished from those of another individual, that moral responsibility can be tracked through the deeds of persons, and that we can arrive at an understanding of what kinds of conduct will bring us happiness and unhappiness. The insight into psychophysical causation will certainly, early Buddhist thinkers maintain, disabuse us of the illusions of an "eternal soul," for it will show that all of our states of sensation, thinking, feeling and acting are dependent on bodily processes and contact with the world, and so none of our experience can be attributed to some immaterial "soul."[10] At the same time, however, the causal regularity of *paticcasamuppada* itself cannot be doubted, for if it were false, then all justifications for both moral life and Buddhist practice would simply fall apart. Given the early Buddhists' intellectual context and framework, then, it is the correct analysis of causality that will prevent us from becoming nihilists.[11]

What the nihilist, as the early Buddhists conceive of one, does not understand in particular about psychophysical life is how "volitional formations" (*saṅkhāra*) not only persist but also accrete in the passage of time, and how, in virtue of this process, they perpetuate the rebirth cycle. We are not, after all, merely sensing and feeling bodies, but also the kinds of creatures that, in response to the things and persons in our environment, build up attitudinal and actional habits. These habituated likes and dislikes, attractions and aversions, loves, hatreds and indifferences lead us to act in increasingly characteristic ways as time proceeds, acquisitively pursuing in some cases, avoiding or battling in others, and ignoring still other experiences as unimportant to us. The constitution of these *saṅkhāra* will be unique to each individual, of course, depending on her past. The two most important features of these psychophysical "formations" from the standpoint of our inquiry are their volitional, or willing, nature and their key role in facilitating the process of rebirth. The *Suttas* of the *Saṃyutta Nikāya* directly define mental formations as the six kinds of volition (*cetanā*) that are associated with each sense, seeing, smelling, hearing, tasting, touching, and inner states of feeling, and that these volitions are sparked by the body's contact with things (Bodhi (trans.) 2005: 337). These complexes of volition, which are also classified into bodily, verbal and mental formations of will, ossify into psychological dispositions, and this is precisely what is meant by *saṅkhāra* (Bodhi (trans.) 2005: 333). Now, when a certain individual dies with a remainder of unresolved, unfulfilled or un-pacified desires still festering, it is precisely these leftover complexes that, with her persisting attachments to the world and life, cause the birth of another individual who inherits them. The character of the new individual's life, their environing circumstances, bodily makeup, desires, attitudes, aims, moral character and so on will all depend on the specific quantities of "light" and "dark" *kamma* or "intended deeds" that have accreted through these volitional formations.[12] It is because intentions and deeds have different degrees of moral value, with those manifesting egoistic and acquisitive desires being "impure" (*akuśala*) and those that are selfless, generous and compassionate being "pure" (*kuśala*) that *kamma* of respectively "light" and "dark" admixtures forms. And so, because they do not understand the nature of causality and how causality operates in persistent psychophysical habits that can lead to either greater or lesser degrees of happiness, "annihilationists" flagrantly disregard morality. And it is for the same reason, the Buddha insists, that "annihilationists" do not accept the reality or appreciate the gravity of the rebirth process, having no regard for the extent to which merely pleasure or power-seeking conduct will, in the long run, cause both frustration for oneself and others in this life and bring about even further, and inestimable, difficulties for sentient beings in future generations. If there is, so to speak, "nothing" beyond the present moment or present life, the will of the body, senses, words and ideas shall make a chaotic havoc out of life.

Nietzsche was not wrong in saying, as was shown above, that Buddhists did ultimately think of both "good" and "evil" deeds as habituated attachments to worldly existence. It was for this reason that he concluded Buddhists exhibited, especially for an otherwise ascetic movement, a remarkable lack of moralistic *ressentiment* toward the "aristocratic" classes compared to Christianity. Indeed, Nietzsche often included in this evaluation the observation that Buddha himself came from the aristocratic warrior class to begin with. However, the fact that Buddhists aimed for release from all desirous attachments did not imply that they showed no preference for intentions and deeds they considered moral over those they considered immoral. They excoriate the "annihilationists" frequently precisely because of their dismissal of morality out of a rejection of consequences. Moreover, it should be stressed, the pinnacle of Buddhist cultivation is the elimination of volitions (*cetanā*), and through this elimination the dissolving of "mental formations" (*saṅkhāra*). The elimination, or "extinguishing" (*nirvāṇa*) of these volitional complexes, the "wills," of a person will bring an entire heritage of causally connected rebirths to an end, and with that, liberation from rebirth. Those, on the other hand, who, whether out of ignorance or willfully, proliferate the continued consolidation and even new formation of volitional complexes shall continue, as the Buddha vividly says, to "tumble down the precipice of birth, aging and death, they tumble down the precipice of sorrow, lamentation, pain, dejection and despair. They…are not freed from suffering" (Bodhi (trans.) 2005: 362).

It is surely the case that the Buddhists saw themselves, in denouncing the doctrines of "eternalists" and "annihilationists," as contesting with other schools of philosophical thought and praxis and thereby establishing some kind of "middle ground" between them. As Hulin (1993: 66) rightly notes, Nietzsche, probably due to the mischaracterizations of other nineteenth century Orientalists, exaggerates the age of Indian civilization and with it the representation of how the Buddhists triumphed over nihilism at a culmination of that long history. Indeed the earliest generations of Buddhists are closer to the beginning of the "age of the ascetics" (*śramana*) than they were to the beginning of it as a matter of history. But what is of greatest import to us in the context of this inquiry is the stance that Buddhists took to what they considered to be "nihilism." To them, nihilism was the naturalistic rejection of causal continuity, of moral consequences and of rebirth that prompted people to value only the present of their present lives. We will not try here to adjudicate which of these two seminal, transformative figures, the Buddha or Nietzsche, had the "correct" interpretation of nihilism. But, given Nietzsche's well-known skepticism about the "reality" of regular causation, his rejection of the "good" and "evil" dichotomy as anything more than the shifting historico-cultural ideas of those vying for power, his spurning of "spiritualistic" ideas like that of the afterlife and his council for human beings to willfully embrace their earthly and painful lives, it is not hard to imagine that, had their chronological lives on the world stage been somehow reversed, Siddārtha Gautama would have branded Nietzsche a "nihilist" too. But Buddhism, he may have in these hypothetically reversed historical circumstances argued, does not take human beings through and past this "stage" of nihilism in their individual or collective civilizational lives, but rather helps them see the errors of nihilism so it can be avoided. The diametrically opposed conceptions of nihilism, and therefore the sharply contrasting ideals for life espoused in early Buddhist and Nietzschean thought should give anyone who wishes to find affinities between them much pause. For all the great limitations of Nietzsche's own comprehension of Buddhism, his perspicacity regarding the underlying motives of their different philosophical orientations made him perhaps a better judge of his relationship to Buddhism than some modern comparativists. For while he had, in his own mind, sound reasons for admiring the tradition, he saw all too well that the *arhant* and the *Übermensch* were most definitely not after the same goals in life.

Nietzsche and Early Buddhism: The Questions of Influence and Resonance

In light of all that we have examined here, there is little danger in saying that the figure of Buddha and the tradition of early Theravāda, at least as far as Nietzsche understood them, did exercise some influence on his works. We can see him wrestling with what he believed to be the relative strengths and weaknesses of the Buddha's teaching for his entire active philosophical life. He surely envisions Buddhism as fitting into his overall picture of the "ascetic life" but definitely as an atypical representative of it, especially to the extent that it seemingly rejects the transcendental ideas of God and the moralistic absolute dualism of "good" and "evil." He strongly suspects that the Buddhist ideal of *nirvāṇa* is the quintessential manifestation of decadent world and life-denial, but comes over time to appreciate that some senses of "nothingness" in the Buddhist tradition, especially those which represent the universe as eternal and therefore not tending toward any teleological end, have some affinity with the way he sometimes thinks of "eternal recurrence." He unquestionably considers Buddhists nihilists, but finds them to be entirely laudable ones right up until the point where they ultimately refuse to willfully embrace the pain of existence and reassert themselves in the world of competing powers. Most importantly, the Buddha and his teachings provide Nietzsche with a template for an historical and transformational "type" of nihilism that surpasses "priestly" forms of nihilism but in its turn is surpassed by his own vision. With the possible exception of Epicurus, no other historical philosopher could fulfill this role, or manifest this "type" of nihilism as the Buddha could. None of this entails that Nietzsche had a studied familiarity with or a reliable understanding of early Buddhist thought. The evidence suggests not merely that he could claim neither of these, but that the resources were abundantly available to him for have learned far more about South Asian Buddhism than he bothered to. In comparison to other seminal nineteenth century Continental thinkers, Hegel read a much greater volume of Orientalist literature than Nietzsche, and Nietzsche was not in his own systematic reflections influenced by Brāhmiṇical or Buddhist thought to anywhere near the degree that Schopenhauer had been. But none of these circumstances obviates the fact, as said earlier, that the Buddha and his teachings remained important for Nietzsche from at least the late 1860's right up until the most unfortunate breakdown of his active life in 1889. One need not, after all, accurately or completely understand a set of ideas in order to be heavily influenced by them oneself.[13] The Buddha was, in many senses of the term, a pivotal figure in Nietzsche's construction of nihilisms old and new, ancient Indian and Greek and modern European.

As was also mentioned at the beginning of this essay, modern scholars such as Nishitani Kenji, Abe Masao, André van der Braak and certainly Graham Parkes have, given the unique classical and recent contours of East Asian Buddhist thought, far more viable grounds to argue for areas of substantive philosophical dialogue between Nietzsche and Zen. But, given what we have covered here, far less affinity seems to obtain between ancient South Asian and Nietzschean thought, perhaps even less than Nietzsche himself believed. One need look no further for the great divergence between early Buddhist values and those of Nietzsche than their respective definitions of "nihilism," their assessments of the possibilities of willing and the projects of their ideal figures, the mendicant renouncer and the creative world-affirmer, to appreciate the starkness of these differences. Indeed, even those facets of Buddhism that Nietzsche admired may well not have as closely approximated his avowed ideals as he hoped. True enough, the early Buddhists did not believe in one divine being, one heaven, one hell and one afterlife; instead they everywhere proclaim the existence of many of each. True, the Buddhists advocated compassion even for evildoers, but that did not prevent them from devoting vast bodies of texts to finely detailing the distinctions between deeds of moral merit and deeds of unqualified impurity, all for the purpose of persuading monks and laypeople to choose the former. True, the Buddhists rejected the idea that the universe was created by any divine being for any specific human-centered purpose, but this did not prevent them from believing that certain acts would eventually bring woe on every person who did them and certain other acts were signs of objectively verifiable virtue for any human being who did them. While it is certainly possible to entertain great admiration for both the Buddha and Nietzsche, and mostly for very different reasons, it is simply too much of a stretch of the hermeneutic imagination, even one which makes all the appropriate qualifications, to envision them as philosophical or practical allies.

Notes

1 This chapter was first published as "The Pivot of Nihilism: Buddha Through Nietzsche's Eyes," in *Nietzsche and the Philosophers*, Mark T. Conard, (ed.), Lanham, Maryland: Lexington Books, 2017, 104–20. The essay is republished here with the permission of Taylor and Francis, L.L.C.

2 When not so indicated through citation, all translations from German or Pāli in this essay are my own.

3 In his early essay on Schopenhauer as his philosophical "educator," Nietzsche (1983: 192) compares European Indologists of his generation in the presence of ancient Indian texts to animals listening to the lyre.

4 This sentiment is expressed in Nietzsche's very late *Nachlass*; quoted in Halbfass (1988: 127).

5 Hulin (1993: 74) notes that the lethal combination of rice and opium in ancient India that leads to such weak characters is paralleled, according to Nietzsche, in modern Europe by the indulgence in pear potatoes and brandy. Nietzsche (1974: 148) does however praise Buddhism for prohibiting intoxicating drink.

6 This definition is explicitly given in the *Avijjapacaya Sutta* (Bodhi (trans.) 2003: 575).

7 From the *Acela Sutta* (Bodhi (trans.) 2003: 545).

8 This is my translation of the formula, which is more commonly rendered "dependent arising" or "dependent origination" by hosts of other scholars. The absolutive *paticca* identifies not just logical conditions, but causal ones, and the "arising" (*uppada*) that these causal conditions bring about is not of lone things, but of things together, or in their collectivity (*sam*). Detailed specificity about

these terms in translation is necessary, in my view, to disambiguate the idea as it is articulated by Buddhist thinkers.

9 This is the well-known, and often chanted, principle: "This existing, that comes to be; this arising, that arises. This not existing, that does not come to be; this ceasing, that ceases." (*imasmim sati idam hoti / imass upada idam upajjati / imasmim asati idam ahoti / imassa nirodha idam nirujjhati /*) from the *Nidānasaṃyutta* (Bodhi (trans.) 2003: 505).

10 From the *Saṃyutta Nikāya* 12:20 (Bodhi (trans.) 2005: 354–5).

11 This is the central message of the one-page but highly valued *Kaccānagotta Sutta*, where the Buddha announces that one who maintains the "middle" view of causally conditioned co-arising will be tempted neither by the eternalist's conviction that existence is some kind of enduring spiritual principle or the annihiliationist's belief that there is nothing whose existence persists for more than one instant (Bodhi (trans.) 2005: 356–7).

12 This is all drawn out in some detail in the *Kammavagga Suttas* of the *Anguttara Nikāya* (Bodhi (trans.) 2005: 155–6).

13 I argued more extensively a decade and a half ago in my study of Schopenhauer's engagement with early Indian thought that "interpretive accuracy" is a fallacious hermeneutic criterion in determining the influence of one thinker on another. I then demonstrated that we need only determine whether a thinker was familiar enough with the ideas of another, and whether that familiarity had some "thematic effect" on the former's wirings, to adjudicate influence (Berger 2004: 1–26).

Bibliography

Anālayo, B. (2017), "The Luminous Mind in Theravāda and Dharmaguptaka Discourses," *Journal of the Oxford Center for Buddhist Studies*, 13: 10–51.

Argawal, M. M. (1992), "Arjuna's Moral Predicament," in B. K. Matilal (ed.), *Moral Dilemmas in the Mahābhārata*, 129–42, Shimla: Indian Institute of Advanced Study.

Ashton, G. (2014), "Role Ethics or Ethics of Role-Play? A Comparative Critical Analysis of Confucianism and the *Bhagavad Gītā*," *Journal of Dao*, 13: 1–21.

Bartlett, F. (1932), *Remembering: A Study in Experiential and Social Psychology*. Cambridge: Cambridge University Press.

Berger, D. L. (1998), "Illocution, No-Theory and Practice in Nagarjuna's Skepticism: Reflections on the Vigrahavyavartani," *The Paideia Archive: Twentieth World Congress of Philosophy*, 24: 7–13. Available online: http://www.bu.edu/wcp/Papers/Asia/AsiaBerg.htm.

Berger, D. L. (2004), "The Veil of Māyā:" *Schopenhauer's System and Early Indian Thought*, Binghamton: Global Academic Publications.

Berger, D. L. (2008), "Relational and Intrinsic Moral Roots: A Brief Contrast of Confucian and Hindu Concepts of Duty," *Journal of Dao*, 7: 157–63.

Berger, D. L. (2010), "Acquiring Emptiness: Interpreting Nāgārjuna's MMK 24:18," *Philosophy East and West*, 60 (1): 40–64.

Berger, D. L. (2011), "A Reply to Garfield and Westerhoff on Acquiring Emptiness," *Philosophy East and West*, 61 (2): 368–72.

Berger, D. L. (2015), *Encounters of Mind: Luminosity and Personhood in Indian and Chinese Thought*, Albany: State University of New York Press.

Bernier, F. (1914), *Travels in the Mogul Empire, A.D. 1656–68*, trans. A. Constable, London and New York: H. Milford & Oxford University Press.

Bhandare, S. (1993), *Memory in Indian Epistemology: Its Nature and Status*, Delhi: Sri Satguru Publications.

Bhattacharya, K., E. H. Johnston, and A. Kunst. trans. (1990), *The Dialectical Method of Nāgārjuna*, 3rd ed., Delhi: Motilal Banarsidass.

Bilimoria, P. (1997), "On Śaṅkara's Attempted Reconciliation of 'You' and 'I' (*Yuṣmadasmatsamanvaya*)," in P. Bilimoria and J. N. Mohanty (eds.), *Relativism, Suffering and Beyond: Essays in Memory of Bimal K. Matilal*, 252–77, Oxford and Delhi: Oxford University Press.

Bodhi, B. (2003), *The Connected Discourses of the Buddha: A New Translation of the Samyutta Nikaya*, Boston: Wisdom Publications.

Bodhi, B., trans. (2005), *In the Buddha's Words: An Anthology of Discourses from the Pāli Canon*, Boston: Wisdom Publications.

Burton, D. F. (1999), *Emptiness Appraised: A Critical Study of Nāgārjuna's Philosophy*, Richmond Surrey: Curzon Press.

Campbell, J. (1997), "The Structure of Time in Autobiographical Memory," *European Journal of Philosophy*, 5: 105–18.

Campbell, S. (2003), *Relational Remembering: Rethinking the Memory Wars*, Landham: Rowman and Littlefield.

Caputo, J. D., ed. (1997a), *Deconstruction in a Nutshell: A Conversation with Jacques Derrida*, New York: Fordham University Press.

Caputo, J. D. (1997b), *The Prayers and Tears of Jacques Derrida: Religion without Religion*, Bloomington and Indianapolis: Indiana University Press.

Chadha, M. (2006), "Yet Another Attempt to Salvage Pristine Perception," *Philosophy East and West*, 56 (2): 333–42.

Chakrabarti, A. (1992), "I Touch What I Saw," *Philosophy and Phenomenological Research*, 52 (1): 107–20.

Chakrabarti, A. (2000), "Against Immaculate Perception: Seven Reasons for Eliminating *Nirvikalpa* Perception from Nyāya," *Philosophy East and West*, 50 (1): 1–8.

Chatterjea, T. (2002), *Knowledge and Freedom in Indian Philosophy*, London: Lexington Books.

Cornell, D. (1992), *The Philosophy of the Limit*, New York and London: Routledge.

Coward, H. (1990), *Derrida and Indian Philosophy*, Albany: State University of New York Press.

Cox, C. (1999), "Saṅghabhadra *Nyāyānusāra*," in K. H. Potter (ed.), *Encyclopedia of Indian Philosophy*, vol. 8 of 9, 650–716, Delhi: Motilal Banarasidass.

Critchley, S. (1999), *The Ethics of Deconstruction: Derrida and Levinas*, West Lafeyette: Purdue University Press.

Derrida, J. (1994), *Specters of Marx: The State of the Debt, he Work of Mourning and the New International*, trans. P. Kamuf, London and New York: Routledge.

Derrida, J. (1995), *The Gift of Death*, trans. D. Wills, Chicago and London: University of Chicago Press.

Derrida, J. (1997), *Politics of Friendship*, trans. G. Collins, London and New York: Verso.

Deurlinger, J. (2003), *Indian Buddhist Theories of Persons: Vasubandhu's Refutation of the Theory of a Self*, London and New York: Curzon.

Deutsch, E. (1973), *Advaita Vedānta: A Philosophical Reconstruction*, Honolulu: University of Hawaii Press.

Dreyfus, G. B. J. (1997), *Recognizing Reality: Dharmakīrti's Philosophy and Its Tibetan Interpretations*, Albany: State University of New York Press.

Engle, S. (1999), *Context Is Everything: The Nature of Memory*, New York: W. H. Freeman Press.

Frauwallner, E. (1995), *Studies in Abhidharma Literature and the Origins of Buddhist Philosophical Systems*, trans. S. F. Kidd and E. Steinkellner, Albany: State University of New York Press.

Frazer, C. (2016), *The Philosophy of the Mozi: The First Consequentialists*, New York: Columbia University Press.
Gandhi, M. K. (2009), *The Bhagavad Gita According to Gandhi*, Berkeley: North Atlantic Books.
Ganeri, J. (2000), "Cross-Modality and the Self," *Philosophy and Phenomenological Research*, 61 (3): 639–57.
Ganeri, J. (2012), "Buddhist No-Self: An Analysis and Critique," in I. Kuznetsova, J. Ganeri and C. Ram-Prasad (eds.), *Hindu and Buddhist Ideas in Dialogue: Self and No-Self*, 63–76, London and New York: Routledge.
Garfield, J. L. (1995), *The Fundamental Wisdom of the Middle Way: Nāgārjuna's Mūlamadhyamakakārikā*, Oxford: Oxford University Press.
Garfield, J. L. (2010), "Taking Conventional Truth Seriously: Authority Regarding Deceptive Reality," in G. Newland and T. Tillemans (eds.), *Moonshadows: Conventional Truth in Buddhist Philosophy*, 23–38, Oxford: Oxford University Press.
Garfield, J. L. and J. Westerhoff (2011), "Acquiring the Notion of a Dependent Designation: A Response to Douglas L. Berger," *Philosophy East and West*, 61 (2): 365–7.
Gascoigne, B. (1971), *The Great Moguls*, New York: Carroll & Graff Publishers.
Graham, A. C. (1964), "The Logic of the Mohist *Hiao Ch'u*," *T'oung Pao*, 51 (1): 1–54.
Gregory, P. N. (1995), *Inquiry into the Origin of Humanity: An Annotated Translation of Tsung-Mi's Yuan Jen Lun with a Modern Commentary*, Honolulu: University of Hawai'i Press.
Guo, Q. (2007), "Is Confucian Ethics a Consanguinism?" *Journal of Dao*, 6: 21–37.
Gupta, B. (1988), *The Disinterested Witness: A Fragment of Advaita Vedānta Phenomenology*, Evanston: Northwestern University Press.
Gupta, B. (2003), *Cit: Consciousness*, Oxford: Oxford University Press.
Habata, H. (2007), *Die Zentralasiatischen Sanskrit-Fragmente des Mahāparinirvāṇa Mahāsūtra*, Marburg: Indica et Tibeta Verlag.
Hakeda, Y. S. (1967), *The Awakening of Faith*, New York: Columbia University Press.
Halbfass, W. (1988), *India and Europe: An Essay in Understanding*, Albany: State University of New York Press.
Halbfass, W. (1992), *On Being and What There Is: Classical Vaiśeṣika and the History of Indian Ontology*, Albany: State University of New York Press.
Halbfass, W. (1993), *Tradition and Reflection: Explorations in Indian Thought*, Albany: State University of New York Press.
Harvey, P. (1995), *The Selfless Mind: Personality, Consciousness and Nirvana in Early Buddhism*, London and New York: Routledge.
Hasrat, B. J. (1982), *Dārāv Shikøh: Life and Works*, New Delhi: Munshiram Manoharlal Ltd.
Hattori, M., trans. (1968), *Dignāga on Perception: Being the Pratyakṣapariccheda of Dignāga's Pramāṇasamuccaya*, Cambridge, MA: Harvard University Press.

Hayes, R. (1988), *Dignaga on the Interpretation of Signs*, Dordrecht: Kluwer Academic Publications.

Herman, A. L. (1983), *An Introduction to Buddhist Thought: A Philosophic History of Indian Buddhism*, Lanham: University Press of America.

Holt, J. C. (1991), *The Buddha in the Crown*, New York: Oxford University Press.

Huang, C. C. (2010), "East Asian Conceptions of the Public and Private Realms," in K.-P. Yu, J. Tao and P. J. Ivanhoe (eds.), *Taking Confucian Ethics Seriously: Contemporary Theories and Applications*, 173–99, Albany: State University of New York Press.

Huang, Y. (2017). "Why an Upright Son Does not Disclose he Father Stealing a Sheep: A Neglected Aspect of the Confucian Conception of Filial Piety," *Asian Studiesī*, 5 (2): 15–45.

Hubbard, J. and P. L. Swanson, eds. (1997), *Pruning the Bodhi Tree: The Storm over Critical Buddhism*, Honolulu: University of Hawai'i Press.

Hulin, M. (1993), "Nietzsche and the Suffering of the Indian Ascetic," in G. Parkes (ed.), *Nietzsche and Asian Thought*, 64–75, Chicago: University of Chicago Press.

Inada, K. K., trans. (1970) *Nāgārjuna: A Translation of His Mūlamadhyamakakārikā with an Introductory Essay*, Tokyo: Hokuseido Press.

Jha, G., ed. (1963), *Padārthadharmasaṅgraha of Praśastapāda with Nyāyakandalī of Śrīdhara*, Benares: Benares Sanskrit University.

Jiang, T. (2006), *Context and Dialogue: Yogācāra Buddhism and Modern Psychology on the Subliminal Mind*, Honolulu: University of Hawai'i Press.

Johnston, E. H., ed. (1950), *Ratnagotravibhāga Mahāyānottaratantraśāstra* by Asanga, Patna: Bihar Research Society.

Jorgensen, J. (2018), "The Radiand Mind: Zhu Xi and the Chan Doctrine of *Tathāgatagarbha*" in J. Makeham (ed.), *The Buddhist Roots of Zhu Xi's Philosophical Thought*, 36–121, New York: Oxford University Press.

Kalupahana, D. J., trans. (1986), *Nāgārjuna: The Philosophy of the Middle Way*, Albany: State University of New York Press.

Kalapuhana, D. J. (1992), *A History of Buddhist Thought: Continuities and Discontinuities*, Honolulu: University of Hawai'i Press.

Kazim, M. M. (1865–73), *Ālamgirnāmah*, eds. M. K. Husain and A. Hai, *Bibliotheca Indica*, vol. 7, Calcutta: College Press.

King, S. B. (1991), *Buddha Nature*, Albany: State University of New York Press.

Kochmuttom, T. A. (1982), *A Buddhist Doctrine of Experience: A New Translation and Interpretation of the Works of Vasubandhu the Yogācārin*, Delhi: Motilal Banarasidass.

Krishna, D. (1991), "Adhyāsa–A Non-Advaitic Beginning in Śaṁkara Vedānta," in *Indian Philosophy: A Counter Perspective*, 156–63, Oxford and Delhi: Oxford University Press.

Krishna, D. (1991), *Indian Philosophy: A Counter-Perspective*, Oxford and New York: Oxford University Press.

Lamotte, É. (1954), "*Sur la formation du Mahāyāna*," in L. Schroeder (ed.), *Asiatica: Festschrift Friedrich Weller*, 377–96, Leipzig: Otto Harrassowitz.
Larson, G. J. (1995), *India's Agony over Religion*, Albany: State University of New York Press.
Liu, Q. (2007), "Confucianism and Corruption: An Analysis of Shun's Two Actions Described by Menciu," *Journal of Dao*, 6: 1–19.
Loy, D. (1987), "The Clôture of Deconstruction: a Māhāyana Critique of Derrida," *International Philosophical Quarterly*, 27 (1): 59–80.
Lusthaus, D. (1997), "Critical Buddhism and Returning to the Sources," in J. Hubbard and P. L. Swanson (eds.), *Pruning the Bodhi Tree: The Storm over Critical Buddhism*, 30–55, Honolulu: University of Hawai'i Press.
Magliola, R. (1984), *Derrida on the Mend*, West Lafayette: Purdue University Press.
Martin, C. B. and M. Deutscher (1966), "Remembering," *Philosophical Review*, 75: 161–96.
Martin, G. T. (1993), "Deconstruction and Breakthrough in Nietzsche and Nāgārjuna," in G. Parkes (ed.), *Nietzsche and Asian Thought*, 91–111, Chicago: University of Chicago Press.
Massignon, L. ([1926] 2003), 'An Experiment in Hindu-Muslim Unity,' in M. Waseem (ed. and trans.), *On Becoming an Indian Muslim: French Essays on Aspects of Syncretism*, New Delhi and Oxford: Oxford University Press.
Matilal B. K. (1986), *Perception: An Essay on Classical Indian Theories of Knowledge*, Oxford: Clarendon Press.
Matilal, B. K. (1990), *The Word and the World: India's Contribution to the Study of Language*, Oxford and Delhi: Oxford University Press.
Matilal, B. K. (1998), *The Character of Logic in India*, Albany: State University of New York Press.
Mayeda, S., ed. and trans. (1992), *A Thousand Teachings: The Upadeśasāhasri of Śaṅkara*, Albany: State University of New York Press.
McDermott, S. A. C., ed. (1970), *An Eleventh Century Buddhist Logic of Exists: Ratnakīrti's Kṣaṇabhaṅgasiddhiḥ Vyatirekātmikā*, Dordrecht: D. Reidel.
Mohanty, J. N. (1993a), "Can the Self Become an Object?" in P. Bilimoria (ed.), *Essays on Indian Philosophy: Traditional and Modern*, 68–74, Oxford and Delhi: Oxford University Press.
Mohanty, J. N. (1993b), "Nyāya Theory of Doubt," in P. Bilimoria (ed.), *Essays in Indian Philosophy: Traditional and Modern*, 101–25, Oxford and Delhi: Oxford University Press.
Mohanty, J. N. (1993c), *Essays on Indian Philosophy: Traditional and Modern*, Delhi: Oxford University Press.
Morrison, R. G. (1997), *Nietzsche and Buddhism: A Study in Nihilism and Ironic Affinities*, New York: Oxford University Press.
Murti, T. R. V. (1960), *The Central Philosophy of Buddhism: A Study of the Mādhyamika System*, London: George Allen & Unwin, Ltd.

Nagao, G. (1991), *Mādhyamika and Yogācāra*, trans. L. Kawamura, Albany: State University of New York Press.

Nandy, A. (1983), *The Intimate Enemy: The Loss and Discovery of Self under Colonialism*, Oxford and Delhi: Oxford University Press.

Ni, P. (2017), *Understanding the Analects of Confucius: A New Translation of Lunyu with Annotations*, Albany: State University of New York Press.

Nietzsche, F. (1964a), *Beyond Good and Evil*, trans. H. Zimmern, New York: Russell and Russell.

Nietzsche, F. (1964b), *The Joyful Wisdom*, trans. T. Common, New York: Russell and Russell.

Nietzsche, F. (1967a), *The Birth of Tragedy and the Case of Wagner*, trans. W. Kaufmann, New York: Random House.

Nietzsche, F. (1967b), *On the Genealogy of Morals / Ecce Homo*, trans. W. Kaufmann, New York: Random House.

Nietzsche, F. (1967c), *The Will to Power*, trans. W. Kaufmann and R. J. Hollingdale, London: Weidenfeld and Nicholson.

Nietzsche, F. (1974), *The Twilight of the Idols / The Antichrist*, trans. A. M. Ludovici, New York: Gordon Press.

Nietzsche, F. (1983), *Untimely Meditations*, trans. R. J. Hollingdale, Cambridge: Cambridge University Press.

Nietzsche, F. (1990), *Sämtliche Werke, Kritische Studienausgabe*, eds. G. Colli and M. Montinari, vol. 10 of 15, München: Deutscher Taschenbuch Verlag.

Olivelle, P., trans. (1996), *Upaniṣads*, Oxford and New York: Oxford University Press.

Olivelle, P., trans. (1999), *Dharmasūtras: The Law Codes of Ancient India*, New York: Oxford University Press.

Phillips, S. H. (1995), *Classical Indian Metaphysics*, Chicago and La Salle: Open Court Publishing.

Potter, K. H., ed. (1981), *The Encyclopedia of Indian Philosophies*, v. 3: *Advaita Vedānta up to Śaṅkara and His Pupils*, Delhi: Motilal Banarasidass.

Priestley, L. C. D. C. (1999), *Pudgalavāda Buddhism: The Reality of the Indeterminate Self*, Toronto: Centre for South Asian Studies, University of Toronto.

Radich, M. (2008), "The Doctrine of *Amalavijñāna* in Paramārtha (499–569) and Later Authors to Approximately 800 CE," *Zinbun*, 41: 45–174.

Ram-Prasad, C. (2012), "Self and Memory: Personal Identity and Unified Consciousness in Comparative Perspective," in Irina Kuznetsova, J. Ganeri and C. Ram-Prasad (eds.), *Hindu and Buddhist Ideas in Dialogue: Self and No-Self*, 129–46, London and New York: Routledge.

Rāmānuja (1992), *Śri Rāmānuja Gītā Bhāṣya*, trans. Swami Ādidevānanda, Madras: Sri Ramakrishna Math.

Rangarajan, L. N., ed. and trans. (1992), *Kautilya: The Arthashastra*, Penguin Classics, New Delhi: Penguin Books India.

Rao, V. S. (1969), *The Philosophy of the Sentence and Its Parts*, New Delhi: Munshiram Manoharial.

Reid, P. (2014), *Buddha Nature Sutras: Translations of the Nirvāṇa Sūtra, Śrimalādevi Sūtra and the Infinite Life Sūtra*, CreateSpace Independent Publishing Platform.

Rhys Davids, T. W., trans. (1890), *The Questions of King Milinda*, vol. 1 of 2, Oxford: Clarendon Press.

Robinson, R. H. (1964), *Early Mādhyamika in India and China*, Delhi, Varanasi and Patna: Motilal Banarasidass.

Rogacz, D. (2015), "Knowledge and Truth in the Thought of Jizang (549–623)," *The Polish Journal of the Arts and Culture*, 16 (4): 125–38.

Rospatt, A. von (1995), *The Buddhist Doctrine of Momentariness*, Stuttgart: Franz Steiner Verlag.

Rukmani, T. S. (1988), "Vijñānabhikṣu's Double-Reflection Theory of Knowledge in the Yoga System," *Journal of Indian Philosophy*, 16 (4): 367–76.

Salvini, M. (2011), "*Upādāyaprajñaptiḥ* and the Meaning of Absolutives: Grammar and Syntax in the Interpretation of Madhyamaka," *Journal of Indian Philosophy*, 39 (3): 229–44.

Sarkar, J. (1912–24), *A History of Aurungzeb*, vol. 2, New Delhi: Oriental Languages Ltd.

Sasaki, R. F. and T. Y. Kirchner (2009), *The Record of Linji*, Honolulu: University of Hawai'i Press.

Sastri, D. N. (1964), *The Philosophy of Nyāya-Vaiśeṣika and its Conflict with the Buddhist Dignāga School*, Delhi: Bharatiya Vidya Prakashan.

Schopen, G. (2000), "The Mahāyāna and the Middle Period in Indian Buddhism: Through a Chinese Looking Glass," *Eastern Buddhist*, 32 (2): 3–24.

Schopenhauer, A. ([1851] 1988), *Parerga und Paralipomena II*, Haffmans-Ausgabe, vol. 5, Zürich: Haffmans Verlag.

Schroeder, J. (2000), "Nāgārjuna and the Doctrine of Skillful Means," *Philosophy East and West*, 50 (4): 559–83.

Sharma, R. N., ed. (2003), *Manusmṛti*, trans. M. N. Dutt, Delhi: Chaukhamba Sanskrit Pratishthan.

Siderits, M. (1980), "The Madhyamaka Critique of Epistemology. I," *Journal of Indian Philosophy*, 8 (4): 307–35.

Siderits, M. (1981), "The Mādhyamika Critique of Epistemology II," *Journal of Indian Philosophy*, 9 (2): 121–80.

Siderits, M. (1997), "Matilal on Nāgārjuna," in J. N. Mohanty and P. Bilimoria (eds.), *Relativism, Suffering and Beyond: Essays in Memory of B. K. Matilal*, Oxford, Delhi and New York: Oxford University Press.

Siderits, M. (2003), "On the Soteriological Significance of Emptiness," *Contemporary Buddhism*, 4 (1): 9–23.

Siderits, M. and S. Katsura (2013), *Nāgārjuna's Middle Way: Mūlamadhyamakakārikā*, Somerville: Wisdom Publications.

Soll, I. (1990), "Pessimism and the Tragic View of Life: Reconsiderations of Nietzsche's *Birth of Tragedy*," in R. C. Solomon and K. M. Higgins (eds.), *Reading Nietzsche*, 104–31, Oxford: Oxford University Press.

Sprung, M., trans. (1979), *Ludic Exposition of the Middle Way: The Essential Chapters from the Prasannapadā of Candrakīrti*, Boulder: Prajñā Press.

Sprung, M. (1993), "Nietzsche's Trans-European Eye," in G. Parkes (ed.), *Nietzsche and Asian Thought*, Chicago: University of Chicago Press.

Taber, J. (2005), *A Hindu Critique of Buddhist Epistemology: Kumārila on Perception: The "Determination of Perception" Chapter of Kumārila Bhaṭṭa's Ślokavārttika*, London and New York: Routledge/Curzon.

Takasaki, J. (1966), *A Study on the Rantagotravibhaga (Uttaramantra): Being a Treatise on the Tathagatagarbha Theory of Mahayana Buddhism*, ed. Estremo Oriente, Rome: Instituto Italiano per il Medio.

Thakur, A. L., ed. (1967), *Nyāyasūtra* with *Bhāṣya* of Vātsyāyana, *Nyāyavārttika* of Uddyotakara, *Nyāyavārttikatātparyaṭikā* of Vācaspati Miśra and *Pariśuddhi* of Udayana, *Nyāyasūtra*, Darbangha: Mithila Institute.

The Koran (1999), trans. N. J. Danwood, London: Penguin.

Tripati, D., ed. (1989), *Ātmatattvaviveka* of Udayana with *Tātparya*, vol. 3 of 3, Calcutta: Calcutta Sanskrit College.

Tuck, A. (1990), *Comparative Philosophy and the Philosophy of Scholarship: On the Western Interpretation of Nāgārjuna*, New York: Oxford University Press.

Van der Braak, A. (2011), *Nietzsche and Zen: Self-Overcoming Without a Self*, Plymouth: Lexington Books.

Van Norden, B. (2009), *Mengzi: The Essential Mengzi: Selected Passages with Traditional Commentary*, Indianapolis: Hackett Publishing.

Walser, J. (2006), *Nāgārjuna in Context: Mahāyāna Buddhism and Early Indian Culture*, New York: Columbia University Press.

Warder, A. K. (1971), "The Concept of a Concept," *Journal of Indian Philosophy*, 1 (2): 181–96.

Westerhoff, J. (2018), *The Golden Age of Indian Buddhist Philosophy*, Cambridge: Oxford University Press.

Williams, P. M. (1981), "On the Abhidharma Ontology," *Journal of Indian Philosophy*, 9 (3): 227–57.

Yadav, B. S. (1992), "Methodic Deconstruction," in S. Biderman and B.-A. Scharfstein (eds.), *Interpretation in Religion*, 129–68, Leiden: E. J. Brill.

Yadav, B. S. (1994), "Vallabha's Positive Response to Buddhism," *Journal of Dharma*, 18 (2): 113–37.

Yadav, B. S. (2000), "Mispredicated Identity and Postcolonial Discourse," *Sophia*, 39 (1): 78–131.

Yadav, B. S. and W. C. Allen (1995), "Between Vasubandhu and Kumarila," *Journal of Dharma*, 20 (2): 154–77.*Bibliography*

Index

Abhidharma Buddhism 68, 70–2, 77, 88
Abhidharmakośa 93
Abhidharmakośabhāṣya 26, 40 n.6, 143 n.11
Acela Sutta 206
Acintyastava 73–4, 96
adharma
 and Nāgārjuna 132–3, 138–9
 as unrighteousness 105, 155
Advaita Vedānta 15–23, 47, 106, 110–12, 177–8, 189, 192–3
agency 19–20, 25–8, 36, 164
 action 15, 30, 45, 117, 125, 130, 133–40, 166–8, 172–3, 178
 agent 27, 35, 104, 111, 117, 206–7
 desireless action (*niṣkāma karma*) 150, 155–7, 166
Akutobhyā 75, 78
al-A'rāf 190
Ambedkar, Bhimrao R. 120–1, 122 nn.3–4, 124 n.25, 145 n.24
Analects (*Lun Yu*) 149, 162
annihilationism 206–8
The Antichrist 200–2
anvīkṣikī 106
aporia 125–9, 133, 140
appearance (*ābhāsa*) 19
Arjuna 149–60, 166–8, 171–3
Arthaśāstra 106, 136, 144 nn.20–21
Āryadeva 83
Ashton, Geoffrey 150, 157–9, 162, 171
ātman 15–23, 24–6, 29–33, 37–8, 65, 68, 102–3, 110–11, 156–8, 177, 181, 192
Ātmavādapratiṣedha 26–7, 39 n.4, 39–40 n.5
ātmology 103, 116
attachment 65, 85, 101, 116, 130–3, 141, 150–1, 179, 181, 183, 198, 200, 208–9
attraction 38, 208
Aurobindo Ghose 112–13
auto-apprehension (*svasaṃvedana*) 25, 27, 44
Avalokitavrata 82
aversion 34, 38, 203, 208
awareness 17, 21, 25, 27, 31–2, 34–7, 41–3, 115, 174–87, 192

Bartlett, Frederic 39 n.3
being 15–16, 21–2, 77, 102, 110–12, 115–20, 130–2, 137, 139–40, 142 n.9, 152, 155, 157, 159, 167–9, 176, 178, 181–7, 204, 210
Benveniste, Émile 141 n.3
Beyond Good and Evil 203
Bhagavad Gītā 149–60, 162–3, 165–7, 170–3
Bhāvaviveka 63, 67, 77–81, 92, 117, 124 n.19
Bilimoria, Purushottama 4, 123 n.15
The Birth of Tragedy 200, 203
bodhisattva 103, 117–20, 138, 186, 204
body 17–19, 23–5, 37–8, 110–11, 155–6
borrowed name (*jia ming*) 75–7, 91
brahman 15, 19–21, 41, 110, 115, 192, 196 nn.10–11
Brahmasūtrabhāṣya 15, 196 n.10
Brāhmin 19, 22–5, 33, 68, 78, 102, 106, 108, 112–14, 137, 139, 149, 151, 188–9, 198, 211
Bṛhadāraṇyakopaniṣad 115
Buddha 60, 65–71, 73–4, 79, 83–8, 91, 96, 105, 116–8, 120, 134, 137–8, 183, 197–212
Buddha Nature 175–7
Buddhaghoṣa 93
Buddhapālita 67, 80, 83, 100 n.10
Buddhapālitavṛtti 77, 78
buddhi 20, 31, 111
Buddhism 24–38, 43–7, 49–51, 59–60, 62–3, 65–9, 82, 89–93, 101–3, 114–21, 125, 130–40, 174–85, 197–212

Buddhist Logicians 42–6
Burton, David 59, 63, 71–2, 99 n.4

Cai Yuanpei 162
Campbell, Joseph 2
Campbell, Sue 40
Candragomin 64
Candrakīrti 6, 25, 59, 63–73, 75–88, 91–3, 97–8, 101–3, 115–17, 135–6
Caputo, John D. 141 n.2, 144 n.22
care 160–1, 169–70
  inclusive care (*jian ai*) 169
    ren 149
Cārvāka Materialism 24–5, 105, 185, 206
caste (*varṇa*) 105, 107, 154, 168
causality 9, 19, 25–31, 39, 60, 63, 88, 114–17, 131, 133–5, 138, 178–9, 201, 206–8, 210
  capacity of a thing to bring about an effect (*arthakrīyakāritva*) 30
  causal capacity (*samārthya*) 34, 131
  causal connection 21, 52
  causal efficacy 30, 32, 130
  causally conditioned co-arising (*pratītyasamutpāda*) 6, 60–9, 71–9, 84–6, 90–7, 99 n.4, 125, 131, 137–9, 207, 213 n.11
  causal power 28, 30–1
  causal root (*gen ben*) 176
  mental causation 27
cause (*kāraṇa*) 52, 95, 114
Chadha, Monima 48, 52
Chakrabarti, Arindam 4
Chakravarthi, Ram-Prasad 4, 38
Chan Buddhism 175–6, 179–80, 182–4, 197, 199, 211
Chāndogya Upaniṣad 8, 17–8, 192
change 16, 21, 31–3, 37–8, 111, 115, 138–9, 178, 184–5, 206
Christianity 200–2, 209
cognition 10–11, 15, 17–8, 20–3, 25–8, 32–8, 40 n.6, 41–53, 81, 86, 107, 111, 123 nn.12–13, 130–1, 177–9, 181
cognitive error. *See* error
cognitive "magic" (*māyā*) 20, 41
combination (*sāmagryā*) 88, 93
commentarial tradition 57, 67, 79–80, 84, 98, 162–3, 189, 194
commonality (*samānya*) 44, 46–7
compassion 140, 160, 168, 170, 184, 204, 208, 211
conceptual analysis 30, 78
conceptual proliferation (*prapañca*) 87, 95, 115
conduct 46, 86, 105, 125, 132–40, 142 n.8, 151–3, 166–8, 174, 184, 206–8
Confucianism 149–50, 160–6, 169–70, 172–3
consciousness 4–6, 11, 15–6, 18–9, 22–30, 32–9, 41–2, 81, 106, 110–12, 131, 143 n.14, 174–86, 192, 206
constructed kind (*upādhi*) 107, 158. *See* natural kind or feature (*jāti*)
continuity 24–5, 28, 33–7, 51, 61, 93, 115, 134, 143 n.16, 168–70, 178, 181, 209
conventionalism 66
conventional or social activities (*saṃvṛti*) 29, 133–6
Coward, Harold 57, 121, 142 n.7
craving (*taṇhā*) 110

dao 76–7, 169–70, 176, 179
Dao De Jing 76
Daoism 99 n.9, 176, 179
Dārā Shukøh 7–8, 188–94
darśana 9, 79, 189
Da Sheng Qi Xin Lun 176
debate 108–9
debt (*ṛṇa*) 125, 133–4
deconstruction 10, 57, 66, 116–21, 125–8, 133, 137, 141 n.4, 142 nn.7–8, 143 n.15
Derrida, Jacques 7, 126–9, 132–3, 135–6, 140, 141 nn.2–5, 142 nn.6–7, 144 n.22
Descartes, René 39 n.2, 120, 123 nn.12–13
designation (*prajñapti*) 58–9, 61–2, 64–7, 93, 138
  depending designation (*upādāya prajñapti*) 64–79, 85, 88, 91, 93–7

reciprocal designation (*anyonya prajñapti, shi she*) 95–6
desire 8, 20, 34, 37–8, 45, 99 n.4, 118, 121, 131, 150, 155–8, 166, 172, 177–9, 184, 200–8
Deurlinger, James 28–30, 39 n.4, 40 n.6
Deussen, Paul 8, 198, 202
Deutsch, Eliot 15, 196 n.10
Dhammacakkapavattana Sutta 205
dharma 48, 71–2, 87, 89–90, 93, 102, 105, 106, 115–18, 131, 136, 143 n.14, 152, 176, 183
as duty 155–6, 165–8, 170–2, 206–7
as righteousness 90, 105–6, 132–3, 136–9, 155
sanātana dharma 114
Dharmakīrti 6, 42–6, 49–53, 105, 119, 124 n.17
Dharmatrāta 115
Dharmotarra 45
differentiation 18, 21–2, 102
Diṅnāga 6, 42–7, 49–53, 81, 83, 95, 119, 122 n.5, 124 nn.17, 21
discerning awareness (*vijñānati*) 26
displacement (*adhyāsa*) 9, 16, 18, 20–1, 110–3
disposition 17, 25–8, 34, 37, 45–6, 49, 170, 178, 208
dispositional habituation (*saṃskāra*) 4, 26, 45, 56, 88, 130, 139, 179, 181, 183–4, 208–9
distinction (*vibhāga*) 62
the doctrine of annihilationism (*ucchedavāda*) 206
donation (*le don*) 127–8
doubt (*saṃśaya*) 108–9
dream 19–20, 177
dualism 15, 19, 21, 37, 112, 117, 192, 210. *See* Sāṃkya
moral dualism 125, 130, 132–4, 139, 141
Dvaita Vedānta 192–3

Ecce Homo 201
effect (*kārya*) 30–1, 95, 207
ego-consciousness (*ahaṃkāra*) 111
emptiness (*kong*) 76–7, 99–100 n.9. *See* emptiness (*śūnyatā*)
emptiness (*śūnyatā*) 58, 60–1, 68, 70, 73–5, 82–3, 88–94, 132, 137–8, 142 n.7
empty terms (*śūnyavāda*) 102, 115, 122 n.7
Engle, Susan 39 n.3
environments (*jing*) 172, 183, 186
Epicurus 211
epistemology 18, 20–1, 42, 81, 102–7, 119, 122 n.5, 123 n.13
equality 101, 103, 108, 120, 126–8
error 16–18, 32, 42, 45, 47, 51–2, 83, 87, 107, 111, 153, 167–8, 202
essentialism 6, 62, 97, 101, 103–4, 107–8, 114–15, 119, 175, 177, 183
eternalism 10, 199–200, 205, 207, 209, 213 n.11
ether (*ākāśa*) 37
ethics 63, 106, 125–9, 134, 138–41, 141 n.4, 163, 172
evil 139–40, 161, 184, 199, 201, 203, 209–12
existence 15–21, 30, 37, 60, 64, 77, 86–7, 103, 106–9, 114–16, 121 n.2, 135, 151, 154, 167, 170, 178, 184, 192, 201, 203–11, 213 n.11
experience 5–6, 8, 10, 17, 19–20, 23–38, 41–53, 61–2, 81, 85, 110–11, 177–9, 181, 183–6, 206–8
external forms (*bāhyākāranimittatva*) 19
external objects (*bahirmukha*) 19

family dependability (*xiao*) 7, 149–50, 161, 172
family duty (*kuladharma*) 149, 151–5, 158
Faxian 82, 100 n.11
form (*rūpa*) 48, 95
Foucault, Michel 121
Four Noble Truths 45, 60, 68, 86, 89–90, 96, 116, 137, 207
Fo Xing Lun 175–6
freedom 11, 38, 125–6, 131–9, 158, 171, 178
free from error (*abhrānta*) 45, 51
friendship 127–9, 153, 171, 201, 203, 204
Fukayama, Francis 126
fundamental incomprehension (*mūlāvidya*) 17

Gandhi, Mohandas K. 121, 124 n.25, 155
Ganeri, Jonardon 29, 39 n.1, 39–40 n.5
Gaṅgeśa 25, 43, 47, 52
Gao Yao 162–4
Garfield, Jay L. 57, 59, 62, 73, 98 n.1, 100 n.10, 143 n.16, 144 n.18
Gautama Siddhārtha 105, 116, 136, 205, 210. *See* Buddha
general characteristic (*sāmānyalakṣana*) 44, 81
generosity 127–9, 208
genuine or real (*zhen*) 76
gift (*cadeau*) 7, 125, 127
God 151, 157–8, 189–194, 195 n.5, 196 n.11, 198, 202, 210
Goebel-Gross, E. 194 n.2
goodness 105, 107–8, 112–13, 125, 127–9, 134, 138–41, 156, 160–4, 172, 186, 199–202, 209–10
the grasped (*grāhya*) 19, 41
the grasper (*grāhakā*) 19, 41
great pronouncement (*mahāvākya*) 17. *See Upaniṣads*
    tat tvam asi 18
Griffiths, Paul 34
Guifeng Zongmi 176, 179
Guo, Qiyong 149–50
Gu Sou 161
Gupta, Bina 15, 20, 41

Halbfass, Wilhelm 3, 87, 122 n.8, 142 n.9, 192, 198, 212 n.4
Hanshan Deqing 180
heaven 105, 157, 167, 169
Hegel, Georg W. F. 57, 211
Huainanzi 179
Hu Anguo 99 n.8
Hulin, Michael 200–1, 204, 209, 212 n.5
Husserl, Edmund 39 n.2, 42

idealism 8–10, 121
identifying terms (*viśeṣasaṃjñā*) 64–5, 72
identity 16–18, 20, 32, 34, 37–8, 69, 102–4, 107–19, 142 n.7, 181
    tādātmya 102
illusion 42, 59, 72, 120, 144 n.17, 207
imagination 6, 20, 41–53, 93, 184, 212
    abhūtaparikalpa 20
    kalpanā or *vikalpa* 10, 41–53
imaginative perception 6, 42–5, 49–53
impermanence 11, 21, 31, 131, 178, 204–7
imprints (*vāsanā*) 28
Inada, Kenneth K. 61, 142 n.8, 143 n.16, 144 n.17
incapable of articulation (*anirvacanīya*) 20
inference 20, 22, 44–5, 50–1, 107–8. *See* means of knowledge (*pramāṇa*)
    for others (*parārtha-anumāna*) 108
inferential mark (*liṅga*) 44
inherence (*samavāya*) 25, 47, 122 n.8
inner instrument (*antaḥkaraṇa*) 18–19
instrumental cause (*kāraṇa*) 52
intention 28, 128, 130, 134, 156–7, 159, 168, 170, 208–9
intercultural philosophy 1–2, 4–5, 8, 58, 63, 97–8, 149
Islam 8, 112, 188–91, 193–4

James, William 28, 57, 62
Janārdana 153–4
Jayanta Bhaṭṭa 48
Jiang, Tao 34
Jiao Shun 163
Jizang 99–100 n.9
The Joyful Science 200
Judaism 202
justice 101, 125–30, 132–3, 137–8, 140–1, 141 n.2, 155, 161, 163–4, 170, 201

kalpanā. *See* imagination
Kalupahana, David 57, 59, 62–3, 115, 123 n.16, 142 n.8, 143 n.13, 144 n.18
kāma 105, 208. *See pleasure*
kamma 208. *See karma*
Kant, Immanuel 3, 8–9, 38, 42
Kārikāvalī 123
karma 7, 22, 61, 89, 93, 96, 105, 114–6, 122 n.8, 125, 130, 133–5, 143–4 n.16, 144 n.17, 150, 155–7, 166–8
    karmic capacities 22, 131, 138
Kaṭha 192–3
Kathāvattu 65, 70

Katsura, Shōryū 61–2
Kauṭilya 106
Kenopaniṣadbhāṣya 196 n.13
knowledge 3, 9, 17, 20, 32, 40 n.8, 50–1, 87, 105–7, 109, 114–7, 121, 123 nn.12–13, 129, 177, 181, 202
Kongzi Jingyu 162
Krishna, Daya 5, 15–16, 18, 21, 23, 112–3
Kṛṣṇa 149–60, 166, 168, 171–3
Kṣaṇabhaṅgasiddhiḥ Vyatirekātmikā 30–2. *See* Ratnakīrti
Kumārajīva 67, 75–7, 79, 91, 96
Kumārila Bhaṭṭa 43, 52, 103–6, 119, 122 nn.8–9

Lamotte, Étienne 82
law (*droit*) 125
Li Ji 162
liberation (*mokṣa*) 22, 62, 112, 130, 133, 209
limb (*aṅga*) 65, 75
Linji Yulu 180, 182–3
Liu Qingping 149–50
Liu Shao 179
locus (*dharmin*) 43, 102
logic 6, 57, 63, 102, 104, 106–12, 114–17, 119–20, 122 nn.5, 7, 123 nn.13, 16, 124 nn.17–18, 127, 212 n.8
Lokātītastava 73–4, 96
love 128, 151–2, 156, 159, 165, 170, 196 n.10, 208
Loy, David 121, 142 n.7
loyalty 7, 127–8, 150, 152, 161, 163, 165–6, 170
luminosity 19, 37, 174–5, 177, 179–80, 186
  of awareness (*prakāśatva*) 19, 37, 174, 177, 180–3, 186
  of consciousness (*prabhāsvaram cittaṃ*) 7, 174, 178–80, 182–3
  pure and luminous awareness (*qing jing xin*) 174, 179–83, 186
  singular, pure mind (*yi ming xi*) 174, 176, 180, 182–3
  spiritual luminosity (*shen ming*) 179
luminous (*prakāśa*) 19, 177
Lusthaus, Dan 124 n.17

Madhyamaka Buddhism 3–4, 6, 10, 57, 59, 61, 63, 65, 72, 80–1, 83, 85–7, 99 n.5, 99–100 n.9, 101, 103, 114, 117, 120, 145 n.24
Mādhyamika Buddhism 9, 25, 57, 60, 63, 70, 81, 83, 91, 99–100 n.9, 102–3, 109, 116, 121 n.1, 122 n.4
Madhyānta Vibhāga 178
Magliola, Robert 142 n.7
Mahābhārata 151, 159, 172
Mahāparinirvāṇa Sūtra 176
Mahāyāna Buddhism 80–3, 88, 96, 100 n.11, 103, 105–6, 119, 125
Majjhima-nikāya 143 n.13
Majma'-ul Bahrain 188, 195 n.3
Martin, Glen 57, 121, 143 n.15
Marxism 128
Masao, Abe 197, 211
Matilal, Bimal K. 9, 42, 51, 57, 87, 104, 143 n.15
Mausala Parva 159
meaning (*artha*) 70–1, 93
means of knowledge (*pramāṇa*) 3, 9, 20–1, 40 n.8, 43, 50, 81, 105, 117
meditative cultivation (*bhavaṅga*) 89, 178, 182
memory 6, 10, 24–30, 33–8, 39 n.3, 43, 45–6, 48–50, 53, 131
Mengzi (Mencius) 7, 149–52, 160–6, 168–70, 172
mere cognition (*vijñaptimātra*) 81
metaphysics 3, 5–6, 9, 21, 33, 63, 103, 122 n.8, 132, 137, 156, 171
methaphysical or epistemological theories (*prameya-pramāṇaśāstra*) 101, 115
the middle path (*madhyamā pratipad*) 61, 64–9, 72–4, 85, 90, 92, 94, 96, 119, 137–8, 199. *See* Four Noble Truths
Milindapañha 65, 70
Mīmāṃsā 38, 41, 43, 52, 101, 103, 104, 106, 177
mind 4, 20–2, 38, 39 n.3, 41, 111, 156–7, 175–6, 179–87
  citta 26
Mohanty, J. N. 1–3, 15, 23, 123 nn.11, 15
Mohism 4, 169, 180
moment (*kṣana*) 33

momentariness 27–8, 30–4, 37, 39, 115
monism 5, 16–7, 21
moral duty 11, 150, 156–7, 168, 207
moral error (*doṣa*) 168
Morrison, Robert G. 197, 204
Mozi 76
Mūlamadhyamikakārikā 58–64, 66–92, 94–8, 99 n.6, 99–100 n.9, 125–6, 130, 133–9, 142 n.8, 143 n.15, 144 nn.17–19, 144–5 n.23
multiplicity of selves 16, 22
Murti, T. R. V. 57, 120

Nāgārjuna 3–4, 6–7, 9–11, 57–63, 65–75, 79–84, 86–98, 98–9 n.1, 99 n.5, 101–3, 109, 114–17, 122 nn.3, 7, 123 n.16, 124 n.18, 125–6, 130, 132–40, 142 nn.7–8, 143 nn.14–15, 143–4 n.16, 144 nn.17–18, 21–2, 144–5 n.23, 197
name (*nāma*) 93
name or word (*ming*) 76, 91
Nandy, Ashis 10, 113
Nāsadīya Sūkta 115
natural kind or feature (*jāti*) 47, 104, 107, 122 n.8
Nehru, Jawaharlal 112–13, 122 n.3
Neo-Vedānta 10, 113, 120
Nietzsche, Friedrich W. 8, 121, 127, 197–205, 209–12, 212 nn.1, 3–5
nihilism 8, 60, 197–9, 201–6, 209–11
nirvāṇa 62, 101, 103, 114, 116–17, 119–20, 125–6, 131–2, 136, 138–9, 141, 198–200, 202, 204, 209–10
Nishitani, Kenji 197, 211
nominalism 59, 63, 66
non-dualism 15–8, 21, 23, 192. *See* Advaita Vedānta, Śaṅkara
non-existence (*asat*) 20
non-existence, absence (*abhāva*) 31, 51, 60–1, 68, 89, 132
non-material ideations (*abhūtaparikalpa*) 41
non-momentary (*akṣanika*) 30
no-self 69–70, 119, 206
nothingness (*wu*) 75–6. *See śūnyatā*
notion
  of the other (*yuṣmadpratyaya*) 16, 111
  pratyaya 19
  of this (*asmadpratyaya*) 16, 111
Nyāya 3–6, 9–11, 17, 24–39, 39 nn.1–2, 41–3, 45–52, 87, 101, 103–4, 106–10, 117, 120, 123 nn.11–13, 124 n.21, 177
Nyāya-Buddhist debate 24–7, 33–5, 37–8, 43, 49–50
Nyāyānusāra 143 nn.12, 14
Nyāyasūtra 34–6, 47
Nyāyasūtrabhāṣya 34, 36, 39
Nyāyavārttika 35
Nyāyavārttikatātparyaṭikā 35

object of negation (*pratiyogin*) 32
On the Genealogy of Morals 200
ontology 10, 25, 37, 51, 107–8, 110, 114, 116–19, 122 n.5, 124 n.18, 141 n.4, 143 n.15
opponent (*pūrvapakṣin*) 31, 49, 60, 82, 86, 89, 91
the other (*taut atre*) 126

pain 11, 28, 34, 37–8, 140, 157, 177, 203, 207
pantheism 193
Paramārtha 7, 82, 175–6, 179–81
Parkes, Graham 211
perceiving (*upalabdhi*) 111
perception 6, 19–20, 26, 36, 38, 40 n.8, 42–53, 104, 107–8, 111. *See* means of knowledge (*pramāṇa*)
  imagination-free perception (*nirvikalpa pratyakṣa*) 42–7, 50, 52
  imaginative perception (*savikalpa pratyakṣa*) 43–7, 50, 52
permanence (*nitya*) 111, 178
person (*pudgala*) 93
personhood 4, 7, 11, 23, 29, 38, 66, 114, 149, 166, 168, 172, 174–5, 177, 206
phenomenology 24–6, 29–33, 39 n.2, 42, 130
phenomenon (*bhāva*) 37, 70–2, 93, 115, 130, 185–6
Phillips, Stephen H. 25, 52

philosophical view (*dṛṣṭi*) 81, 87
philosophy of language 59, 62–3
Platform Sūtra 176
pleasure 34, 37–8, 157, 177, 208. *See kāma*
pluralism 20
Potter, Karl H. 196 n.9
Prajñāpāramitā 114
Prajñaptivāda Buddhism 69, 72, 83, 95–6, 99 n.5
prakāśatva. *See* luminosity
Prāsaṅgika Buddhism 69, 74, 77, 80, 101, 103, 109, 117, 120
Prasannapadā 64, 67, 75, 81–2, 85, 116, 124 n.21, 135
Praśāstapāda 38
Priestley, Leonard 71, 92–3
primordial
  consciousness (*shi*) 179
  materiality (*prakṛti*) 17–19, 167–8 (*see* Sāṃkhya)
    qi (*yuan qi*) 179
Pudgalavāda Buddhism 40 n.6, 69, 74, 83, 93–5
Puggalapaññatti Aṭṭhakathā 93

Qingmu 75–7, 91, 96
quality (*guṇa*) 25, 49, 104, 107, 122 n.8, 167–8, 170–1
Qunqiu Hu Shi Chuan 99 n.8
Qur'ān 188–91, 193, 195 n.6

Ratnagotravibhāga Sūtra 175–6
Ratnakīrti 5, 30–5, 37
Ratnāvali 83, 125
realism 5, 9–10, 47, 62, 97, 103–4, 109, 121
rebirth 22, 91, 93, 131, 135, 156, 178, 185, 207–9. *See saṃsāra*
recognition 24–5, 27, 30, 32–3, 35–6, 42, 46, 49, 53, 122 n.8, 128, 184
    pratyabhijñā 24, 32, 36, 49
recognitional capacity (*saṃvid sāmarthya*) 48
recollection (*pratisaṃdhāna*) 24, 26, 28, 32, 36, 39 n.3, 44
reductionism 4, 29, 39 n.2, 76, 200
relations 16, 21–2, 25, 32, 38, 48, 70, 73, 94, 112–13, 125, 134

Renou, Louis 196 n.13
resemblance (*sādṛṣya*) 26, 46
respect 168
responsibility 127–9, 153–4, 157–8, 160, 163–4, 170, 172, 207
Robinson, Richard 57–8, 65
Rogacz, Dawid 99–100 n.9
Rospatt, Alexander von 33–4
Roy, Ram Mohan 112–3

Salvini, Mattia 64, 98 n.1, 99 n.4, 100 n.12
Sāṃkhya 5, 15–23, 112, 167, 177, 181, 201
Sāṃkhyakārikā 22, 179, 181
Saṃmitīya 83, 93
saṃsāra 101–2, 114, 117, 120, 131–2, 141
Saṃyutta Nikāya 208, 213 n.10
Saṅghabhadra 143 nn.12, 14
Śaṅkara 5, 7–9, 11, 15–23, 106, 110–12, 123 n.15, 189, 192–3, 196 nn.9, 11
Sannayabhedaparacantacakra 95
Sāriputrābhidharma 175
Sarvāstivāda Buddhism 83, 93, 102, 115, 130, 132–5, 138, 143 nn.12, 16
Sautrāntika Buddhism 26, 33, 40 n.6, 93, 115–6, 143 n.11
Sautrāntika-Vaibhāṣika 34
Schmidt, Carl 141 n.3
Schmithausen, Labert 34
Schopen, Gregory 82
Schopenhauer, Arthur 2–3, 8–9, 194 n.2, 198, 200, 203, 211–13 n.13
secret (*rahasyam*) 193
self 5, 10, 15–9, 21–7, 29–39, 39 nn.3–4, 39–40 n.5, 40 nn.6–8, 41, 61, 69–70, 75, 85–6, 102, 104, 110–13, 119, 123 n.13, 155, 177, 181, 192, 206. *See ātman*
    jīva 15, 17
  multiplicity of selves 16, 22
  self-consciousness 24–6, 29–30, 32–9, 39–40 n.5, 40 n.6
  transcendental self 18, 22
self-characteristic (*svalakṣana*) 25, 44, 81

selfhood 5, 10, 30, 32, 34, 116, 123 n.13, 156–7, 177
Sengzhao 99 n.9
sensations 10, 19, 28, 38, 46, 49–51, 104, 177
sense organs 18, 44, 51, 180
servant (*śudra*) 107–8, 113
Shah Jahan 191
shame 168
Shouwen Jiezi 76
Shun 160–6, 169
Siderits, Mark 57, 61–2, 78, 81, 123 nn.12–13, 124 n.19
Sima Guang 164
Sirr-i Akbar 188–94, 194–5 n.2, 195 n.7
skandha 66, 70–1, 78, 86, 88, 93–4, 99 nn.4, 6, 116
social change 23
social duty 7, 150, 155
social justice 101, 108, 113–14, 120–2
social rightness 170
Soll, Ivan 203
space 9, 37
spirit (*puruṣa*) 17, 22, 177. *See* Sāṃkhya
spirit (*shen*) 180
Sprung, Mervyn 57, 59, 61–3, 65, 136, 198
Śridhāra 43
Śrīharṣa 10, 25
Śrīmālādevīsiṃhanāda Sūtra 176
standards and laws (*fa*) 163
Stawson, Peter F. 42
storehouse consciousness (*ālayavijñāna*) 34, 179, 181
subjectivity 5, 16–17, 23, 32, 112, 177–8, 181
substance 17, 22, 25, 31, 33, 37, 40 n.6, 49, 102, 104, 107, 111, 115–6, 130, 177–80, 185
substance (*dravya*) 40 n.6, 47, 115, 122 n.8
success, prosperity (*artha*) 93, 104–5
suffering 45, 108, 119–20, 138–40, 155, 168, 172, 204, 207, 209
surname (*you shi*) 76
svabhāva ('own-nature') 25, 64–5, 72, 77, 85, 90, 93, 96, 99 n.5, 102, 109, 115–6, 130–2, 138, 142, 143 n.14, 168, 170
svadharma (own-duty) 168, 170
svakarman ('own-action') 168
Svātantrika Buddhism 102
Śvetaketu 8, 18

Tantravārtika 122 n.9
Tao Ying 162–3
Tarka-saṃgraha 123 n.10
Tathāgata 66, 70–1, 73, 88, 102–3, 114–20, 121 n.2
Tathāgatagarbha Sūtra 175–6, 182
Tathāgataparikṣa 70
Tawhid, the doctrine of God's unity 190, 193–4
testimony 20, 107, 136, 144. *See* means of knowledge (*pramāṇa*)
theory of the momentariness (*kṣanavāda*) 28
thesis (*pratijñā*) 87, 122 n.7, 124 n.18
time 9, 22, 31–2, 61, 69–70, 93, 114–15, 131
to guide (*dao*) 77
to lead (*yin*) 77
training (*yong*) 183
transcendence 16, 18, 22, 118, 199, 204
Triṃśatikā 39–40 n.5
true doctrine (*saddharma*) 90
truth (*satya*) 18, 20, 45, 51, 62, 107–9, 112, 117, 119
  conventional truth (*samvṛti satya*) 78, 86
  paramount truth (*paramārtha satya*) 20, 62, 117, 143 n.14
  truth of conventional transaction (*vyavahāra satya*) 62
  worldly conventional truth (*lokasamvṛti satya*) 86
Tsongkapa 63
Tuck, Andrew 58, 142 n.8

Übermensch 197, 204, 210
Udayana 10, 40 n.8, 43, 119
Uddālaka 8, 18
Uddyotakāra 5, 10, 35
Upadeśasāhasrī 123 n.14
Upaniṣadbhāṣya 192
Upaniṣads 3, 7–8, 17, 20, 41, 110, 155, 189–94, 196 nn.8, 11, 13

Vācaspati Miśra 6, 10–11, 15, 35, 43, 46–50, 52–3
vāda-vaitaṇḍika 102, 109, 119, 143 n.15
Vaibhāṣika Buddhism 130–5, 138, 143–4 n.16
Vaiśeṣika 26–7, 38, 41, 87, 177
values 108, 112–3, 127–8, 151, 198–204, 208, 211
van der Braak, André 197, 211
Vasubandhu 5, 7, 26–30, 33–6, 39 n.4, 39–40 n.5, 40 n.6, 41, 119, 122 n.8, 143 nn.11–12, 178–9, 181–2
Vātsyāyana 5, 10, 34–6, 106, 119
Veda 105–6
  Rigveda 115
Vedānta 3, 8, 10, 15, 17, 22–3, 177, 181, 192–3
Vetullaba 100 n.11
Vidyāraṇya 18, 41
Vigrahavyāvartanī 73–4, 81, 86–7, 96, 122 n.7, 124 n.18, 125, 143 n.15
Vijñānavāda Buddhism 7, 9, 20, 34, 81, 83, 174, 176, 179, 181–2
vikalpa 42–3, 45, 53
virtue 127, 132–3, 140, 172, 178, 184–5
Viśiṣṭādvaita 189, 192–3
Viśvanātha Nyāyapañcānana 123 n.10
volition (*cetanā*) 208–9
volitional formation (*saṅkhāra*) 207–9. *See saṃskāra*
vyavahāra 29, 62, 86, 125, 133–6, 139, 144 nn.20–1

Walser, Joseph 59–60, 64, 67, 72, 74, 82–3, 92–5, 98–9 n.1, 100 n.10
Wang Anshi 164
Wang Bi 179
warrior (*kṣatriya*) 107, 152, 154–6, 158, 167–8, 171, 209
whole (*avayavin*) 104
will (*icchā*) 37–8
witness (*sākṣin*) 36
Wittgenstein, Ludwig 57, 62
world 37, 41–2, 60, 85–6, 91, 102–3, 106–12, 114–20, 130–1, 138–9, 152–8, 164–6, 170, 179, 184, 203–11
  loka 86, 117

Xiang 160–1, 165
Xing Bing 162
Xuanzang 80, 82, 95
Xunzi 76, 162

Yadav, Bibhuti S. 3, 6, 11, 57, 101–21, 121 nn.1–2, 122, nn.3–6, 8, 123 nn.12–13, 124 nn.17–19, 22, 142 n.7, 145 n.24
Yang Shi 163–4
Yizi 169–70
Yoga 47, 177, 181, 189
Yogācāra 41, 99 n.5
Yogācāra-Sautrāntika Buddhism 102, 117, 124 n.17
Yoga-Vāsiṣṭha 195 n.3

Zen Buddhism 61, 142 n.7, 197, 199, 211
Zhao Qi 163
Zhong Lun 75, 77
Zhuangzi 76, 180
Zhu Xi 162
Zuozhuan 76, 99, 162

www.ingramcontent.com/pod-product-compliance
Lightning Source LLC
Chambersburg PA
CBHW062215300426
44115CB00012BA/2078
* 9 7 8 1 3 5 0 2 5 3 9 9 5 *